Modernising the Labour Party

Modernising the Labour Party

Organisational Change since 1983

Thomas Quinn
Lecturer in Government
University of Essex

First published 2004 by
PALGRAVE MACMILLAN
Houndmills, Basingstoke, Hampshire RG21 6XS and
175 Fifth Avenue, New York, N. Y. 10010
Companies and representatives throughout the world

PALGRAVE MACMILLAN is the global academic imprint of the Palgrave Macmillan division of St. Martin's Press, LLC and of Palgrave Macmillan Ltd. Macmillan® is a registered trademark in the United States, United Kingdom and other countries. Palgrave is a registered trademark in the European Union and other countries.

ISBN 1–4039–3584–X

This book is printed on paper suitable for recycling and made from fully managed and sustained forest sources.

A catalogue record for this book is available from the British Library.

Library of Congress Cataloging-in-Publication Data
Quinn, Thomas, 1972–
   Modernising the Labour Party : organisational change since 1983 / Thomas Quinn.
      p. cm.
   Includes bibliographical references and index.
   ISBN 1–4039–3584–X (cloth)
      1. Labour Party (Great Britain)–History. 2. Labour Party (Great Britain)–Reorganization. I. Title.

JN1129.L32.Q85 2005
324.24107–dc22   2004051506

10   9   8   7   6   5   4   3   2   1
13   12   11   10   09   08   07   06   05   04

Printed and bound in Great Britain by
Antony Rowe Ltd, Chippenham and Eastbourne

For my father

Contents

List of Figures

List of Tables

Acknowledgements

Samuel Johnson once said, 'A man will turn over half a library to make one book.' This book was no different, and the arguments presented in it owe much to the growing bodies of literature on the British Labour Party, the theory of party organisation and rational choice theory. However, my academic and personal debts go much further than the authors I have consulted. This book began life as a PhD thesis completed at the London School of Economics, where its main ideas were tested in numerous seminars. I would like to thank all the students and staff who, despite not being Labour Party specialists, read my papers and subjected them to detailed and constructive criticisms. My examiners, Joanna Spear and Mark Wickham-Jones, also made useful suggestions for improvements. Mark has subsequently been a valued friend and a source of advice on all matters concerning the Labour Party. The members of the PSA's Labour Movements Group have always shown a keen, if critical, interest in my papers at PSA conferences. I also owe special thanks to Richard Heffernan, who read earlier versions of Chapters 3–8 and made some excellent suggestions. Any remaining errors are my responsibility.

My greatest academic debt is owed to Keith Dowding, who supervised my thesis, advised on the writing of this book, and served as a general intellectual mentor. He introduced me to the black arts of rational choice theory, which I studied first as a sceptic and later as a convert. Working at the LSE was particularly useful, since it is one of the few institutions in the UK where rational choice theory has taken off. Many of my ideas about rational choice methods were shaped by the seminars and workshops I attended, as well as the undergraduate classes I taught.

My ideas about Labour's policy-making structure were clarified by discussions with head office party officials, and with Ann Black, who is currently a member of the party's national executive. I would like to thank all concerned who generously gave of their time to talk with me.

Some of the arguments in this book have already appeared in print. I am pleased to acknowledge that one section from Chapter 2 and three sections from Chapter 3 first appeared in a slightly different form in my article, 'Block Voting in the Labour Party: A Political Exchange Model', *Party Politics*, Volume 8, Number 2, March 2002 (© 2002 Sage

Publications, London). Much of the material in Chapter 6 first appeared (again in a different form) in my article, 'Electing the Leader: The British Labour Party's Electoral College', *British Journal of Politics and International Relations*, Volume 6, Number 3, August 2004 (© 2004 Political Studies Association and Blackwell Publishing, London).

Thanks are also due to Alison Howson and Guy Edwards of Palgrave Macmillan, who navigated me through the production process and showed great patience.

Finally, my main debt of gratitude is owed to my father, Tom Quinn senior, without whose support over the years this book would not have been possible. He offered encouragement during the dark days when it seemed the thesis would never be completed, and the pride he took in my accomplishments always spurred me on to achieve more. As a token of my thanks, it is to my father that I dedicate this book.

Thomas Quinn

List of Abbreviations

AEEU	Amalgamated Engineering and Electrical Union (previously AUEW, now Amicus)
ALC	Association of Labour Councillors
AM	Assembly Member (of the National Assembly of Wales)
ASTMS	Association of Scientific, Technical and Managerial Staff (later MSF, now Amicus)
AUEW	Amalgamated Union of Engineering Workers (later AEEU, now Amicus)
CAC	Conference Arrangements Committee
CBI	Confederation of British Industry
CCD	Campaigns and Communications Directorate
CIR	Contemporary Issue Resolution
CLP	Constituency Labour Party
COSLA	Convention of Scottish Local Authorities
CSC	Campaign Strategy Committee
CWU	Communication Workers Union
EETPU	Electrical, Electronic, Telecommunications and Plumbing Union (later AEEU, now Amicus)
EPLP	European Parliamentary Labour Party
FBU	Fire Brigades Union
GC	General Committee (of CLP)
GMB	GMB is the name, not abbreviation, of the general workers union (previously, *inter alia*, GMWU)
GMWU	General and Municipal Workers' Union (now GMB)
ILP	Independent Labour Party
JPC	Joint Policy Committee
LGA	Local Government Association
MEP	Member of the European Parliament
MP	Member of Parliament
MSF	Manufacturing, Science and Finance Union (previously ASTMS, now Amicus)
NCC	National Constitutional Committee
NEC	National Executive Committee
NPF	National Policy Forum
NPP	National Parliamentary Panel
NUM	National Union of Mineworkers

NUPE	National Union of Public Employees (now Unison)
NUR	National Union of Railwaymen (now RMT)
NUS	National Union of Seamen (now RMT)
ODOV	One-delegate–one-vote
OLOV	One-levypayer–one-vote
OMOV	One-member–one-vote
PCS	Public and Commercial Services Union
PFI	Private Finance Initiative
PLP	Parliamentary Labour Party
PPC	Prospective Parliamentary Candidate
PRG	Policy Review Group
RFMC	Rank and File Mobilising Committee
RMT	Rail, Maritime and Transport Union (previously NUR and NUS)
SCA	Shadow Communications Agency
SDP	Social Democratic Party
SOGAT	Society of Graphical and Allied Trades
SPD	Sozialdemokratische Partei Deutschlands
TGWU	Transport and General Workers' Union
TUC	Trades Union Congress
TUFL	Trade Unionists for Labour
TULO	Trade Union and Labour Party Liaison Organisation
TULV	Trade Unions for a Labour Victory
USDAW	Union of Shop, Distributive and Allied Workers

Introduction

'Parties that do not change die, and this party is a living movement not an historical monument. If the world changes and we don't, then we become of no use to the world.'
Tony Blair (address to the Labour Party's Annual Conference, 1994)

In 1983, in the aftermath of its worst postwar election defeat, the Labour Party had, in the eyes of many, become a byword for extremism, illegitimate trade union power, class warfare and ineffectual leadership. On being elected to government in 1997, Labour was widely seen as a slick electoral machine that sought the votes of the middle classes, preferred the advice (and the money) of businessmen over union leaders, and had stolen the policies of the Conservatives. There is an element of caricature in each of these descriptions, but many people believed them, and in parliamentary democracies numbers matter: 8.5 million people voted for the 1983 model but 13.5 million lent their support to the 1997 version. The condition for this spectacular turnaround was a sweeping transformation of Labour's policies, structures and strategy during the intervening wilderness years. Under the tenures of Neil Kinnock and John Smith, steps were taken to reform the party, but it was with Tony Blair's accession to the leadership in 1994 that the pace of change quickened. Only then did a majority within the Labour Party finally accept that the choice was, as Blair would later tell the TUC, to modernise or die.

For the advocates of change, the term 'modernisation' conveyed the forward-looking nature of the project to broaden Labour's electoral appeal. For opponents of change, it was a pejorative term applied to a process in which the party lost its soul. It has also been used in a more neutral and descriptive sense (see Seyd and Whiteley, 2002), and the present study follows suit. The focus of this book is one of the major dimensions of Labour's modernisation: the comprehensive transformation of its organisational structure. Institutional reform was a prerequisite for many other changes, including those of policy and strategy, because it was the principal means by which internal opponents of policy and strategy change were defeated.[1] Later chapters analyse the main areas of organisational change, including the reconstruction of Labour's relationship with its affiliated unions. This introduction provides the background to modernisation and sets out the remit of the book.

The background to Labour's modernisation

In common with all social democratic parties that eschewed revolution for the pursuit of change by parliamentary means (Przeworski and Sprague, 1986), Labour's principal measure of its performance is provided by election results. Parties wishing to implement policies must win elections. Parties that continually lose elections must change their policies, their leaders, their organisational structures, or all three, which Labour did in the 1980s and 1990s. It was Labour's catastrophic defeat in 1983 that created the conditions for change. A period of left-wing ascendancy had followed the party's ejection from office in 1979, culminating in arguably the most leftwing policy programme in its history, together with organisational reforms that increased the power of activists. A group of high-profile MPs from Labour's right wing abandoned the party to form their own (the Social Democratic Party), and the period was one of internecine conflict between left and right. However, the left took the blame for the fiasco in 1983, as the election was fought and lost on a manifesto famously described by Gerald Kaufman as 'the longest suicide note in history'.

Labour's modernisation began under Neil Kinnock, who was elected as leader in the aftermath of the general election defeat. The delicate balance of forces in the party, together with the year-long miners' strike in 1984–85, ensured that little changed during the first couple of years of Kinnock's leadership. However, the defeat of the strike signalled a realignment of party factions (see Chapter 3), as the moderate 'soft left' acknowledged the limits of extra-parliamentary strategies and backed Kinnock's plan to reform the party. Policies were moderated and the parliamentary leadership assumed greater control over the party than at any previous time in opposition. However, the changes were insufficient to prevent Labour suffering in 1987 a third consecutive election defeat, with only modest improvements on the 1983 result, though the secondary goal of vanquishing the SDP was achieved. The constituency for reform grew larger and a major policy review was undertaken between 1987 and 1989, in which many unpopular policies were abandoned. *Inter alia*, the party accepted most of the Conservative government's industrial relations legislation, which restricted the rights of trade unions, to demonstrate to voters that Labour would not take Britain back to the strikes of the 1970s. Kinnock also began the process of reforming Labour's organisation to shift power away from the leftwing activists in the constituency parties. Changes were made to the processes of choosing parliamentary candidates, with individual party members enfranchised (see Chapter 5). By the time of the 1992 general election, Labour was confident of winning, or at least preventing the Conservatives from winning, so it was a shock to the entire party when John Major's government was returned, albeit on a reduced majority.

After Labour's record fourth consecutive defeat, Kinnock resigned and was replaced by John Smith, a respected politician from the old right of the party. Smith's tenure in charge proved to be an interregnum because he died after only two years in the post and did not lead Labour into a general election campaign. These two years are best remembered for Smith's ultimately successful battle to introduce a series of reforms to Labour's organisation, which eroded the power of the trade unions. The issue of union power had arisen in 1992, when key modernisers claimed the party's institutionalised links with the unions played a major role in the election defeat. Smith was never entirely convinced by the modernisers' case but he did accept that Labour had to dispel lingering doubts among voters about union influence, something that had been an issue during his own successful leadership bid. Even with these reforms, leading modernisers such as Tony Blair and Gordon Brown were worried Labour had not changed enough to convince voters to put their trust in it. However, with Smith's death from a heart attack in 1994, they got their chance sooner than they anticipated. It was ultimately Tony Blair who ran as the modernising candidate, and his emphatic victory in all sections of the electoral college confirmed there was finally, after four elections defeats, a constituency for change that encompassed not just a majority of MPs, but also a majority of individual party and union members.

With his accession to the leadership, Blair made a conscious attempt to break with the past. He and his allies redefined the party as 'new Labour' (though its name was never formally changed)[2] and contrasted it to 'old Labour' (see Mandelson and Liddle, 1996). Whereas 'old Labour' represented sectional interests and higher taxes and spending, 'new Labour' was fiscally conservative and spoke for 'middle England' (see Smith, 2000; Fielding, 2000). Blair told the party it had to come to terms with a changed and changing world. The shrinkage of Labour's traditional manual-working-class electoral base, together with partisan dealignment, made it necessary for the party to broaden its electoral appeal (Crewe, 1991). Thatcherism had transformed the social and economic landscape of Britain through privatisation, council house sales, legislative attacks on the unions, and a free-market assault on the postwar consensus of full employment, corporatism and the welfare state. Globalisation was changing the nature of the world economy, and demanded flexible labour markets and a preparedness to work with the market rather than against it. In response, Labour would need to overhaul its policies and electoral strategy, which demanded leadership control of the party organisation. Blair's period as leader has marked a further centralisation of power, together with a straining of Labour's relationship with the unions. After three years of arguing the case for modernisation, Blair led Labour to its first general election victory in 23 years. Modernisers presented the landslide triumph of 1997, followed by another in 2001, as vindicating their strategy. Moreover, Blair told his followers on the night of his first election victory that the party had been elected as 'new Labour' and would govern as 'new Labour'. Few would dispute that he was true to his word.

Structure of the book

This book focuses on the main areas of institutionalised decision-making in parties, namely candidate selection, leadership elections and policy-making. The unitary nature of the UK state ensures that the national decision-making institutions of the Labour Party are pre-eminent, though local bodies are important in the selection of parliamentary candidates. Changes to Labour's regional structure are not considered because it has traditionally been of lesser importance. Recently, regional bodies have been given a boost, first through devolution and second, through their representation at Labour's new national policy forum. They are likely to become the focus of future research on the party's organisational structure.

Before discussing the Labour Party, some theoretical issues are addressed. One of the distinguishing features of this book is its use of rational choice models to analyse institutions and institutional change in the Labour Party. Although the book contains some historical narrative, the emphasis is on the systematic analysis of intra-party institutions, in terms of their functioning and incentive structures rather than every twist and turn on the road to modernisation. Chapter 1 provides a short account of the rational choice approach used in the book. Critiques of both the approach in general and its previous application to the Labour Party are evaluated. Chapter 2 turns to the theory of party organisation, beginning with a brief assessment of some existing theories, before setting out a rational choice 'exchange' model of politician-activist relations. To campaign for office, politicians need labour and finance from party members, and in return, they offer policy promises. However, this exchange is non-simultaneous, with resources supplied by members months or even years before politicians can deliver on their promises. Therefore, party members demand internal institutional controls to guard against possible opportunistic behaviour by politicians, though the precise degree of autonomy that politicians enjoy is subject to bargaining and external circumstances. Chapter 3 begins the analysis of the Labour Party by applying the exchange model to Labour's pre-modernised organisational structure. The principal form of political exchange is that between the parliamentary leadership and Labour's affiliated trade unions, and it is shown that the block voting system was an efficient means of institutionalising exchange.

Chapters 4–6 examine the three key areas of institutional reform in the Labour Party since 1983: policy-making, the selection of parliamentary candidates and the electoral college for leadership contests. In each case, the *status quo ante* is described and its consequences for the internal distribution of power assessed, before the reformed structures are analysed. Two general phases of reform are identified: first, a process of centralisation under Kinnock's leadership, in which power was taken away from leftwing activists in the constituency parties; and second, the 'legitimisation' of Labour's structures under Smith and Blair, whereby union influence was reduced, in tandem with further centralisation. Chapter 7 addresses the issue of Labour's organisational resources, beginning with a description of trends in funding and membership levels, before moving on to how Labour deploys its resources in election campaigns. Chapter 8 concludes by reflecting on Labour's modernisation and its consequences for the future. It is argued that power is now so centralised, there are serious questions as to whether individual members and affiliated unions have sufficient incentives to continue pursuing their political goals through the agency of the Labour Party in the absence of a new institutional settlement.

1
Aims and Methods

A welcome development in the academic study of the Labour Party in recent years has been a greater willingness among party specialists to think theoretically about their subject. Studies of individual members have utilised incentives-based models of party membership and activism (Seyd and Whiteley, 1992, 2002); students of Labour's economic policies regularly discuss the applicability of theories of social democratic strategy (Hay, 1999; Wickham-Jones, 1996); and the party-union relationship has been interpreted in terms of social norms and values (Minkin, 1992; see also Shaw, 2003). In this spirit, the Labour Movements Specialists' Group of the UK Political Studies Association convened, in July 2001, a conference on interpretations of the Labour Party. The organisers' aim was to 'revisit and re-evaluate the relative strengths and weaknesses of key interpretative approaches' to the study of the party, and thereby 'better understand Labour's past, present, and possible future'.[1] The present book is a contribution to this undertaking.

A key feature of this study is its use of rational choice models to examine Labour's organisational reforms since 1983. Rational choice theory has proved particularly useful in the analysis of institutions and institutional change. Self-interested actors seek institutions that maximise their utility, but if other actors prefer different institutions, conflicts may emerge. In the case of the Labour Party after 1983, the office-seeking party leadership sought reforms that diminished the influence of leftwing activists and trade unions, the latter having long provided Labour with most of its funds and (affiliated) members. The power of the unions was such that they were able to forestall serious change for a decade.

The clash of interests is not how most academic observers of the party view its internal workings, especially in relation to the unions.

1

The most famous account of the party-union link is Lewis Minkin's 'sociological' interpretation (1992), which views it in terms of shared values and restrictive norms (see below). The party-union link is permeated by a culture and ethos (Drucker, 1979) that expresses itself in myths, icons and 'understandings' about what constitutes acceptable behaviour in given circumstances. However, although norms and values exist in the party, the present book argues they are like a lush covering of ivy on an old mansion: they provide the structure with its character but not its foundations. The cornerstone of the party-union link is the exchange of money for influence over policy. The Labour Party exists because of a hard-headed, rational assessment by politicians and unions that labourism – 'the institutionalized duo of *electoralism/parliamentarism* and *economism*' (Elliott, 1993: xi, emphasis in original) – offers the best organisational means of pursuing social democracy and trade union interests in Britain. Historically, it has been a relationship of interdependence, with Labour financially dependent on the unions, and the latter politically dependent on the party. It is a history punctuated with conflicts – Minkin aptly calls it 'the contentious alliance' – but these tensions are built into the party's structure.

The aim of this chapter is to establish the utility of the rational choice approach for the examination of organisational change in the Labour Party. It begins by setting out the general methodological approach used in this study, before addressing some of the main criticisms of the approach, particularly in regard to party dynamics. The chapter ends with a critique of the rival sociological approach to the study of the Labour Party.

Rational choice theory and the study of institutions

It is unnecessary to engage in an exhaustive discussion of rational choice theory, not least because the widespread and increasing use of rational choice models is a testament to the utility of the approach. Nevertheless, it would be useful to recall the key assumptions employed in rational choice analyses.[2]

Rational choice models are based on the interaction of individuals, who are generally seen as the bearers of preferences, but who are confronted by economic, institutional and informational constraints. 'Rationality' in rational choice theory refers to individuals' means rather than ends, though certain conditions are laid down about preferences. First, preferences must be *complete* in that all options can be ranked better than or equal to each other. Second, individual preferences must be *transitive*, or, logically consistent – if I prefer x to y and y to z, I should also logically prefer x to z. Third, preferences must be translatable into action, so that if I prefer x to y, then given a choice between x and y I will undertake action to bring about x (Dowding and Hindmoor, 1997: 455; see also Downs, 1957: 6).

An individual's preferences are usually assumed to be fixed (see below), and the interest for the analyst concerns whether the individual chooses from the available courses of action that which secures his highest attainable preferred end. Rational individuals act this way to maximise their *utility*, an analytic concept through which preferences can be assigned numerical values. Each individual has a utility function that captures his choice behaviour under institutional and informational constraints. A rational actor will not choose a course of action that leads to a lower payoff than he could obtain by acting differently. Moreover, actions are chosen to achieve certain goals (instrumentalism) rather than being pursued for their own sake; only the accomplishment of the actor's goals enables him to attain utility. Action involves the expenditure of scarce resources and thus involves costs. Some rational choice theorists have relaxed the assumption of instrumentalism by allowing a role for expressive motives, whereby the performance of certain actions can itself provide utility (Brennan and Lomasky, 1993; Chong, 2000; Schuessler, 2000). In their surveys of Labour Party members, Patrick Seyd and Paul Whiteley (1992, 2002) claim such benefits are a major reason for joining. However, most rational choice theorists are uneasy about modelling expressive motives, because there is the danger they can be invoked to 'explain' discrepancies between a model's predicted outcome and the observed outcome. Expressive benefits are excluded from the model of party organisation developed in Chapter 2.

Strictly speaking, utility maximisation is not the same as self-interest. An altruist maximises his utility by performing generous acts for others, but these acts could entail personal costs and not be in his selfish interest (Margolis, 1982). However, most rational choice models assume self-interest, which is usually introduced through 'auxiliary assumptions' (Kavka, 1991: 373) that supersede utility maximisation. Entrepreneurs seek to maximise profits, politicians votes, and bureaucrats budgets. In the present study, utility maximisation and self-interest are assumed to be synonymous, unless otherwise specified. This work deals principally with institutional actors rather than specific individuals. This distinction corresponds to the type/token contrast, in which a type is a general class of object or actor, whereas a token is a specific example of a given type (Dowding, 1991: 11). The focus here is on general types – 'party leaders', 'activists', 'trade union leaders', and 'voters'. Such actors are defined by their institutional position or role rather than by any personal tastes that may enter into their utility functions. Even when a token individual, such as Neil Kinnock, is discussed, he is so in his former capacity as the leader of a vote-seeking party and not as an individual with a personal history and idiosyncratic quirks.[3]

The type/token distinction is relevant to another feature of rational choice theory. Methodological individualism is the doctrine that all outcomes and events are to be explained in terms of individuals' actions. Sociological critics of rational choice theory have long complained about its focus on individuals at the expense of social structures and institutions (Hindess, 1988). However, much of this critique is misplaced. The emphasis on type rather than token actors ensures institutional and structural elements are incorporated into rational choice models through actors' preference schedules and constraints. Viewing politicians as office-seekers means importing structural features of the competitive party system into explanations of individual acts. Most rational choice models are structuralist, not anti-structuralist (Dowding and Hindmoor, 1997: 453).

Besides, individualism does not have to be methodologically so (Dowding, 1991: 10). Rational choice theorists contend that although events *can* be explained in terms of individuals, it is often otiose, because institutional-level explanations may suffice. We can discuss the behaviour of 'parties' or 'interest groups' without referring to individuals, because even though such collective bodies never have their own preferences (only individuals have desires), we can often refer to them as a shorthand for aggregates of individual decisions that take place within such bodies. In principle, a party's electoral strategy could be explained by reference to the countless individual decisions taken in devising it, but this degree of detail is unnecessary. All that matters for the individualist is that we could so explain if we desired.

Critics of rational choice theory may respond that this framework of analysis and the narrow characteristics of *homo economicus* offer a pared-down conception of individuals, and demand in its place a more 'realistic' view of human behaviour. However, rational choice theorists do not believe all people are self-interested in every sphere of their lives. Instead, they claim that the simplifying assumptions of rational choice theory enable us to *model* scenarios, in which extraneous factors are filtered out and the explanatory work is performed by a few concepts. It is not inherently objectionable to simplify matters; all science is reductionist, explaining the complex in terms of the simple. However, some things inevitably are left out of our models; if they were not, the 'models' would be merely descriptive.[4]

Nevertheless, good models and assumptions illuminate key patterns, processes and mechanisms. In his model of party competition, Anthony Downs (1957: 30) assumed unapologetically that '[p]oliticians in our model are motivated by the desire for power, prestige, and income ... their primary objective is to be elected.' This assumption provides politicians with an instrumental attitude to policy and ideology, and gives the model considerable analytical purchase. The assumption is a simplification: real politicians are as likely as anyone else to have their own intrinsic preferences (more so, since they have found their ways into political careers). According to Downs, office-seeking politicians 'choose an ideology which will win votes, not one they believe in, since their objective is the acquisition of office, not the creation of a better society' (Downs, 1957: 111). This blunt statement not only posits the primacy of office-seeking motives, but also acknowledges politicians may have different *personal* views. However, even if politicians have radical private preferences, the success of their careers depends on their *parties'* policies. A party leader who sticks dogmatically to his own private preferences may find himself forever out of office, or, more likely, removed by his colleagues.

This book employs the general assumption of politicians as office-seekers. It does not preclude politicians expressing support for radical policies to an intra-party audience in leadership or candidate selection contests. Instead, it provides a useful approximation of the incentive structures of politicians in the British parliamentary system during the period under review. These incentives were framed by a largely two-party system in the House of Commons. Moreover, the 'Westminster model' of a strong single-party executive governing a unitary state ensures that the only way of wielding real power is to win a general election.[5]

Rational choice theory is most fruitful when applied to types rather than tokens, involving specific institutional arenas in which political actors' goals are clear, and the rules of interaction are precise (Tsebelis, 1990: 32–3). Douglass North (1990: 3) defines institutions as 'the rules of the game in a society or, more formally, ... the humanly devised constraints that shape human interaction'. Rational individuals pursue their interests subject to institutional limitations. Furthermore 'those seeking to change an institution have some result in mind when they try to do so' (Alt and Shepsle, 1990: 2). Just as political actors have preferences over policy, they also have preferences over institutions because the latter present alternative utility streams: an actor may have more chance of achieving his goals under institution A than institution B. Rational choice institutionalism is thus concerned with the related questions of equilibrium within institutions and equilibrium institutions (ibid.).[6]

The remainder of the present book fleshes out this approach to institutions to explain why different actors in the Labour Party had divergent preferences over its structure. It argues that the existence of party organisations *per se* reflects the mutual interdependence, but conflicting preferences, of elected politicians and party members. The argument is built on simple assumptions about how different types of actors interact with each other in institutional settings. An important component is the spatial, or 'Downsian' model of party competition. Given the importance of this model for the present work, and its recent invocation by Labour-studies specialists, it is worth examining briefly.

The Downsian model and the study of the Labour Party

The Downsian model of two-party competition provides the backdrop to the exchange model of party organisation developed in Chapter 2.[7] The model is positive, explaining what is, rather than what ought to be. Supporters of rational choice theory commend it for explaining and analysing, rather than merely describing and judging (Shepsle and Bonchek, 1997: 5–35). By contrast, much work in the Labour-studies literature is informed by strong normative commitments. This observation most clearly applies to the various Marxian analyses of the Labour Party, which bemoan its failure to become a vehicle for socialism, and condemn its conservatism *vis-à-vis* the existing political and social order (Elliott, 1993; Miliband, 1972; Nairn, 1964). Labour's recent modernisation has spurred a fresh wave of academic assaults from the left on the party's leadership (Hay, 1994, 1999; Taylor, 1997). Even Robert McKenzie's (1964, 1982) famous analysis of the distribution of power in the Labour Party was informed by the normative belief that parties' policies should not be determined by extra-parliamentary bodies, such as Labour's annual conference. The present book offers no normative recommendations. Instead, it explains why coalitions of actors in the Labour Party undertook organisational changes. The focus is on the 'how, what and why' of party change rather than the 'should or should not'.

Nevertheless, some critics of rational choice theory claim it is irredeemably tainted by an ideological association with the new right (Self, 1993). There is widespread suspicion of rational choice theory in the Labour-studies literature, particularly in relation to the Downsian model, which is seen as informing Labour's electoral strategy in the 1990s. As Colin Hay (1999: 76) observes, '[a] quite startling range of authors have ... been impressed by the similarities of Labour's "politics of catch-up", with its studious targeting of the "median voter", and the Downsian logic of electoral rationality and/or expediency'. However, this recognition of the model's importance is usually filled with dismay and regret. More often than not, the Downsian label is applied disapprovingly, as Labour is condemned for pusillanimity or even treachery. The Downsian model is seen as a siren song to seduce the leaders of socialist parties into abandoning progressive policies. How sympathetic should we be to these fears?

The Downsian two-party model is an informal statement of Duncan Black's (1958) more rigorous median-voter theorem. The latter shows that if the members of a group have single-peaked preferences, the ideal point of the median voter has an empty winset.[8] One of Downs' contributions was to relate informally the importance of the median voter to two-party electoral competition. His model consists of two types of actors, voters and parties (the latter coterminous with politicians), with parties offering policy promises in exchange for citizens' votes. Voters have single-peaked policy-preference schedules, which are mapped along a unidimensional ideological scale. The latter is based on attitudes towards government control of the economy, with leftists in favour of nationalisation, and rightists preferring free markets. (Present-day versions of the model would map attitudes to taxation and government spending, with leftists preferring more of each and rightists less.) Downs assumed voters are 'normally distributed' along this scale, with most in the political centreground, though there is nothing to rule out voter distributions skewed to the left or right. Parties are concerned solely with the aim of winning governmental office, with policies being means to an end: '[p]arties formulate policies in order to win elections rather than win elections in order to formulate policies' (Downs, 1957: 28). Downs assumed politicians are *vote-maximisers* though it is better to view them as *office-seekers* or *vote-seekers*, pursuing only as many votes as are needed to win an election.[9] Figure 1.1 depicts two parties, A and B, each seeking to win a majority

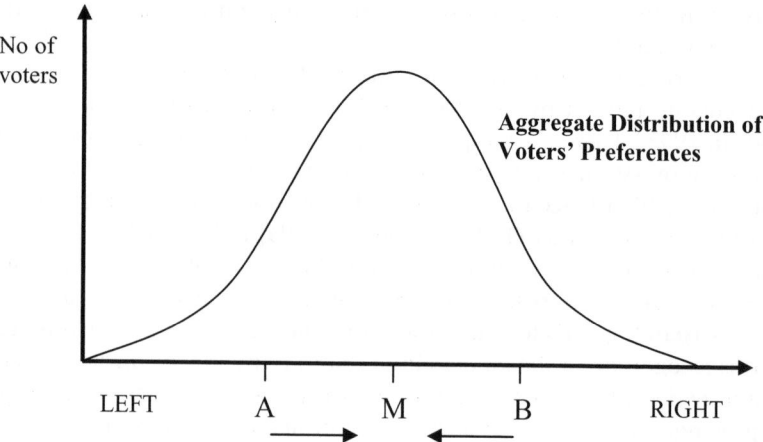

Figure 1.1   Downsian Model of Party Competition

of votes. Each voter supports the party nearest him in policy space. Whichever party captures the median voter (M) will win the election. Each party can thus steal a competitive advantage by moving closer than its opponent to M, and in equilibrium they converge at this point.

The parties converge because point M has an empty winset. It is possible for a party to win the election even if it does not occupy point M, provided that the other party is even further away from M. However, most discussions of the 'pure' Downsian model assume the parties converge at M. It is this equilibrium result that has worried, among others, many critics of Labour's electoral strategy under Blair.

Such fears and hostility are misplaced. It is possible for a theory to be used as intellectual cover for a political programme, but that fact alone is not sufficient to damn the theory. Moreover, it is unfair to claim that Downs advised that parties *should* adopt centrist policies. In fact, the model (when formalised) is purely axiomatic, stating that if a given set of axioms is satisfied (two parties, unidimensional scale, single-peaked preferences, proximity voting, and so on), parties will converge on the median-voter position (Barry, 1991: 216). The model does not offer predictions for given countries' political systems, not least because its assumptions are so pared-down. Relaxing any of them can create alternative outcomes. Extensions of the model assuming incomplete information have generated equilibria in which parties diverge: trusted and credible extremists can sometimes defeat untrusted moderates (Hinich and Munger, 1997: 122–7), and less trusted candidates can harm their prospects by shifting from extreme to moderate positions (Berger et al., 2000). Neither does the Downsian model provide normative advice on electoral strategy. In this book, it is used as an analytical device that helps us understand why Labour's parliamentary leaders have usually pursued moderate policies.

The confusion of positive and normative elements pervades the whole of Hay's critique of the model and its impact on Labour. His caution about what he revealingly calls 'the dangers of Downsianism' (Hay, 1999: 102) throws into relief the normative content of the term – a debased strategy of selling out socialist principles in the search for votes. Hay discusses Downs' book as if it were entitled, 'How to Win Elections: A User's Manual'. It is not. The apparent belief that Downs is offering prescriptive advice to politicians underlies Hay's assertion that although the Downsian model is a useful description of Labour's electoral strategy in the 1990s, it fails to explain that strategy. From Hay's perspective, to concede that the model explains Labour's centrist shift is tantamount to endorsing that shift.

The critique of the Downsian model by Labour-studies specialists entails a number of points, two of which are considered briefly. One criticism is that it is too simplistic to assume politicians are office-seekers. Many radical critics might agree that a particular leader was 'motivated by the desire for power, prestige, and income', as Downs puts it, but their objection would be that leaders of socialist parties *should not* be so shallow. Instead, they should argue their case and win support for socialist policies.

However, viewing politicians as policy-seekers has little impact on the two-party Downsian model because even here parties experience a centripetal pull (Barry, 1978: 149–50; Calvert, 1985). Assume the party leaders positioned their respective parties at their ideal policy points towards the left and right extremes of the policy continuum. The leader of the leftist party would have an incentive to shift marginally towards the median voter because, although it is a small distance from his preferred position, it is enough to defeat the rightist party, whose policies are detested by leftists. Similarly, the leader of the rightist party would shift closer towards the median voter, and at the limit the two parties would be in equilibrium at the median-voter position. Thus, whether as office-seekers or policy-seekers, the competitive dynamics in a two-party system are the same.

A second response of the critics is to attack the assumption of fixed preferences. Most rational choice theorists assume fixed preferences to give their models predictive power. If preferences were not fixed, any change from the *status quo ante* could be 'explained' by a change in preferences (Becker, 1986: 110). If a party loses votes in an election, it could be depicted as a (largely unobservable and unmeasurable) change in voter preferences, rather than as a change in the parties' relative policy positions. This explanation is unsatisfactory. Assuming fixed preferences helps stabilise models. Even so, few rational choice theorists believe preferences are permanently fixed, and the trend has been to endogenise preference formation (Dunleavy and Ward, 1991; Grafstein, 2000; Ward, 2000; cf. Stubager, 2003).

The fixity of preferences is a prime target of Hay and illustrates his confusion of axioms and normative prescriptions. Hay does not explain the purpose of assuming fixed preferences, instead criticising what he sees as its normative content – that parties should pander to voters' prejudices, a process he terms, following Patrick Dunleavy and Hugh Ward (1991), 'preference accommodation'. Hay wants parties to lead, not follow public opinion. This 'preference-shaping' strategy entails winning votes with the force of argument.

At this point, some clarifying remarks need to be made about these two terms. In a hostile assessment of the Downsian model's applicability to British politics, Richard Heffernan (2001: 101–27) reaches a similar conclusion to Hay: parties have the ability to shape voters' preferences, which implies they need not converge in the political centre-ground. Heffernan seeks to make a 'clear distinction' between preferences and choices: 'an elector casts a vote for one party rather than another not necessarily because that party meets his or her preference but because that is the choice made available to them'. He adds, 'always a preference is constrained by the choices that can be made' (2001: 104–5). Quite so, yet rational choice models assume not that an actor always chooses his ideal preference, but merely that he chooses *from among the available options* the one he ranks highest in his preference schedule. This choice is clearly the one facing voters in Downs' spatial model, because there are innumerable voters but only two parties, each adopting one point on the ideological continuum. Those voters whose ideal policies are not offered by either party (which implies the vast majority of voters) must choose between the more preferred of two positions, neither of which represent their ideal points.

The misleading term 'preference accommodation' may be the source of the confusion. This term is assumed to capture the electoral strategy of a conventional 'Downsian' party, whereas preference shaping refers to parties' alteration of voters' preferences. Preference shaping involves changing the *aggregate* distribution of voters' preferences, but preference accommodation is the process whereby parties seek to satisfy the preference of the median voter only. 'Preference accommodation' is an unhappy choice of term, not least because all parties accommodate preferences – those of the voters whose position they happen to share (which might not be the median voter).

The 'preference-shaping-versus-preference-accommodating' debate in Labour studies is normative.[10] From the perspective of individuals with radical policy preferences, a strategy that involves 'accommodating' the preferences of centrist voters will involve a 'betrayal'. Only a strategy that changes preferences will secure voter support for radical policies. Interestingly, in their first survey of the opinions of Labour's individual members in the 1990s, Seyd and Whiteley (1992: 167) suggested that those members on the most radical wing of the party, the so-called 'hard left', were most set against electoral compromise. The authors compared the attitudes of the hard left to all other members. Faced with the statement, 'The Labour Party should adjust its policies to capture the middle ground of politics', which is the essence of so-called 'Downsianism', the hard left were six times more likely than other party members to disagree strongly (36 per cent to 6 per cent). They were also more likely to agree strongly that the party should stick to its principles (52 per cent compared with 19 per cent for other members). The reason for these differences is that 'members of the hard left have their own distinctive analysis of Labour Party electoral strategy' (Seyd and Whiteley 1992: 166). This strategy involves viewing politics as revolving round class struggle, so Labour should adopt policies favourable to workers. Manual workers are a minority of the electorate in Britain, as elsewhere, creating problems for electoral strategies based on class mobilisation (Przeworski and Sprague, 1986). In response, many socialists have argued white-collar workers should be classified as working class. Given the considerable differences between blue- and white-collar workers, only an aggressive 'preference shaping' electoral strategy would induce a majority of voters to identify themselves as members of the working class and supporters of the hard left.

Here is not the place to discuss the feasibility of such a project, though it would probably require industrial mobilisation on an enormous scale, involving increased white-collar unionisation and/or widespread fear of job losses. The point is that in a two-party system, radicals on both the left and the right face a struggle. 'Preference shaping' offers the hope of overcoming these problems, though even then it is easier for governments than oppositions to achieve, because the former have access to the resources of the state. Shifting policies towards the centreground usually involves fewer political costs and promises speedier electoral rewards. It is this reality that the Downsian model recognises, rather than opposing radical policies on normative grounds.

Neither Hay nor Heffernan fully define what they mean by 'preference shaping', and each fails to distinguish it from 'persuasion' (see Dowding, 2003: 321, n.26). In Dunleavy and Ward's initial discussion, preference shaping generally referred to the systematic transformation of individuals' material *interests* and the very structure of society, as through the policy of selling council houses in the 1980s. However, both Hay and Heffernan usually appear to be referring to persuasion, which involves furnishing voters with *information* rather than altering their material incentives. Thus, Hay (1999: 60) describes preference shaping as 'the politics of advocacy', while Heffernan (2001: 121) claims the preference shaping model 'assumes that voters can be persuaded to alter their electoral preferences'.

With these clarifications in mind, we can usefully employ the Downsian model in the analysis of Labour's modernisation. It provides the backdrop to the intra-party exchange model developed in the next chapter. Internal exchange implies a check on vote-seeking behaviour because policy-seeking party members are often less ready than politicians to trade-off policy for votes. Nevertheless, the Downsian model alerts us to the fundamental competitive dynamics that characterise two-party systems and provides the context in which intra-party conflicts are set.

Sociological explanations of the Labour Party

A standard criticism of rational choice theory is that it is too simplistic to see individuals as the embodiment of *homo economicus*. From this perspective, viewing actors as utility-maximisers pursuing their self-interest involves omitting too many important factors, such as social norms, values and culture; a more 'sociological' approach is therefore required. In fact, there are a number of rational choice analyses of these phenomena. David Kreps (1990) offers an account of corporate culture (which can, in principle, be generalised to non-corporate settings) in which conventions and reputations provide imperfectly-informed actors with common focal points on which they can co-ordinate their activity. Ken Binmore's (1998) game-theoretic account of the social contract views norms of fairness as equilibria of repeated games. Dennis Chong (2000) combines individuals' material incentives with their social and moral dispositions, seen as psychological and social investments acquired within groups over the course of time, to produce a model of value formation and change. Introducing incentives into the discussion of norms and values gives the rational choice approach an advantage over sociological and psychological theories in explaining how and why such deeply-rooted phenomena can change. The difficulty of explaining change within a purely norms-based framework is evident in the Labour-studies literature. This 'sociological' approach is closely identified with Lewis Minkin's book, *The Contentious Alliance* (1992), which, according to Eric Shaw (2003: 180), shows '*homo sociologicus* ... has much more to offer than does *homo economicus*' in the study of the Labour Party. Minkin's book is probably the most frequently-cited source on the party-union link, so it is worth examining his argument.

Minkin's explanation of party-union relations

Minkin's aim was to explode the myth, as he saw it, that trade union leaders (or, 'barons', as they were described by Labour's opponents) run the Labour Party. This 'baronial thesis' was enjoying a revival in the late-1970s and early-1980s, as the unions assumed a more central role in intra-party affairs. However, Minkin argued that although the unions theoretically possess great power in the party, they have usually been inhibited from using it: '[r]estraint has been the central characteristic of the trade union-Labour Party relationship' (1992: 26). Restraint was essential because, according to Minkin, four major factors regularly caused tensions in the party-union relationship. First, ideological differences arose over the meaning of 'socialism', and how it related to economic policy in particular. Second, despite being formed to defend trade union interests, Labour usually found itself advancing the national interest, especially in government. Third, social tensions marked relations between a working-class union leadership and an increasingly middle-class parliamentary Labour Party (PLP). Fourth, the party and the unions frequently pursue different strategies because they have different functions. Labour must appeal beyond trade union members if it is to win elections, while the unions need to protect their members' interests under governments of all political colours, necessitating a degree of mutual detachment (1992: 9–22, 105–48).

These tensions might have been terminal were it not for the willingness of party and union leaders to adopt a flexible approach to their management. Minkin claims this accommodation led to an intra-party power structure that emphasised the distinction of functional roles between party and unions, and which was regulated by a complex series of informal norms of behaviour, or what he rather confusingly calls 'rules'. Although rarely codified, the 'rules' were a powerful restraining force on union domination. According to Minkin, the 'rules' derived from the long-standing trade union values of 'freedom', 'democracy', 'unity' and 'solidarity', and the 'working principle' of 'priority'.

First, 'freedom' reflected the union movement's desire for autonomy from the state, as expressed in the right to strike, collective bargaining, and other union prerogatives. In the Labour Party, it led to a 'rule' that Labour governments should do nothing to hinder the unions' pursuit of their industrial interests; the unions, in turn, should not use their financial and constitutional power to sanction the party if it fails to deliver the policies they want.

Second, 'democracy' entailed a deep respect for majority decision-making, particularly in a delegatory form, and was expressed in affection for the party conference. However, it had to be squared with the conventions of British parliamentary democracy, so a 'rule' permitted the PLP to choose the 'time and method' of giving effect to conference decisions (see Chapter 3). The unions should not use their control of the party constitution to bring the PLP into line with union demands. There were also 'rules' prohibiting the unions using financial sponsorship to influence MPs' voting behaviour in parliament, or of mentioning sponsorship in selection contests (see Chapter 5).

Third, labour-movement 'unity' reflected the desirability of consensus, essential for collective action. 'Rules' derived from it limited factionalism in the party. Thus unions should be represented by size in party decision-making bodies, irrespective of their ideological leanings, which meant the big unions always voted for each other's candidates in national executive committee (NEC) elections. The NEC's union section was a loyalist bloc for the PLP leadership, intervening only when vital union interests were threatened.

Fourth, 'solidarity' between unions, especially when in dispute with employers, was a *sine qua non* of trade unionism. In the Labour Party, this value was expressed in the mutual support that PLP and union leaders offered to one another. For the unions, it meant playing a stabilising role, as with the 'rule' of ballast, whereby the unions sheltered the PLP from the left at the party conference and on the NEC.

Fifth, supplementing these values was the 'working principle' of 'priority', which encouraged pragmatism in the quest for union objectives. Unions adopted 'a trade union perspective' rather than a factional one in their dealings with the party, and focused on goals that were immediately attainable in the political sphere rather than utopian aspirations.

The party's 'rules', and the values from which they sprang, were maintained through the continual socialisation of union officials and politicians. According to Minkin, they are essential for understanding how the party-union link survived the powerful forces that buffeted it for a century. The 'baronial thesis' suggests that self-interested union leaders should intervene in party affairs and impose their preferred policies. However, the system of shared norms and values encouraged them to cede autonomy to the party and to exercise self-restraint, even when it harmed their interests. In turn, the PLP was always expected to consult with the unions and not to attack their vital interests (Minkin, 1992: 27–48).

Assessing Minkin's sociological framework

Any fair-minded reading of Minkin's book would have to conclude that it succeeds in its principal goal of demolishing the 'baronial thesis' of power in the Labour Party. It is clear from the mass of information Minkin presents that the unions do not 'run the Labour Party', in the sense of imposing policies on the PLP. Restraint does indeed appear to have long been an important feature of the party-union link. The question is whether Minkin's sociological analysis provides the right explanation. Problems arise over the causal role of values, the conservative bias in his 'rules', and the ambivalent position of interests in his account.

Explaining outcomes in terms of social values is notoriously tricky (Barry, 1978: 89–98). Assuming that Minkin has correctly identified the labour movement's values, it must still be demonstrated that they explain the existence of the restraining 'rules'. There is nothing inherently wrong in saying that values have a causal effect; it is another matter entirely to say that they enjoy explanatory primacy. Values must be reproduced, and although socialisation is one aspect of this process, it is not the only one. The performance of the PLP, especially in government, must surely play a significant part in the reproduction, or otherwise, of the labour movement's shared values.[11] If Labour governments deliver benefits to the unions, the effect will be to foster among union members and officials values conducive to restraint in the party-union link, as well as increasing support for restraint and for the link in general. A successful performance by Labour in office can thus help maintain the link and restraint within it, both directly, and indirectly through strengthening values. Equally, if Labour governments antagonise the unions, the link may be damaged and restraint can break down, as it did under the Wilson government in 1969 and the Callaghan government in 1978–79. If this general approach is accepted, it is clear that values are part of the explanation but not all of it, or even most of it; governmental performance seems to be the crucial factor (which itself depends on economic conditions and other factors). Minkin does not show that his labour-movement values are either necessary or sufficient to explain party-union restraint. Indeed, one could as easily claim that the party's values and 'rules' were the result of the historical need for restraint. Both party and unions had an interest in stability, which would have helped the growth of values conducive to it.

There are further questions about the values Minkin claims are important for understanding the origin of the 'rules'. Minkin introduced his four values and the principle of 'priority' to link the political and industrial wings of the movement (see Minkin, 1997: 286–7). However, he does not provide a satisfactory account of how the politicians are inculcated into these values, especially as the PLP has become more middle class, with little or no direct experience of working-class culture and trade unionism. Even on the union side, the restraining 'rules' often have tenuous connections to their parent values. It is one thing to say unions want autonomy in industrial relations, but another to claim the originating value of 'freedom' also encourages unions to permit autonomy to the PLP, and that it crystallised into a 'rule' prohibiting unions from using intra-party sanctions to punish Labour governments. Similarly, is the 'rule' of union ballast such an obvious expression of 'solidarity', or a rational realisation that the left would lead the party to electoral oblivion?

In contrast to the set of general values and principles Minkin outlines, the 'rules' he identifies are more akin to social norms, being (negatively) prescriptive. A trap to be avoided in norms-based explanations is that of using as evidence for a norm's existence observations of behaviour the norm is supposed to explain, which is simply to offer a redescription of that behaviour (Barry, 1978: 90–1; Chong: 2000: 36). Not all of the 'rules' are fallacious in this way; however, Minkin occasionally observes an instance of restraint and concludes there must be an unwritten 'rule' explaining it, rather than demonstrating long-standing normative commitments. His 'rule' against the unions unilaterally altering Labour's constitution falls into this category, as does the 'rule' of ballast.

A second problem with sociological models is their tendency to focus excessively on stability. If individuals act out pre-assigned roles, internalising values and following norms, how do we explain change? Exogenous shocks account for some changes, but norms-based models tend to provide less room for self-interested behaviour bringing about change in a deliberate way (Chong, 2000: 36–7; 229). Minkin holds an ambivalent position on change in the Labour Party. On the one hand, there are the four destabilising factors discussed earlier, which can create tensions in the party-union link, leading to change. On the other, Minkin has a tendency, repeated throughout *The Contentious Alliance*, to play down the extent of changes from the *status quo ante*. The clearest example is his attempt to minimise the role of the unions in the left's campaign to reform Labour's institutions after the fall of the Callaghan government. Minkin claims that given the closeness of the votes at the party conference on the left's reforms, the *union* majority must have been slim or non-existent, with the CLPs strongly in favour of the changes (1992: 195). Yet the CLPs controlled only 10 per cent of the conference votes, compared with 90 per cent for the unions. No measure could get through the conference without a considerable degree of union backing. To obtain this support for such a vital shift in power away from MPs in the aftermath of the election defeat of 1979 was a clear indication that restraint had broken down. If this move does not count as an attempt to 'sanction the PLP', it is hard to see what would.

Minkin was right to identify the importance of restraint in the party-union link, but he occasionally ignores the extent to which it was a contingent, not a permanent, feature of the relationship.[12] The effect is to give his account of the link a conservative bias. Something else must explain the changes that periodically occur. In a recent defence of Minkin, Shaw claims change can be understood within his analytical framework:

> [O]rganisations can be conceived as arenas characterised by the ongoing processes of negotiation and bargaining, where 'rules', roles and relationships constantly evolve in response to shifts in the balance of power, in the pattern of political alignments, and in the face of conflicting interests and priorities and environmental shocks. (Shaw, 2003: 177)

Yet this description sounds more like instrumental rationality and the clash of interests. 'On-going processes of negotiation and bargaining' are not what we usually associate with norms and values, and if the latter 'constantly evolve in response to shifts in the balance of power', they are merely descriptive concepts rather than analytical ones. Norms tend to survive only when there are clear incentives to follow them, such as the willingness of individuals to enforce them, and the unavailability of strong competing norms (Chong, 2000: 45–75). The latter may depend on whether norms are reasonably aligned with individuals' material interests. The experience of the last decade has been that the unions' incentives for restraint have gradually eroded, as the Blair government has shown a willingness to confront 'vested interests' in the public sector. The old inhibitions are breaking down on both sides, with some unions cutting funds to the party – a considerable breach of the old 'rules' (see Chapter 8).

Minkin's attitude to the role of interests in the party-union link is also rather ambivalent.[13] He acknowledges that differences of interest exist between the party and the unions, but his emphasis is on how the 'rules' held the subsequent tensions in check. For Minkin, the unions' restraint in the party vitiates the claim that their behaviour is instrumentally rational, a position he equates with the 'baronial thesis'. If union leaders were not socialised into the 'rules', and acted solely in their self-interest, they would dictate Labour's policies. Restraint would no longer be the principal feature of the party-union link.

Jon Elster (1989: 98) claims that norms, on the strictest definition of the term, are not instrumental: people follow them, not to bring about outcomes, but because they have been socialised to see such behaviour as 'proper'. Minkin's 'rules' of restraint fall into this category. Restraint is a valued end in itself. However, Minkin's own discussion of the party's values and 'rules' suggests that they do have instrumental purposes. Freedom in the industrial sphere is beneficial for the unions; union ballast for the PLP leadership stops the left imposing unpopular policies; fixing union votes for NEC elections prevents outbreaks of damaging factionalism. If restraint stabilises the party and enhances its electoral prospects, the inhibiting 'rules' are rational means to an end. An important aim of the present book is to demonstrate, *pace* Minkin, that union restraint has an instrumental purpose, and that other peculiar features of the party-union link, such as block voting, are also rooted in rationality.

Conclusion

This chapter has set out some of the theoretical building blocks of the present work. The defence offered for the rational choice approach is that it generates interesting questions and equips us with the tools to answer them. One of the principal arguments of this book is that the traditional organisational structure of the Labour Party and the changes it has undergone in the last twenty years are best understood using rational choice theory. Specifically, Labour's institutional links with the trade unions are usefully conceived in terms of self-interested political exchange. Both the politicians and the unions see tangible benefits in the liaison, and if these benefits are eroded it becomes more likely that one or other side will prefer to end the institutional relationship. Much of this book is about how the relationship has transmuted as the party suffered multiple electoral defeats.

The examination of the Labour Party begins in Chapter 3, but first it is necessary to set out the theoretical framework for understanding internal relations in political parties. The next chapter constructs a political exchange model of party organisation and party change.

2
Political Exchange and Party Organisation

Despite political parties being one of the most important organisational forms in modern societies, the rational choice literature on party organisation is underdeveloped. There is a classic literature on party organisation dating from a century ago (Ostrogorski, 1902; Michels, 1962), together with important later contributions (Duverger, 1964; Epstein, 1980; Panebianco, 1988). Yet, significant as these works are, there is still a dearth of work on the micro-foundations of parties. This chapter sketches such micro-foundations. The model developed follows the 'exchange' approach, in which politicians are assumed to offer policy promises to activists in exchange for campaign resources. Parties as organisations have changed enormously over the past century, so our models must be able to account for party change. In this respect, exchange models are particularly useful.

The present chapter begins with a justification for using the exchange approach rather than other models of party organisation, and describes the basic exchange between activists and politicians. The next two sections demonstrate how transaction costs create the need for formal organisations. Parties' internal institutions can give politicians the necessary autonomy from activists to win elections. The final substantive section outlines an exchange model of party change.

Political exchange and party organisation

To analyse organisational change in the Labour Party, we need a model of party organisation and party change. The most common approach is to take organisational ideal-types and relate them to historical periods in the development of democracy. The main types in this 'developmental' model (Maor, 1997: 99–113) are the cadre, mass, catch-all, electoral-professional and cartel parties. The cadre party was prevalent in the era of restricted suffrage and consisted of small groups of elites lobbying for the support of other elites, out of public view. European socialists devised the mass party to mobilise working-class voters after the extension of the suffrage early in the twentieth century. The emphasis was on recruiting members who would finance the party through subscriptions and campaign for it. A branch structure enabled it to break the membership down into smaller, manageable units and eased socialists' collective action problem (Duverger, 1964). The catch-all, electoral-professional and cartel parties arose in the postwar period of prosperity and class dealignment. Catch-all parties abandoned ideological baggage, centralised power, downgraded individual members, appealed to voters across social classes and sought links with a variety of interest groups (Kirchheimer, 1966: 190). The electoral-professional party went further, developing capital-intensive campaign technologies and employing campaign professionals rather than relying on bureaucracies (Panebianco, 1988). The cartel party is the latest party form, arising in an era in which the basis of party competition is technocratic, with parties offering similar policies and competing on managerial expertise. Most parties find themselves in government before long, and politics becomes simply another profession rather than a means of pursuing social reform. Parties thus become a 'cartel', dividing the spoils of office among themselves (Katz and Mair, 1995: 16–23).

The developmental model provides useful comparisons for real parties. However, it is of limited use for analysing the minutiae of changes that took place in a single party over a twenty-year period, which is the task before us. A more fine-grained approach to the study of party organisation and party change is required. In this respect, the rival 'exchange' model of party organisation is particularly helpful. A principal argument of this book is that the internal organisation of parties, and their relationships with voters, is usefully comprehended in terms of political exchange, the exchange of votes and/or resources for policy promises. We need to be clear about what is meant by 'exchange'. Most democracies make it illegal for individuals, businesses or interest groups to pay directly for policies or other government decisions, and the UK is no different. British trade unions have occasionally been reprimanded by parliament for overstepping the mark, such as when seeking to instruct sponsored MPs how to vote. What is meant by 'political exchange' is something less formal but no less significant. It is the provision of resources in the hope (at minimum) or expectation (at best) that certain benefits will be delivered in return. Unlike economic contracts, a disinterested third party (the state) will not enforce political 'contracts', and political actors will rarely describe their deals as such. Enforcement is by means of either, refusing to provide more resources if past promises are broken, or alternatively, constructing intra-party institutions, as is shown later. There are other transaction costs attached to political exchange, including difficulties in measuring what is being exchanged, and problems caused by the fact that such exchanges are usually non-simultaneous, with votes, favours, donations and labour supplied now in return for promises of *future* benefits.

Nevertheless, exchange models shed light on the micro-foundations of political organisations and help explain why certain institutions arise. Political exchange is a feature of rational choice models of party competition. The Downsian model consists of voters and parties engaging in electoral exchange, in which policy promises are traded for votes. However, Downs did not examine exchanges that occur inside parties, between intra-party actors. Parties appear as 'black boxes' in his model, being cohesive teams of office-seekers rather than organisational complexes:

> [A] political party is a team of men seeking to control the governing apparatus by gaining office in a duly constituted election. By *team*, we mean a coalition whose members agree on all their goals instead of just part of them. (Downs, 1957: 25, emphasis in original)

Downs' intention was to explore the dynamics of party competition in a simplified setting, so he assumed away internal divisions in parties. However, opening up the 'black box' reveals that party organisation is a response to transaction costs that attend party-voter exchange, most notably, costs covering organisation, mobilisation, and the collection and transmission of information. Thus, parties have incomplete information about voters' preferences; hence the need for polling and focus groups. However, a party's most important activity is election campaigning, the pursuit of votes through persuasion and propaganda. The latter implies incomplete information among the voters, which parties can exploit. Voters have only a basic idea of party programmes, relying on free information from the mass media, using ideologies as information-economising devices, and seeking information cues from elites (Downs, 1957; Lupia and McCubbins, 1998). Party campaigning requires leaflets, posters, opinion polls, spin doctors and other professionals. To cover these costs (and others, such as transportation and rent), politicians need financial contributions and labour from their supporters. The extent of these costs gives individual politicians incentives to pool their resources in parties to surmount these otherwise considerable barriers to entry. Campaigning is costly but can exhibit economies of scale, and it is easier for politicians to raise funds as a group because greater numbers lend greater credibility (Laver, 1997: 85).

Party organisation is a response to the imperfections that characterise politician-voter exchange. However to persuade individuals and organisations to supply the money and labour required to campaign for votes, party leaders must offer incentives; in doing so, they create a new set of exchange relations.

Intra-party incentive structures

Since Downs' definition of a party is inadequate for the present study, we need an alternative one. Alan Ware offers the following:

> A political party is an institution that (a) seeks influence in a state, often by attempting to occupy positions in government, and (b) usually consists of more than a single interest in the society and so to some degree attempts to 'aggregate interests'. (Ware, 1996: 5)

This definition avoids assuming party members are united in their beliefs and goals. It also enables a distinction to be drawn between parties and interest groups. It does not, however, mention participation in elections, because it is intended to cover parties in one-party states, as well as liberal democracies. For present purposes, participation in competitive elections and the pursuit of government are essential attributes of parties. Combining these points produces a conception of parties as politicians and activists interacting within an institutional setting.

Exchange models of party organisation focus on exchange between politicians and activists, whereby activists agree to campaign for politicians to help them get elected, in return for policy concessions or other benefits. The most important exchange models are those of Joseph A. Schlesinger (1984) and Kaare Strøm (1990), both of which strongly inform the model developed here.[1] The remainder of this section assesses Schlesinger's model, which looks at incentives within parties. The following section turns to Strøm, who focuses on institutions. Throughout this chapter, the discussion of politician-activist exchange relates to a two-party system with a unidimensional ideological scale. The conclusions derived apply to systems conforming to these restrictions.

Schlesinger examines the organisational incentive structure of a party embedded in a two-party system, in which politicians are assumed to be office-seekers. His account is based on a distinction between parties and other types of organisation, such as firms, interest groups and bureaux.[2] He compares them in terms of three variables: (1) how they obtain key resources; (2) the nature of the organisation's principal output; (3) the mode of compensation of the organisation's participants. Parties and firms are similar on the first of these counts, since both obtain key resources through market exchange. Parties measure their success by the market criterion of winning elections. By contrast, interest groups have greater freedom to define their own goals and standards of success. They can lobby governments for particular policies, and if they are successful, they can turn their attention to other goals. They might put up candidates in an election to target certain incumbents for removal, but winning elections is not the *raison d'être* of an interest group. Whereas parties are office-seekers, interest groups are policy-seekers. Similarly, bureaux obtain resources from governments, maintaining their existence if they convince governments to continue funding them.

Thus parties and firms both need to be competitive, but in two other respects they differ. On the nature of their respective outputs, firms produce private goods, but parties, like interest groups and bureaux, seek to supply collective goods. Private goods are divisible, easy to measure, and individuals who refuse to pay for them can be excluded from consuming them. Revenues generated from sales are used to compensate directly the firm's workers, who are recruited in the labour market. Given the material incentives firms provide to their workers, the latter can happily produce their employer's output without having any desire to consume it. By contrast, parties produce collective goods (policies), which cannot be divided among individuals, which are not easily measurable, and which cannot be restricted to those who pay for or produce them. Collective goods generate no revenue, which implies that parties must recruit labour (and obtain financial donations) by offering non-financial incentives.[3] Whereas politicians receive social and material benefits from attaining office, activists receive solidary and purposive incentives in return for their voluntary labour (Clark and Wilson, 1961).[4] Solidary incentives include such factors as friendship and status, which are social-outcome benefits, though they can also be negative, such as avoiding ridicule and ostracism. Purposive benefits are the payoffs an individual receives from seeing certain policies implemented or ideological goals achieved.[5] As Schlesinger observes, these benefits are collective and thus confront the free-rider problem. Those individuals attracted to parties by purposive incentives tend to be the young and inexperienced, who lack sufficient information to be able to calculate the relative costs and benefits of joining groups. Such incentives lack staying power and there is likely to be a high rate of membership turnover, as those who gain experience realise their marginal influence and quit the party, being replaced by new recruits. Those individuals who stay have usually become attracted to the social benefits of membership. Nevertheless, the existence of purposive incentives means that party members, unlike employees in a business firm, have preferences over the type of output their organisation produces (Demsetz, 1990). They thereby have an interest in the institutional configuration of power in the party, because it partly determines which policies are adopted.

This point leads to Schlesinger's third variable, the mode of compensation offered by the organisation. Firms pay their workers monetary rewards, but parties generally do not pay their members and activists; on the contrary, they look to their members to supply the party with finance. Direct payment allows firms to recruit workers from the full-time labour market and exercise control over them once they are hired, making sure they comply with the conditions of their employment. Moreover, it allows the firm to rationalise its workforce, producing the most efficient division of labour. By contrast, parties recruit members from the leisure market, and there is the constant risk they may be diverted by other pursuits. The absence of financial remuneration prevents parties from controlling their low-level personnel to the extent that firms do. Party members' contributions are voluntary, so they cannot be ordered around under the threat of dismissal. Most members are likely to make no active contribution at all, other than paying their annual subscriptions. Party leaders are thus prevented from rationalising their organisations as efficiently as entrepreneurs. Perhaps most important, parties must offer their members other rewards, namely, policies and candidates. Since the latter are a party's principal output, its competitiveness in the electoral market may be damaged if the members' preferences are not aligned with the median voter's.

Schlesinger's account of incentive structures in parties forms a central part of the exchange model deployed in this book. Empirical studies of British Labour Party members found that incentives of a broadly purposive nature were the most important reason members gave for joining the party. Seyd and Whiteley (1992; see also 2002) devised a general incentives model of party membership, fairly similar to that described above. They identified three classes of reasons for joining a party: rational (collective and selective incentives, whether process- or outcome-oriented), altruistic and social norms. *Inter alia*, they claim 42 per cent of Labour members joined for altruistic reasons, and a quarter joined for collective incentives (positive and negative). However, the distinction between the two is rather hazy. Collective incentives referred to support for certain policies, or a desire to defeat the Conservatives. The most important altruistic motives for joining were a belief in socialism, to help the working class, and to create an equal society (1992: 74). Both categories relate to ideology and policy, and fall under the heading of purposive incentives; in which case, two-thirds of Labour's members had broadly purposive motives for joining.

Schlesinger discounts the long-term significance of purposive incentives because they are collective, and he invariably assumes office-seeking politicians face few impediments from activists (1984: 387–8). There would appear to be little 'exchange' taking place inside parties, certainly over policies. Yet this conclusion sits uneasily with the important recruiting role of purposive incentives and the ubiquity of ideological struggles inside real-life parties. Purposive incentives can be accorded an important role in rational choice models once we realise the impact they have in combination with social incentives. The latter conform to Mancur Olson's (1971) broad definition of selective incentives, as private benefits that accrue only to joiners, because only by participating in a party's activities can individuals secure friendship, status and the opportunity to meet like-minded people (see Chong, 1991: 31–72; 2000). In his critique of exchange models, Ware (1992: 81–3) complains that they sideline social incentives, yet there is no reason why the latter should not be integrated into the model. Social incentives buttress purposive incentives. Theoretically, people may join a party just for social incentives, while having no sympathy for its policy goals, but they are unlikely to find friends in a party whose members are hostile to their own views (Chong, 1991: 34). Social incentives are important when a party is out of government and unable to implement policies, though their relative importance has diminished in the postwar period. In the era of the mass parties, many people joined parties for access to their cultural and social functions. Access to other sources of leisure, particularly through the mass media, has reduced the appeal of these types of clubs, yet party activists still benefit in the narrower sense of meeting like-minded people. Seyd and Whiteley (1992: 74) showed that nearly a quarter of Labour's members joined for selective process incentives, mainly of a social nature.

Social incentives are particularly important for *activist* retention. Negative social incentives can persuade activists to continue working hard for a party. Since activists are volunteers, they cannot be 'sacked' if they shirk, as employees can. Whereas employment contracts set out duties and penalties for unfulfilled obligations, party constitutions rarely detail the responsibilities of activists other than specifying an annual membership fee. There are never provisions setting out activist's duties. This lacuna is due to the collective goods output of parties and the voluntary nature of party membership. There seems to be nothing to stop activists from shirking on their labour contributions. However, negative social incentives, such as ridicule or ostracism from colleagues, may help control shirking. Those activists seeking to occupy elected positions in local parties will not want reputations for shirking. Social benefits are more likely to accrue in small groups, where individuals' efforts are noticed by others, so it is not surprising that much activism is organised locally. A branch structure breaks up a national collective action problem into thousands of small collective action problems, which can be overcome as social incentives and conditional cooperation flourish (Bendor and Mookherjee, 1987). Nevertheless, social incentives are most useful for existing activists. They do not accrue to inactive (and often fleeting) members, who normally comprise the majority of a party's membership. The activists form a self-selected core that dominates intermediate-level party structures.

Indeed, the relatively small numbers of individuals joining parties, and the even smaller number who become active, has led many political scientists to suggest that activists are different from most voters, and here we can see the true significance of purposive incentives. The most famous expression of this idea is John May's 'law of curvilinear disparity' (1973), which predicts that activists will be politically more radical than voters and politicians. May's law is based on two assumptions: first, party members can be horizontally divided along organisational fractures, and second, each subgroup's members face different incentives and receive different types of payoffs. The subdivision of the members is along a continuum ranging from low to high 'organisational status', with leaders filling high positions, activists holding intermediate positions, and the party's supporters occupying low positions. May claims there is a 'curvilinear disparity' of incentives and preferences between high-, intermediate- and low-status levels.

Politicians strive for material and social incentives, such as the financial rewards and status of holding office and power, whereas activists are attracted mainly by purposive incentives. Only the most zealous people will undertake the tedious administrative chores of local party organisations. To gain office, party leaders prefer moderate policies aligned with ordinary party supporters' preferences, whereas activists are more likely to have radical preferences, producing leftwing extremists in socialist parties and rightwing extremists in conservative parties (Figure 2.1).

May's law has been criticised on theoretical and empirical grounds, but some of its weaknesses stem from the model of party competition on which it is based. It is sometimes said that May's law is founded on the Downsian model (Iversen, 1994: 158), but this claim is not true; May assumes most voters are *pre-committed* to one or other party (1973: 139, n.1). Two recent tests of May's law (Iversen, 1994; Norris, 1995b) followed May in focusing on the preferences of parties' mean partisan supporters, and purported to show the lack of any great differential between these voters and party activists. However, reformulating May's schema on the Downsian model draws our attention away from partisan supporters and towards the median voter overall, since it is the latter that parties must capture. If a party attracts its activists from one side of the median voter divide, the median activist will always be more radical than the median voter, regardless of whether the activist body is dominated by extremists. It is, therefore, unnecessary to make strong psychological assumptions about activists (Kitschelt, 1989) to show they are radical.[6]

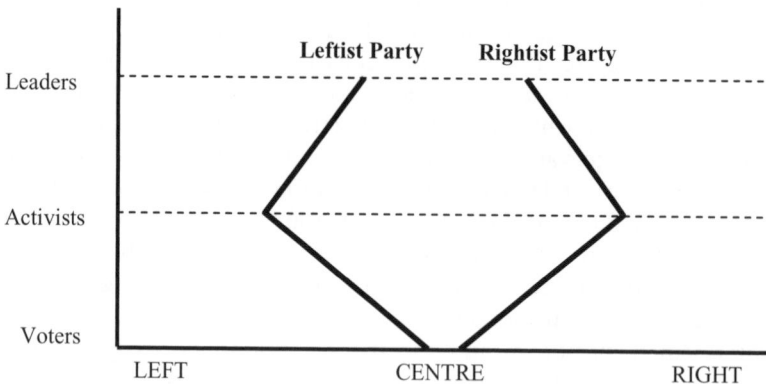

Figure 2.1   Curvilinear Disparity

Thus a genuine exchange model of parties stipulates two parallel spheres of political exchange: an internal sphere, between politicians and activists; and an external realm, between politicians and voters. *Pace* Schlesinger, the exchange of policy promises for labour/finance inside parties is important, and we cannot assume that such internal exchange is always trumped by politician-voter exchange.

At this point, two problems arise. First, politicians make the same policy promises to all activists, yet if an activist is not happy with these policies, he would appear to have little incentive to engage in the exchange. How can parties retain activists whose preferred policies are not adopted as party policy? Second, even if activists unite behind a policy, politicians face a choice between accommodating their preferences or the median voter's. Politicians might signal to activists that moderation could be abandoned once an election is won, but the risk remains they will renege. These problems are discussed next.

Party organisations as governance structures

The black box status of parties in rational choice models of party competition mirrors the way in which the firm was regarded as a production function in neo-classical economics.[7] Organisational economists' attacks on this conception of the firm point the way forward in reconceptualising parties. Oliver Williamson (1985) argues that firms are *governance structures*, in which some transactions are organised more efficiently than they would be in markets. The key elements are: (1) imperfect information, since not everything can be known in advance; (2) opportunism, which is 'self-interest seeking with guile'; (3) asset specificity, or, the degree to which investments made during the course of a trading relationship are dependent on the continuation of that particular relationship (Williamson, 1985: 30–2). Some exchanges can take place through the market, without the need for other institutions, because the goods being traded can easily be put to alternative uses if the exchange breaks down. Such exchanges involve unspecific assets. By contrast, highly specific assets are vulnerable to opportunistic behaviour in market exchange, such as *ex post* attempts to renegotiate contracts, so they are more efficiently organised in firms through a process of 'vertical integration'. It might be efficient for the supplier of components to a large manufacturer to situate its own premises nearby, but it could fall victim to *ex post* opportunism, and find it too expensive to switch to other manufacturers, because of higher transportation costs. Locating elsewhere would prevent economies being realised, so a buy-out by the manufacturer would solve the problem.

Political parties are similar to the Williamsonian conception of firms. Given the nature of the transaction costs attending exchange between politicians and activists, it is best organised within an institutional framework, providing it with durability. When politicians offer policy promises in return for a tangible resource, such as a vote or a donation, the exchange is normally non-simultaneous. This point (following Weingast and Marshall, 1988) forms the centrepiece of Strøm's exchange model of party organisation (1990). Strøm observes that when activists campaign for politicians, they usually supply their labour in the months and years before an election, after which they hope to obtain favourable policies from the newly-elected politicians (the same applies to financial donors). We may add that non-simultaneity also characterises politician-voter exchange, because when voters cast their votes, they do so hoping policy promises will be enacted in the future. In each case, politicians may face a *commitment problem*, because once voters or activists have supplied votes or finance/labour, the politicians could decide to renege on their promises. Thus, politicians might promise radical policies to activists to secure their campaigning efforts, but once in office they could renege. If activists anticipate this problem, they will undersupply campaign resources (Strøm, 1990: 576).

Commitment problems in non-simultaneous political exchange are similar to the problems caused by high asset specificity in economics (for example, donated labour or finance cannot be retrieved and reinvested elsewhere). In the case of politician-activist exchange, the solution is similar: to institutionalise exchange in a rules-based governance structure – a party. Strøm (1990: 577–9) lists three institutional means to promote credible commitments in parties: (1) intra-party democracy, which allows decentralised policy-making; (2) internal recruitment policies that favour existing activists, permitting them to pursue careers; (3) personnel accountability of leaders to members, enabling activists to replace shirking politicians. Each is a means, whether direct or indirect, by which activists can influence party policy and strategy, and limit politicians' autonomy.

Institutionalising exchange in organisational structures assigns enforcement powers to activists and reduces their fears of elite shirking. Institutions are efficient because they permit exchanges that otherwise might not take place, due to the transaction costs that attend them. Strøm also observes that the severity of commitment problems for politicians can vary according to the technology of campaigning that is deployed (1990: 575–6). Labour-intensive mass parties will be most affected, because they depend on activists, whereas capital-intensive parties, which rely on mass media campaigns, can comfortably afford shirking by activists. Other things equal, office-seeking politicians may thus prefer capital-intensive technology, because it eases their reliance on policy-seeking activists. This dynamic element in the exchange model is discussed later.

Political exchange between politicians and voters is mediated by institutions such as electoral systems, voter registration and term limits. However, formal organisations, whose functions and activities occur much more regularly than quadrennial election days, are not required, despite the non-simultaneity of politician-voter exchange. The frequency of exchange is an important dimension of asset specificity, with infrequent exchange less needful of costly governance structures (Williamson, 1985: 72–3). An individual voter has little incentive to form extra-electoral institutions to reduce the costs of exchange, because his vote is but one among millions and is cast once every four years. By contrast, activists make much higher political investments of labour and donations, which are wasted if politicians shirk; hence, institutional guarantees of control are required.

Strøm's model fits well with the incentives-based approach set out earlier, and forms an important part of the exchange approach adopted here. However, there would appear to be a problematical feature with the story thus far. The unstated assumption has been that activists seek a single set of policies from the politicians; after all, a party can occupy only a single position on the policy continuum at any point in time. However, activists' preferences range along the ideological spectrum, even if the distribution is usually skewed towards the radical end. In which case, why is one set of policies chosen rather than another? Furthermore, will those activists who do not receive their most favoured policies from politicians decide to exit? An exchange model must be able to address these problems.

Preference heterogeneity among activists

Simple exchange approaches focus on 'horizontal' divisions within parties, between the elite at the top and the activists at the bottom. This dichotomy has been dismissed by critics as too simple to capture all the important elements in parties (Kitschelt, 1989). However, recognising the existence of preference heterogeneity within the activist body allows us to go beyond simple exchange models, because a role is created for vertical (factional) fractures running through parties. While retaining the assumption that, on average, activists are more radical and politicians are more moderate, both sets of actors display a range of policy preferences. Moreover, elites and followers with similar preferences can band together in their own factions. Figure 2.2 presents a simple illustration of crosscutting hierarchical and factional divisions in a social democratic party. The moderate faction (shaded light) is a 'top-heavy' coalition, consisting of the bulk of the political leaders and a minority of party members. The radical faction is a 'bottom-heavy' coalition, mainly of ordinary members, together with a minority of the politicians. This example is a simplification, but according to May's law, it is the normal configuration in major parties. Moderate coalitions are top-heavy, whereas radical coalitions are bottom-heavy, though all coalitions exhibit tensions between leaders and followers.

Many authors use the concept of 'dominant coalition' to describe the subset of actors that controls a party (see Panebianco, 1988; Harmel and Janda, 1994). Rival factions challenge the dominant coalition or can be coopted into it. Vertical and horizontal cleavages crosscut because each faction includes politicians and activists. A subgroup of activists can attempt to control party policy by installing a subgroup of politicians. The excluded activists can, in turn, promote another subgroup of politicians. Likewise, politicians outside the dominant coalition will compete against it or be co-opted into it. A constraint on incumbent party leaders straying too far from the preferences of most activists is that they could be replaced by an alternative group of poli-

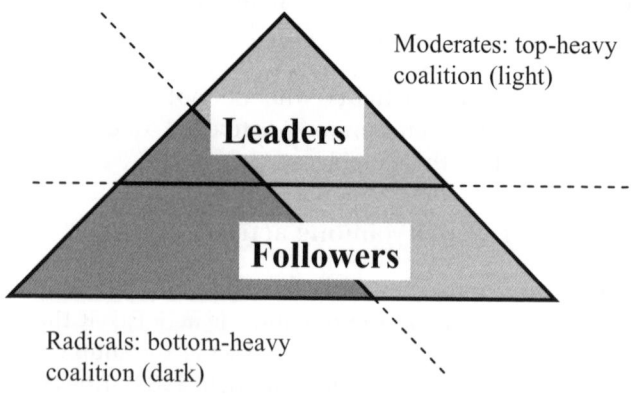

Figure 2.2   Horizontal (Hierarchical) and Vertical (Factional) Cleavages

ticians. The parliamentary body contains many politicians seeking to pursue their own interests, and the most effective way of doing that is to hold key leadership positions in the party. Rival politicians have incentives to monitor the leaders and expose shirking, in the hope of being called upon to replace the incumbents (see Laver, 1997: 68–88). Thus vertical cleavages are very important. However, major intra-party organs are usually in a hierarchical relationship. It is rare to find institutions deliberately divided by vertical fractures, with a body reserved for the party's left wing and another for its right. This latter configuration must be distinguished from horizontally divided bodies that happen to be dominated by one or other faction, such as local party branches dominated by radical activists. The assumption of horizontal cleavages inside party organisations, together with May's law, suggests there is a systematic tendency for party organs at given organisational levels to have particular distributions of preferences, such as parliamentary bodies dominated by moderates and local branches controlled by radicals.

These points raise questions about the institutionalisation of politician-activist exchange. Since a party's leadership can set party policy at only one point on the policy continuum, and given preference heterogeneity among activists, leaders cannot recruit activists by offering them all their most preferred policies. Why, then, would activists remain in a party if their preferred policies were not adopted, given their considerable investments of money and labour? The answer is that party institutions aggregate members' preferences and permit enduring preference heterogeneity among members and politicians. Through their procedural and voting rules, institutions agglomerate conflicting activist demands and prioritise a single policy position. Policy-making conferences allow activists to choose policies they collectively want party leaders to pursue. It necessarily means that not all activists are exchanging resources for promises of their most preferred policies; only some activists are in this position. Thus, rather than being directly offered policy promises *per se*, activists are instead offered *institutions*, as a means of *influencing* policy. Intra-party institutions serve as a substitute for the explicit exchange of policy promises for resources. This point is crucial because even if a subset of activists fails to secure its most preferred policies, it can use the institutions to try to change policies. These activists, therefore, have incentives to remain in the party, because they can fight again, building new coalitions and forcing new votes. Institutions also provide the means for activists to bargain with politicians, through their elected representatives on committees. Thus institutions and the distribution of preferences co-determine party policy. Finally, party constitutions usually set out procedures by which the institutions themselves can be changed, so that even if groups of activists are disadvantaged under current rules, they have incentives to stay, if they believe they could introduce more favourable institutions. Just as actors have different policy preferences, so they may have different institutional preferences.

In summary, Strøm's exchange model provides insights into how party organisation helps reduce commitment problems between politicians and activists. However, we identified a second function of institutions – to aggregate members' preferences – which forces us to reconceptualise the exchange approach to parties. Intra-party institutions for policy-making and candidate selection substitute for the explicit exchange of activists' resources for policy promises. However, the degree to which institutions can enforce deals is itself variable. Parties engage in electoral exchange with voters, which means that politicians must have some autonomy to navigate a course between the respective preferences of activists and voters.

Elite autonomy and the policy-votes trade-off

Politicians must offer popular policy promises to voters to win elections, and thereby satisfy their own office-seeking desires. Politicians also require activists if they are to win votes, and in return, activists require institutions through which they can pursue their own interests and exert influence over politicians. However, the median activist and the median voter have different preferences, presenting politicians with a strategic dilemma. Activists also face tough choices, since they know that their favoured policies can be implemented only if their party wins the support of the median voter. If they burden the party with radical policies, they may hand victory to the opposing party, whose policies they dislike even more. It is, therefore, too simplistic to regard them as pure policy-seekers, who have no interest in electoral considerations, though the rational choice literature normally views them this way (Robertson, 1976; cf. Kitschelt, 1989). Activists face a trade-off between doctrinal purity and electoral viability, so it is more realistic to regard them as *constrained* policy-seekers; in other words, there is a minimum acceptable probability of electoral success that any policy package must have before being adopted. (Determining such probabilities is likely to be achieved through trial and error.) Activists may voluntarily dilute their demands if their preferred policies fail to offer a high enough chance of electoral success. Intra-party institutions are important as sites of bargaining between politicians and activists. Whether in delegate conferences or committee meetings, politicians and activists' representatives can agree a policy package that wins votes, but which also contains some policies favoured by the activists. Such compromises are usually possible, given imperfect information among voters. Politicians can 'becloud their policies in a fog of ambiguity' (Downs, 1957: 136; see also Alesina and Cukierman, 1990; Shepsle, 1972) to capture centrists, while retaining the support of radicals. Such strategies are more likely to sway voters than better-informed activists.

Politicians need some autonomy from activists, with freedom to expound and interpret policies. Since electoral politics is characterised by constant flux, with new issues and events arising, politicians generally do require some – and prefer more – discretion over policy and its presentation. Institutional accountability and control mechanisms provide safeguards for activists, and may encourage them to permit autonomy. However, granting discretion carries risks for activists, because opportunistic politicians can exploit it to tweak policies through presentation. This possibility becomes likelier if the party gains office, because governments can use the resources of the state and are more independent of activists.

Many intra-party tensions can be traced back to elites' exploitation of their autonomy. This autonomy is greatest when politicians are in government, and we often find that activists attempt to impose stricter controls on politicians after their ejection from office, especially if there is a perception that the government reneged on promises to activists. It is costly for politicians to shift policy in the face of activist opposition, because it can cause 'voice' and 'exit' (Hirschman, 1970). 'Voice' ranges from public disquiet, to attempts to implement new policies or enforce institutional reforms. If a subgroup of activists realises it has no hope of changing party policy, its members may decide to exit. Voice and exit among activists are more likely to occur when politicians have considerable autonomy. If politicians were completely controlled by activists, the latter would bear full responsibility for the party's performance. However, if politicians have discretion to shift policy, activists are more likely to believe they are being ignored when policy does not reflect their own preferences. Politicians must weigh up the electoral costs of voice and exit. Voice is costly because voters are repelled by divided parties, though closing down channels of voice, such as embarrassing conferences, may encourage members to exit. Exit is costly if it leaves politicians with insufficient activists for campaigning: politicians may be compelled to offer new policies or institutional reforms to stem the outflow of activists or to attract new ones (see below).

Some degree of leadership autonomy is a reality in most parties, which reminds us that political institutions have distributive, as well as efficient, consequences. Party organisation is efficient if it provides politicians and activists with payoffs higher than they could achieve in non-institutionalised exchange. Party organisation offers activists some protection from the threat of shirking by politicians, and institutionalises the supply of resources to politicians. However, numerous institutional configurations are compatible with this constraint. Which will be chosen cannot be determined *a priori*, as it depends on the relative bargaining power of politicians and activists. Such disputes are distributional conflicts, as politicians and activists seek to maximise their payoffs.

If politicians and activists prefer different policies, they may disagree over institutions. Conflicts over institutions are even more intense than conflicts over policies, because institutions have longer time-spans and represent investments by actors (Tsebelis, 1990: 92–118). Institutional change is an ever-present possibility in parties. Generally, politicians prefer institutions that give them more autonomy, whereas activists prefer structures that provide them with greater means of controlling politicians. It is easy to think of examples of institutions with different distributive consequences. Party leaders have more autonomy when challengers must surmount onerous nomination barriers to stand in leadership elections. Parliamentarians have less autonomy if they face compulsory reselection meetings run by activists. If a party's executive has no veto power over local selection contests, the activists can exert more control over their MP. Generally, the more discretion politicians enjoy, the greater the potential commitment costs will be, because activists will suspect that promises could be broken, leading them to undersupply resources. Party organisation reduces commitment problems but does not eradicate them.

Campaign technologies

The high probability of leader-activist disparities over policy gives politicians incentives to develop ways of campaigning that permit a reduction in their reliance on activists' services. This incentive introduces a dynamic element into the exchange model. The postwar period has seen a strong shift in liberal democracies towards capital-intensive communications techniques, based on the electronic media and increasingly involving computerisation (see McNair, 1999; Farrell and Webb, 2000). Intra-party conflicts are not the only motivation to develop new technologies, but they are an important one. Mass parties before 1945 were based on labour-intensive techniques, relying on activists to ascertain voters' desires and communicate the party's policies. The activists were in a powerful position as conveyers and collectors of information, which was filtered through their own policy preferences. The growth of media campaigning, through television interviews and political marketing, enabled politicians to communicate directly with voters. These developments, together with the rise of modern opinion polling, helped reduce the significance of labour-intensive methods. By reducing their demand for activists, politicians alleviate policy-vote trade-offs: capital makes no policy demands. Politicians still require finance to pay for polling and marketing, but there has been a progressive shift to different sources of funding, such as interest groups, firms and the state. State funding eases parties' reliance on the financial donations of activists and interest groups, and reduces constraints on party elites.

Party leaders have incentives to reduce their dependence on party members by seeking alternative sources of funding and by adopting capital-intensive communications technologies. However, capital can only partly substitute for labour (Ware, 1992), and some technology, such as PCs and telephones, requires activists to operate it. The revival of constituency campaigning in the UK (Denver and Hands, 1998; Seyd and Whiteley, 2003) points towards a continued role for activists, and with it, the need for intra-party channels of accountability and control. Yet, the undoubted importance of spin doctors, pollsters and other professionals, has consequences for the internal organisation of parties. Media-based campaigns require centralised command structures, with short lines of communication, so that decisions can be taken quickly and actors can respond to a fast-changing environment (Kavanagh, 1995: 108). This development has distributive consequences, facilitating leadership autonomy, because informal communications groups usually operate outside of parties' formal constitutional structures, making it difficult for them to be controlled 'from below'. In contrast to the mass parties, it is now the strategists and spin doctors, accountable directly to party leaders, who control information flows, undertaking polling, interpreting the data (a powerful resource during policy debates) and spinning the party's message to the voters.

Institutional change in vote-seeking parties

A satisfactory model of parties must explain how and why they change. Developmental models adopt a long-term perspective, particularly those variants that point to socio-political change as the motor of party change. An exchange model of party change must be based on micro-foundations. Therefore, we need tools for understanding short- and medium-term changes, based on politician-voter and politician-activist exchanges. Vote-seeking politicians prefer changes that directly or indirectly improve the party's electoral standing. Much party change centres round the opportunities that institutions offer for elite autonomy from party members.

There is a consensus that the principal conditions prompting organisational change in vote-seeking parties are shocks that affect their electoral performance or sharpen tensions between politicians and activists (Harmel and Janda, 1994; Koelble, 1996; Panebianco, 1988: 243). When a vote-seeking party loses elections, it is usually because it offers extreme policies relative to those of its opponents, or policies lacking credibility after an unsuccessful spell in government. Popular policies are essential for success, but adopting such policies can also entail costs. Some of these costs are external, such as credibility costs, as voters lose trust in the party. Significant policy shifts often need to be accompanied by major changes in personnel, with new leaders untainted by extremism or failure. Other costs are internal, stemming from intra-party impediments to policy change. Radical activists may control important decision-making organs and use them to block policy change. In short, electoral defeat creates pressure for organisational change that promotes policy flexibility and/or reduces the costs of vote-seeking. Electoral defeat is bad for all intra-party actors, since only governments can implement policies. Even activists may accept the need for party change to improve electoral performance, but if, as often, this course involves reducing their own power, they will resist it at first, though their opposition usually diminishes with each successive election defeat. Change is less likely (but not impossible) when electoral performance is good. Parties are conservative organisations, and they undertake potentially costly changes only when necessary (Harmel and Janda, 1994: 278). There are exit and voice costs, as opponents of change resist it or leave the party; furthermore, opportunity costs arise, such as missed opportunities to campaign or attack the opposing party, because time and energy is invested in party change.

Electoral failure prompts different types of change, but the most common is overtly redistributional, as one group tries to increase its power over others. Robert Harmel and Kenneth Janda (1994: 266–7) argue that in addition to the goal-motivated change identified above (whether that goal is policy or office/votes), parties also undergo power-motivated change. Such redistributive institutional change can be *consolidating*, whereby the dominant coalition tries to entrench its position, or it may be *'new deal'*, designed to entrench a new coalition (Tsebelis, 1990: 110–15). Redistributive reforms typically centre on institutional sites of contact between politicians and members, such as candidate selection, leadership election and policy-making procedures, as well as control over rule-making and disciplinary procedures. The argument is principally over how much autonomy the politicians should have. Politicians prefer more institutionalised power to pursue votes, free of control by policy-seeking activists. Redistributive change instigated 'from above', by party leaders, is usually intended to increase their autonomy from party members.

This tendency characterises not only top-heavy dominant coalitions, but also bottom-heavy (activist-dominated) ones. Even party leaders who are supported by a minority of MPs and a majority of radical activists will be tempted to dilute radical policies if it offers the only realistic way of winning office. Any such 'shirking' risks splitting the dominant coalition and could end in the leadership forming a new coalition, buttressed by centralising reforms. This conjuncture occurred in the Labour Party when the centre-leftist, Neil Kinnock, was elected as leader in 1983, with little support from shadow cabinet members, but with overwhelming backing from activists and trade unions. Yet in the following years, Kinnock successfully shifted the party towards the centreground, forming a new coalition with the Labour right, as it sought electoral respectability. As in this case, change is more widely accepted by activists if it is deemed necessary for electoral success. Similar centralising changes occurred in the German SPD in the 1990s after consecutive election defeats, and the process of change has also begun in the British Conservative Party, with moves to assert greater central control over candidate selection. However, politicians must not increase their own power so much that commitment costs are too high, otherwise activists will undersupply resources. A further recent lesson from Labour is that although redistributive change from above normally consolidates the dominant coalition, it is occasionally 'new deal' in nature. Labour's traditional dominant coalition of parliamentary and trade union leaders was partly dismantled by Tony Blair, because the unions were seen as an electoral liability.

Whereas party leaders prefer autonomy from activists, the latter desire to control them. The lower the degree of elite discretion, the harder it becomes for politicians to renege on deals with activists. However, activists must be careful not to bind politicians too tightly, otherwise the party may end up with policies that reflect activists' preferences, but which harm its electoral chances. Nevertheless, redistributive change instigated 'from below' by party members, is usually intended to reduce politicians' opportunities to shirk by shrinking their autonomy from members. An obvious way to achieve such change is through decentralising decision-making to activists, or strengthening enforcement mechanisms. Labour activists in the 1970s fought for the mandatory reselection of MPs to reduce the latter's security of tenure by increasing activists' leverage over them. However, redistributive change can be subtler. Parties' preference aggregation methods can be the subject of fierce battles. There is no perfect way of democratically aggregating the preferences of a group of individuals (Arrow, 1951), so institutions affect outcomes. In 1980–81, Labour was split by an argument over the weighting of votes in its new electoral college for leadership contests (Kogan and Kogan, 1982), and in later years, controversy arose over reform of the block voting system (see Chapter 6).

Redistributive change 'from below' can involve activists who are part of a bottom-heavy dominant coalition reasserting control over leaders; more often, it is 'new deal' in nature, constituting a challenge to the dominant coalition. As with change 'from above', redistributive change 'from below' normally follows electoral failure, but this time it tends to follow an unsuccessful spell in office. A perception of government 'failure' by party members, followed by electoral defeat, increases the likelihood of attempts 'from below' to introduce 'new deal' institutions and/or reduce leadership autonomy. In these circumstances, the first instinct of the activists is to bring the politicians to heel by implementing changes that reduce their autonomy, in the expectation that it will make them listen to the activists. The watchword of such reforms is usually 'accountability'. Labour's activists pushed through reforms of the party's constitution after the defeat of James Callaghan's Labour government in 1979. To a lesser extent, Tory grassroots organisations demanded membership participation in Conservative leadership contests, after their party's ejection from office in 1997. Another example is the leftist-inspired reforms in the German SPD, after its ejection from office in 1982 (Koelble, 1987, 1996). However, reforms can go too far, replacing elite independence with stifling controls that prevent any flexibility, and result in the adoption of 'extremist' platforms. This fate befell Labour after its reforms of 1979–81, leading to the election defeat of 1983. If such reforms fail to turn the party around after one election, strong pressure emerges for greater elite autonomy, as there was in the Labour Party after 1983 and the SPD in the 1990s (Koelble, 1996: 256).

Redistributive reform – changing the distribution of power between institutions – is the major type of change undertaken in parties, reflecting attempts by coalitions to secure control of policy-making and candidate selection. However, there are other forms of party change, which have distributional consequences, but which cannot simply be subsumed under this heading. First, institutional change can be introduced to increase the supply of resources to the party (a point often overlooked in exchange models). If a party does not have sufficient funds or activists to undertake campaigning, it will fare badly irrespective of its policies. Institutional change can provide incentives for people to join the party or for interest groups to affiliate to it. Party 'democratisation' can encourage individuals to join, knowing they will receive the selective benefit of participation rights in decision-making (Pennings and Hazan, 2001: 268). Affiliated membership can help encourage interest groups to institutionalise their relationship with the party, thereby providing a firmer commitment. Party change intended to attract activists may erode politicians' autonomy. Alternatively, the extension of state funding for parties could result in greater control by politicians, as they are less dependent on activists. Even if some activists decide to exit, the impact on the party's campaigning capabilities will be lessened.

Second, institutional change can be introduced to facilitate new communication technologies. Capital-intensive techniques ease politicians' reliance on activists, thereby reducing the costs of activist exit following a centralisation of power (though alternative sources of funding may be needed). Moreover, such techniques require centralised command structures, further undermining activists and their representatives on committees.

Third, institutional change can be introduced if voters are repelled by a party's existing institutional structure. This type of change is rare, but as is shown in this book, it was an important dimension of Labour's transformation in the 1990s. In his taxonomy of parties, Angelo Panebianco (1988) distinguishes internally and externally legitimated parties. The former are parties in which the leadership's legitimacy is based within the party, usually through a mass individual membership, whereas externally legitimated parties are formed by, or organisationally responsible to, an external body. There are two main types of externally legitimated parties: the old West European communist parties, which were responsible to the Comintern in Moscow; and labour parties, which were formed by, and remained connected to, sponsoring trade unions. A problem arises for such parties if their external sponsors undergo legitimacy crises. The collapse of communism in Eastern Europe reverberated on Western communist parties, and most underwent significant reform, including name changes, in the early 1990s. By contrast, the world's labour parties do not share a common extra-national source of legitimacy, but are connected to national trade union movements. Most of the major labour parties reassessed their links with trade unions in the 1980s and 1990s, partly in response to changes in electoral demography, and partly because of globalisation and the demise of corporatism. However, the scale of the changes and the depth of the legitimacy crisis were greatest in the British Labour Party.

British trade unions fell into public disrepute in the 1970s, as industrial relations soured and strikes proliferated. The defining moment was the 'winter of discontent' in 1978–79, when a spate of public sector strikes fatally damaged the Labour government and undermined the credibility of the Labour Party for over a decade. The unions' preponderant position in the party was put under the spotlight, and the sight of demonised union leaders wielding block votes at Labour's annual conference gave the impression of a party under the thumb of its paymasters. Even as public attitudes towards the unions mellowed, unease remained over their role in the party. Labour's organisation lacked legitimacy and engendered distrust. Thus, even when Labour moderated its economic policies, a credibility gap remained, because many voters suspected that the moderate policies would be abandoned in government, as the unions cashed in their investments. The only way it could effectively counter these fears was to reduce the party's dependence on the unions, thereby demonstrating to the public that Labour could be trusted. However, it is difficult to persuade external sponsors to continue contributing funds while giving up power; consecutive election defeats were needed to secure union acquiescence to change.

Finally, party change can sometimes appear truly independent of electoral considerations, such as that following the death or health-related retirement of an incumbent leader (Harmel and Janda, 1994:

280). The death of John Smith in 1994 was the catalyst that sparked a major transformation of the Labour Party, as the modernising candidate, Tony Blair, was elected as Smith's successor. Nevertheless, underlying Blair's subsequent reforms was the realisation among MPs, individual members and trade unionists that if Labour were to emerge from its electoral wilderness, it needed a leader, a structure and a set of policies that appealed to floating voters. Thus electoral imperatives were crucial.

To summarise, vote-seeking parties are acutely sensitive to poor electoral performance, which is the major precipitant of change. It is usually expressed in the form of intra-party power struggles over policy and strategy, which lead coalitions of actors to rearrange party institutions to their benefit. Most of the aims and antecedents of change discussed above are evident in the forthcoming analysis.

Conclusion

This chapter has integrated and extended existing rational choice arguments about party organisation. Political parties are a response to the problems inherent in politician-activist exchange, with institutions substituting for explicit 'market' exchange. Institutions enable politicians to ease their commitment problems with activists, and make it possible for parties to recruit and retain activists with differing preferences. However, parties also engage with voters in electoral exchange, which mediates politician-activist relations. Politicians require discretion if they are to satisfy activists and win votes, and institutions can provide this autonomy. Questions of organisational efficiency, therefore, co-exist with distributional conflicts, as politicians prefer more discretion whereas activists prefer less.

The model of party change is based on an intentional approach to institutional transformation: as Harmel and Janda (1994: 261) argue, 'party change does not "just happen"'. Specific changes are undertaken for reasons, and the actors who implement them are motivated by self-interest. In the long run, parties may approximate the ideal-types derived by the developmental model, but many changes reflect the dual necessities of winning votes and maintaining activists. Any given institutional configuration allocates resources to politicians and activists, and they can use those resources to bring about change. The bargaining power of actors also depends on the party's electoral success (or otherwise). Individual real-life parties differ in all these respects, so individual parties always diverge from the ideal-types of the developmental model.

The exchange model provides the basis for the analysis of institutions and institutional reform in the Labour Party. It is shown that the entire basis for institutionalising political exchange in the party has been transformed over the last twenty years. Before these changes are analysed, it is necessary to examine Labour's structure prior to its modernisation.

3
The Pre-Modernised Labour Party

It was shown in the last chapter that two important functions of party organisation are to aggregate members' preferences and to help intra-party actors alleviate their commitment problems. This chapter turns to the analysis of the Labour Party and shows how it tackled both these problems and entrenched political exchange in the party before its modernisation. The device it used was the block vote, an institutional means by which trade unions dominated Labour's decision-making bodies, and one of the most controversial aspects of the party-union link. Despite the efficient and distributional qualities of block voting, trade unions have rarely been able to control completely the actions of the parliamentary Labour Party. Understanding the logic behind the block vote, and its limitations as a means of overcoming union-PLP commitment problems, enables us to recognise how far-reaching recent reforms have been. The events that ruptured the party-union link in the 1970s are then recounted, and the chapter closes with some reflections on the coalitions for change that assembled in the party in the 1980s and 1990s.

The development of political exchange in the Labour Party[1]

The exchange approach developed in Chapter 2 envisaged office-seeking politicians recruiting activists to campaign for them, and offering policy and social benefits in return. However, the most important type of political exchange in the British Labour Party has always been between politicians and trade unions rather than individual activists. This form of exchange has distinguished Labour from most continental European socialist parties, which were based on individual mass memberships and had few institutionalised links with unions. European socialist parties generally developed before their national union movements, but early industrialisation ensured that the process was reversed in Britain, where the union movement acquired organisational strength in the nineteenth century. Political and judicial hostility persuaded British unions of the need to seek allies in parliament, and after the extensions of the suffrage to working class men in 1867 and 1884, there was a potential constituency for union-backed candidates. Rather than embark on the risky strategy of forming a party, major unions, such as the miners and cotton workers, struck deals with local Liberal Party associations to put up candidates in areas of working-class strength. The first such union candidate was elected to parliament in 1874 and several more followed in the 1880s and 1890s. These MPs became known as Lib-Labs and functioned as a parliamentary pressure group seeking to influence industrial relations legislation. Lib-Labism best served the interests of unions with geographically concentrated memberships, but by the 1890s large general unions, such as the transport workers and municipal workers, had emerged, recruiting across a range of industries and over a wider geographical territory. Lib-Labism was not as attractive to them and by 1899 the number of Lib-Lab MPs stood at only eleven. Yet the unions found themselves under greater attack than ever, both from employers in the workplace, and in the courts. Many in the unions started to think about forming their own party (Lovell, 1991; Moore, 1978).

Meanwhile, the same period saw the emergence of socialist groups, such as the Fabian Society and the Independent Labour Party (ILP). The latter tried to build an individual mass membership along the lines of the German SPD and fielded candidates in elections, but it quickly became clear that the ILP could not challenge the existing party system, which was centred on Liberal-Conservative competition. Winning votes requires a well-resourced organisation to campaign on the ground, but attracting members and funds cannot be achieved overnight. The ILP therefore sought an organisational alliance with the unions: large-scale collective action is easier to organise by drawing together existing groups than by starting from scratch, because it dramatically lowers mobilisation costs (Chong, 1991: 36).

The result was that the unions and socialist groups coalesced to form the Labour Representation Committee in 1900 (becoming the Labour Party in 1906). The unions and socialists had different interests, and the new party represented a compromise for all involved. Its foundation was 'not so much a birth as a marriage' (Pelling and Reid, 1996: 4). However, the new party was completely dependent on union finance, and so the unions dominated its organisation, while their policy preferences took priority. The socialists were needed because their personnel tended to be more middle class, better educated and better versed in administrative tasks than working-class trade unionists. For this reason and others, including the high opportunity costs facing busy union leaders participating in parliamentary politics, the ILP and the Fabians provided most of the leadership of the new parliamentary Labour Party. To ensure they retained control, the unions dominated the party's annual policy-making conference and its national executive committee, as well as furnishing the backbench ranks of the PLP. Political exchange consisted of a commitment by the socialists to pursue policies beneficial to the unions, in return for the right to piggyback on the unions' organisational and financial resources.

Labour enjoyed some early success, both in the electoral arena, where it had 42 seats by 1910, and in terms of policy concessions from the Liberal government, especially the repeal of the Taff Vale judgment of 1901, when the House of Lords had ruled that unions could be sued for damages for loss of earnings resulting from strike action. It also secured the Trade Union Act 1913, which partly reversed the Osborne judgment of 1909, another House of Lords ruling, which prohibited unions from spending money on political activities. However, Labour's electoral breakthrough came in the 1920s when, after another extension of the franchise, it supplanted the Liberals as the main challenger to the Conservatives. In 1923, Labour formed its first government, a minority administration that lasted a year, and by 1929 it was the largest party in the House of Commons. From this time on, however, there was a permanent tension between the office-seeking instincts of the PLP leadership and the policy-seeking motives of the unions. This strain was revealed during the economic crisis of 1931 that brought the Labour government and the unions to loggerheads over government attempts to cut unemployment insurance at a time when unemployment had soared above two million. The PLP's exchange with the unions replicated some features of the earlier exchange between the unions and the socialist societies, in that the unions wanted the PLP to pursue legislation favourable to their interests. However, the unions themselves now had to consider modifying their policy demands because the party was set on winning elections and found its incentives structured by the two-party system.

Federalism and block voting in the Labour Party

Labour was an example of an 'indirect membership' party (Duverger, 1964), in which the party's 'members' were organisations rather than individuals. An individual who wished to join the party could to do so only indirectly, through an affiliated trade union or socialist society. In 1918, a system of constituency Labour parties (CLPs) was established to increase Labour's campaigning capabilities after the extension of the franchise (until then, the party relied mainly on local union branches to mobilise supporters).[2] The new system permitted individuals to join the party independently of affiliated bodies, though their membership was, and remained, dwarfed by that of the unions (see Table 3.1). This innovation diluted the indirect nature of Labour's membership structure, but not considerably so, because the unions continued to dominate the extra-parliamentary party and provide most of the funds. Party leaders had considered restructuring the party on a direct membership basis as part of Labour's broader electoral appeal, but they decided it could not survive financially without the unions. Thus, the indirect structure was entrenched and, with a few important exceptions, remained unchanged until the 1980s (see Appendix).

Table 3.1   Labour Party Membership, 1900–2000 (Selected Years)

Year	Individual members[a]	Trade union members[b]	Socialist and coop. societies	Total membership[c]
1900	0	353,000	23,000	376,000
1910	0	1,394,000	31,000	1,431,000
1920	n/a	4,318,000	42,000	4,360,000
1930	277,000	2,011,000	58,000	2,347,000
1940	304,000	2,227,000	40,000	2,571,000
1950	908,000	4,972,000	40,000	5,920,000
1960	790,000	5,513,000	25,000	6,328,000
1970	680,000	5,519,000	24,000	6,223,000
1980	348,000	6,407,000	56,000	6,811,000
1990	311,000	4,922,000	54,000	5,287,000
2000	311,000	n/a[d]	n/a[d]	n/a

Sources: 1900–90: Tanner et al. (2000: 394–7); 2000: Labour Party Head Office.

a. No individual members until 1918, and no count made of them from 1918 to 1927. The method of counting individual members changed in 1980 (explaining the sharp fall in membership that year), but CLPs continued to cast a minimum of 1000 votes at the annual conference (until the reweighting of votes in 1993 and 1996). For individual membership figures for all years from 1980 to 2003, see Figure 7.2 in Chapter 7.

b. 'Contracting-in' from 1928 to 1946; 'contracting-out' before and after.

c. Total membership figures for 1900 and 1910 include members of Co-operative and Women's Labour League.

d. In 2002, there were 2,769,437 affiliated trade unionists and 21,486 affiliated members of socialist societies (as well as 248,294 individual members). Source: Labour Party Head Office.

The exchange model developed in Chapter 2 needs modifying when applied to a party in which the 'members' are interest groups. Purposive incentives are important for unions, but social incentives are not. The resources that a union donates have a more noticeable impact than the efforts of an individual activist. Another difference is that a union is controlled by a dominant coalition, ranging from elected elites to their lower-level supporters. Controlling the union enables this coalition to engage in exchange with Labour politicians, supplying funds in return for policies. However, unions have their own internal decision-making and selection structures, so potentially they can be captured by new coalitions, which then demand different policies from the party.

Despite these differences in political exchange in indirect parties, the important elements are similar. Mutual commitment problems attend the trade between politicians and unions, stemming from the non-simultaneous exchange of union resources for policies. Resources are constantly needed, but policies may not be delivered until years later. By then, the politicians may have incentives to supply different policies. The risk of shirking by the PLP could encourage unions to undersupply resources, to the detriment of both the party and the unions themselves, since Labour would be less able to fight for union policies. Institutions are needed to enable politicians and unions to make credible commitments to each other and to reduce the scope for PLP shirking.

However, rather than just one union funding the Labour Party, there was a multiplicity of unions, each with different preferences and priorities. One consequence was to increase the supply of funds to the party, and spread the burden over many contributors. However, it also created the possibility of inter-union opportunism, whereby individual unions might free-ride on the financial contributions of other unions. If a number of unions decided to undersupply donations in the hope that other unions would compensate, the party's finances would be damaged, hindering its ability to campaign. The party needed a means of preference aggregation that protected its funds from inter-union opportunism.

The solution was institutions that linked financial contributions to decision-making power. Labour's first constitution, published in 1918, formalised the federal structure that was in operation before the First World War. The party's annual conference aggregated and channelled the affiliates' policy preferences. It was dominated by union delegates, and, as well as deciding policy, it was Labour's supreme decision-making body. The unions also controlled the NEC, which ran the party between conferences. The unions had complete autonomy in their own internal decision-making procedures – another reflection of the federal principle. The PLP, its ranks swollen by union placemen, was expected to introduce legislative Bills that reflected the resolutions passed at the conference.

To give unions an incentive to maintain the supply of funds, they were allocated votes at the conference in direct proportion to the money they donated. This connection was achieved through the *political levy*, a small sum that trade union members pay with their normal union fees. Each union affiliated to the party its own members who paid this levy, even though not all these members were usually aware that they were financing the party in this way. A system of 'contracting out' ensured that, unless levypayers specifically stated they did not wish to pay the levy, it was automatically deducted from their wages. Inertia and ignorance have always ensured that only a small minority 'contract out': 19 per cent in 1975, falling to 15 per cent in 2001 (Ewing, 2002: 13).[3] For each trade unionist whose political levy went to the party, his union received one vote at Labour's annual conference. Big unions affiliated more members and thus obtained more votes.[4]

Although a necessary condition for the unions to maintain their commitment to continue supplying funds, the political levy was not sufficient, because the temptation to free-ride remained. A union might affiliate 150,000 levypayers, but the latter would have widely differing policy preferences, as would the delegates representing them at the party conference. If the union's 150,000 votes were divided among its delegates, under a system of 'one-delegate–one-vote' (ODOV), it would be the delegates, rather than the individual unions qua organisations, that would hold power. Preference heterogeneity among delegates would lead to delegates from the same union cancelling out each other's votes on the conference floor. If three-fifths of these delegates supported a policy resolution, and the other two-fifths voted against, the union's 150,000 votes would be split 90,000 to 60,000 in favour, leaving only 30,000 'effective' votes. Although the union has paid affiliation fees for 150,000 members, only one-fifth have any net effect on the outcome of the vote. Certainly, the same could happen in other unions, but the greater the differential between those delegates in favour and against a policy, the higher a union's effective vote would be. A small union would have more effective votes if there were a consensus among its delegates, whereas big unions with vocationally heterogeneous memberships would be prone to greater opinion diversity and fewer effective votes.

A system of ODOV, or any other form of intra-union vote splitting, would give big unions incentives to reduce their affiliation levels and, thereby, their supply of funds to the party. A union with a finely split delegation could substantially reduce its affiliation level, with only a marginal impact on its effective votes, because all factions would be equally affected. Alternatively, internal decision costs could rise, as union leaders expended resources on reducing the strength of rival factions to increase the union's effective votes. Such practices divert time and energy away from other activities and could necessitate offers of patronage to pull individual delegates into line. To minimise these problems, Labour adopted an 'indirect' federal structure, whereby the unions qua organisations were regarded as the party's members. Each affiliate spoke with a single voice, which in turn facilitated the dominance of the big unions and safeguarded their commitment to continued funding. This system was institutionalised through *block voting* at the party conference.

Block voting involved each organisation casting all its allotted votes as a single unit. Each organisation arrived at a decision and casts its votes unanimously in favour of that decision. Minority opinion was not represented. Thus, a union with 150,000 affiliated levypayers would cast a single block of 150,000 effective votes at the party conference, whether in favour of a policy or against it. Although not specified in Labour's constitution, block voting was a consistent feature of the party since its formation in 1900 (it was first used by the large unions at the TUC in 1895). Until 1953 there were provisions for unions to split their block votes at the conference, but they were rarely used, and even then mainly by federal unions with regional divisions, such as the miners' union (Minkin, 1992: 283). Before 1953, block votes were printed on cards, which were held up by union leaders at each vote. However, with the televising of the conference, party leaders were anxious about audiences' response to this practice, so 'secret' balloting was adopted. Where unions previously required just one voting card, they now needed eighty (forty 'for' and forty 'against'), and it was deemed impractical to give each delegate a book of voting cards (see Minkin, 1992: 283–6). Block voting institutionalised the link between financial contributions and voting power, reducing the risk that the big unions might resent their financial burden.

Since block voting compelled each union to adopt a single position on each policy issue rather than allowing individual delegates to cast

equal votes at the party conference, the policies adopted by the conference did not necessarily reflect the preferences of individual conference
delegates. This point can be illustrated by looking at a simplified conference consisting of two unions (see Figure 3.1). Union A is leftwing
and has 400,000 votes, while Union B is rightwing and has 500,000
votes. Assuming that each union takes up its constitutional entitle-

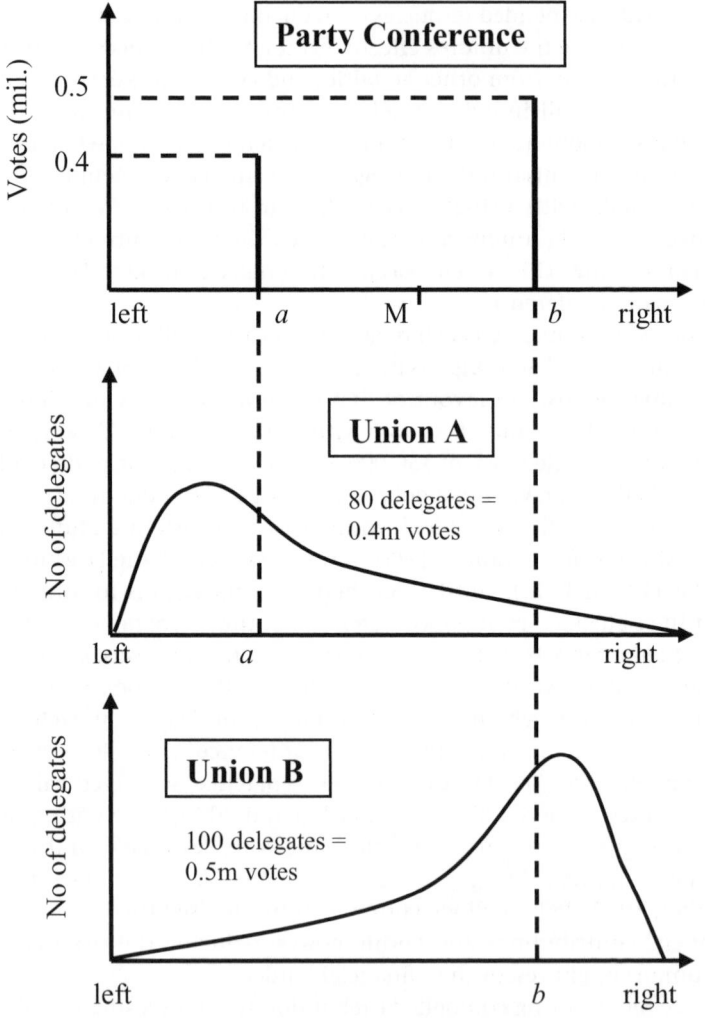

Figure 3.1 Distributional Consequences of Block Voting

ment of one delegate per 5000 votes, Union A will have 80 delegates and Union B 100. Under a system of ODOV, the overall distribution of opinion is more important than that within each union, so the median delegate at the conference is at point M in the upper panel, which is where conference policies are positioned. However, block voting ensures that the preferred position of each union's median delegate is the preferred position of that union as a whole: point a in the case of Union A, and point b for Union B. However, since Union B has more votes that Union A, it can unilaterally decide policy at b, which is a significant distance from M. In this example, the rightwing union wins. Until the 1970s, most union leaders were from the centre-right of the party (reflecting their concern with its electoral fortunes) so block voting disadvantaged the left.

The left was also hindered by the intra-union distributional conse-quences of block voting. At the turn of the twentieth century, when liberals dominated the unions but socialists were growing in influence, block voting prevented socialists in the unions voting with the left-wing socialist societies, and later the CLPs, at the party conference. The latter also wielded block votes, though they were much smaller than the unions' (typically 1000 votes per CLP), and collectively the CLPs rarely controlled more than 15 per cent of the conference votes. If it were ever to capture the party, the left would need concentrated support in the big unions. Block voting enabled centre-right union leaders to control the left by imposing upon it high mobilisation costs. Factional conflict had to be waged within organisations as well as between them, so minority factions first needed to win majorities inside individual unions – a significant undertaking. Under an ODOV system, factional conflict would be mainly extra-organisational, with majority and minority factions within each union affecting the confer-ence's factional balance. A mandating system or some form of 'whip-ping' would be needed to bind all delegates to union policy, but it might not be sufficient. Mandating exists in the Labour Party, with union executives or conferences laying down the policies of their unions, which then form mandates for union delegates to the party conference. However, the sheer volume of policy resolutions submitted to the conference meant that a union's 'official' attitude to a given res-olution could be hard to discern. It is costly trying to write complete contracts or mandates, because the future is uncertain. Block voting reduced these measurement costs by providing a means of voting the preferences of the unions' dominant coalitions. Mandates could con-tinue to exist on all the major issues, as a safeguard, but beyond that they were not always necessary. Trade unions at the Labour Party conference were usually directly mandated on a third of issues, partly mandated on another third, and not mandated at all on the final third (Harrison 1960: 167; Minkin, 1992: 294). Moreover, measurement costs were increased further by the system of compositing resolutions (merging together different resolutions to reduce the number of issues debated). Composites frequently contained elements that a union supported and other elements that it opposed, making it difficult to use mandates as a guide to which way to vote (Minkin, 1980: 164). Block voting circumvented these problems by letting union delegations decide among themselves.

Block voting reduced the costs of exchange between unions on the conference floor by facilitating vote trading. The latter is ubiquitous in voting bodies, but it consumes time and resources that could be profitably employed in other ways. By concentrating voting resources, block voting enabled union delegations and PLP leaders to organise deals quickly. Three or four big unions could collude to ensure their preferred resolutions were passed. Vote trading was particularly prevalent during NEC elections, with the big unions normally voting for each other's candidates. Moreover, it was usually easy to monitor the voting record of the major unions because each controlled such a large proportion of the votes. Deals were thus more likely to stick, because if a union reneged on a promise to vote for another union's resolution, it could face retaliation in later votes. By contrast, vote trading under ODOV would be laborious, entailing high opportunity costs. Hundreds of individual delegates would have to be canvassed, yet each would have only a small chance of being pivotal to the result of a vote. Furthermore, even if they did promise their votes, it would be impossible to determine how they voted in the secret ballot.

Nevertheless, the block voting system could become unstable once the factions were more evenly balanced, as they were from the 1960s onwards. Thus, the amalgamation of unions – a steady feature of the postwar years – impacted on conference votes. If a small rightwing union merged with a larger leftwing union, the left would take the combined block vote of the new union, increasing its share of the conference vote without a single delegate's opinion having been changed (Crouch, 1982: 180). Similarly, small shifts within a single delegation could alter the stance of its union and that of the party conference. One of the most important instances occurred in 1979, when the conference was balanced between left and right. The AUEW, with 928,000 votes, was the pivotal union, but its delegation was split. On the whim of one floating AUEW delegate, Labour's conference adopted mandatory reselection contests for MPs, but rejected a wider franchise in leadership elections (McSmith, 1996: 118–21, 139–40).[5]

The thrust of the argument has been that big block votes translated into an ability to bring about outcomes, yet voting resources and outcome power are not synonymous (Shapley and Shubik, 1954). If the conference were factionally divided among unions, each coalition as a whole might have an incentive to buy more votes and gain a majority. However, each union within the coalition could free-ride, letting its allies buy the extra votes from which they would all benefit. By the same reasoning, unions might be tempted to reduce their affiliation fees and thereby harm the financial position of the party. We should therefore be wary of viewing unions as vote-*maximisers*. Nevertheless, there are good reasons for supposing that such free-rider problems might not be overly serious. The large- and medium-sized unions probably comprised a 'privileged group', in the Olsonian sense of a group whose members have incentives to contribute towards the supply of their desired collective good – a solvent party (Olson, 1971). Moreover, empirical evidence suggests concentrated voting power at the conference *was* positively correlated with outcome power. A power index analysis of the Labour conference in the mid-1980s showed that the 'power' of the TGWU, then the biggest union, was considerably greater than that of medium and small voting bodies. Each 1000 votes cast by the TGWU was worth 23 per cent more on the Shapley-Shubik power index than 1000 votes cast by a CLP (Leech, 1992: 250).[6]

Unions thus had incentives to maintain their affiliation levels, because their voting power was related to their ability to bring about outcomes. Block voting ensured that unions considering cutting their contributions would be reducing their own voting power at the conference, making them less able to ensure their preferences were prioritised by the party. Block voting thus helped insulate the party from financial threats by its affiliates. Intuition suggests that unions unhappy with party policy would have an incentive to cut their funding. In fact, if the opposing faction's majority were not great, it could be rational for dissatisfied unions to *increase* their affiliations, thereby increasing funds to the party. (The incentive would be weaker if either faction had a large majority.) In the 1970s, NUPE, a leftwing union angered by the Labour government's spending cuts, increased its affiliated membership from 100,000 in 1974 to 600,000 by 1980. These votes helped narrowly pass a leftwing package of reforms to the party constitution. In response, some rightwing unions considered choking off funds to the leftwing NEC, but pulled back because a reduction in funds would reduce their voting power at the conference, further entrenching the left (Minkin, 1992: 518).[7]

In conclusion, block voting eased the commitment, measurement and bargaining costs that distort political exchange between the politicians and the unions. It weakened incentives for unions to free-ride on the contributions of others, and gave them a considerable degree of control over the extra-parliamentary party. Block voting was an important means of institutionalising political exchange in the Labour Party and reflected the specific nature of that exchange. The focus above was mainly on block voting at the party conference, though it was also an important feature of NEC elections and the electoral college from 1981 to 1993. Block voting was formally precluded in parliamentary candidate selection by a rule against mandating delegates to selection meetings, though union delegates invariably voted as blocks. Since votes at the local level were also allocated on the basis of affiliated membership, and thereby, financial contributions, there were the same pressures to maximise 'effective votes' (see Chapter 5). However, the relationship between the parliamentary and extra-parliamentary parties has been glossed over. The unions' commitment to supply funds is dependent on the PLP's commitment to supply policies, but office-seeking politicians prefer autonomy so that they can offer attractive policies to the voters. As we shall see, enforcement problems have plagued the supply of policies from the PLP to the unions.

The autonomy of the PLP and party-union tensions

Labour's institutions were intended to solve two sets of commitment problems: that among the unions not to free-ride on each other's financial donations, and that of the PLP to supply the unions' preferred policies. Historically, the institutions were more successful in solving the first of these problems. Even with block voting, the annual conference's lack of direct elective control over MPs deprived it of enforcement powers and ensured that the unions could not simply instruct MPs to vote for certain policies in parliament. Labour's constitution locates sovereignty in the conference: '[t]he work of the party shall be under the direction and control of party conference...' (Labour Party, 2003a: Clause VI.1).[8] More specifically, the '[p]arty conference shall decide from time to time what specific proposals of legislative, financial or administrative reform shall be included in the party programme' (Clause V.1). The PLP is not mentioned but these clauses seem to imply that it should implement conference policies. This position was ambivalently affirmed by a resolution passed at the 1907 annual conference, which stated that the PLP should decide 'the time and method of giving effect' to conference resolutions (McKenzie, 1964: 396). On the question of what happens should the PLP refuse to implement conference policies, the constitution is silent. No enforcement mechanisms or sanctions are specified. This lacuna has resulted in disagreements and spawned a long-running debate about whether it is the party conference or the PLP[9] that has ultimate authority over policy.[10] The debate centres on Robert McKenzie's famous thesis (1964, 1982) that the PLP is dominant, as the British constitution prohibits parliament being held accountable to outside bodies save the electorate. McKenzie acknowledged that the PLP must carry the party with it, but assumed union block votes would be put at the service of the party leadership: 'it is this bond of mutual confidence between the parliamentary leaders and a preponderant part of the trade union leadership which is an essential key to the understanding of the functioning of the Labour Party' (McKenzie, 1964: 505).

The McKenzie thesis appears to fit with much of Labour's history, particularly when Labour was in government, when it often ignored conference decisions. Even in opposition, the PLP leadership has rarely come under great control by the conference (cf. Kavanagh, 1985). However, there is a major problem with the thesis: McKenzie's assumption that the union leaders will always rally to the PLP's defence when faced with leftwing demands. With hindsight, the 'bond of confidence' between the PLP and the major union leaders was, as Minkin asserts, 'a contingent and not an endemic feature of the pattern of power within the Party' (Minkin, 1980: 321). The 'Praetorian Guard' of rightwing unions crumbled in the 1960s and 1970s, as the major unions shifted to the left. McKenzie underestimated the extent to which Labour was run by a PLP-union *coalition*.

The party-union conflicts of the 1960s and 1970s showed that union acquiescence to the PLP is not inevitable, but neither could the unions impose their own wishes on the government. The exchange model offers a way of understanding relations between Labour and the unions. Ever since Labour replaced the Liberals in the 1920s as the main challenger to the Conservatives, the unions have inevitably faced difficulties forcing policies on the PLP. To maintain its electoral competitiveness, Labour has had to change from being a trade union policy-seeking party into primarily a vote-seeking (but union-funded) party. If parliamentary and union leaders had different preferences, the

PLP leadership would face a choice between keeping the unions happy but losing votes, or winning elections with policies opposed by the unions. Yet if the policies offered by the Conservatives are more antithetical still to the unions, the latter may have no alternative but to accept centrist policies from Labour. Contemplating these mutual dilemmas directs us to some questions posed by Minkin:

> If so many features of the Labour Party implied and facilitated the initiative of the unions and their leadership, why did they not control Labour Party policymaking on a permanent basis? ... In casting block votes in [the TUC and the Labour Party,] ... why did union leaders not command similar policies and strategies in both? Paying both pipers why did they not call identical tunes? (Minkin, 1992: 7)

Minkin's explanation is in terms of labour-movement norms that engender restraint (see Chapter 1). The inhibiting force of the movement's unwritten 'rules' encourages union leaders to permit autonomy to the PLP. For Minkin, interest-based explanations are a subset of the 'baronial thesis' and cannot explain restraint. Indeed, Minkin specifically rejects 'an economic model of power maximisation' and denies union leaders are 'power hungry "politicians" seeking to control both the Labour Party and the Government' (1997: 242, 273). Similarly, Shaw states that rational actors generally are best able to pursue their goals when they have more power, and so 'securing power is, for the rational actor, the overriding objective'. In relation to the party-union link, he claims rational choice models predict 'that union leaders would routinely use their entrenched position within the party structure to determine its policy' (Shaw, 2003: 169, 170).

However, these arguments are unconvincing. It is not true that securing, let alone maximising, power is the 'overriding objective' for rational actors. Instead, they want to maximise utility, which is a vector measurement of *all* the things individuals value.[11] Union leaders need to further their members' interests (or face being supplanted), but it is not clear that the way to achieve this goal is to impose policies on the PLP. Rational union leaders will cede autonomy to party leaders and refrain from imposing their preferred policies if they entail electoral costs. In other words, union restraint is rational under certain circumstances (but see below). The unions are policy-seeking interest groups, which lobby governments but, as was shown in Chapter 2, such organisations do not usually measure their success in electoral terms. In Britain, however, the unions are the main sponsors of a polit-ical party competing in a two-party system. For Labour to be successful, they must allow it to adopt a vote-seeking electoral strategy, which means they may not always get the policies they want. It explains not only the unions' restraint, but also the fact that they have tended to play a 'negative' role, setting limits to the politicians' autonomy rather than prescribing policy. The unions often appear restrained because they operate within an organisation where votes are the criterion of success. Thus, they acquiesced to the party's abandonment of its op-position to the industrial relations legislation of the Thatcher govern-ment, because it was a prerequisite for broadening Labour's appeal. Brenda Dean, the former leader of the printers' union, SOGAT, summed up the unions' dilemma, in 1985:

> I don't necessarily think it's good for the Labour Party to be run by the trades unions. In fact, I think it's counterproductive ... [T]he people who put the party in are the five per cent don't knows. If don't knows see that the party is dominated by any one group that's going to hurt its election chances. Politics is about power, about being in government – and we've got to make sure we provide the means for the Labour Party to get elected. (Cited in Taylor, 1987: 293)

Since the 1920s (with the exception of the tumultuous period 1979–83), Labour's vote was always greater than the TUC's affiliated membership. In 1997, Labour won 13.5 million votes at a time when the TUC had 6.8 million affiliated members. Even this statistic does not tell the whole story, because a large minority of trade unionists consistently fails to vote for Labour. Labour's electoral support among union members fluctuated around the 50 per cent mark in the 1960s, but fell in the 1970s. In 1983, only a third of union members voted for Labour, though the figure rose thereafter (Webb, 1992a: 126). This merely moderate propensity of union members to support Labour has reduced the attractiveness of a class-based electoral appeal, and in-hibited union leaders from seeking to impose such a strategy.

Minkin claims that respect for the 'rules' of restraint is as much a feature of the PLP as it is of the union leaders. However, even some of his defenders acknowledge that this proposition lacks credibility in the era of 'new Labour' (Shaw, 2003: 178). Self-restraint is not as inherent in the PLP's incentives, particularly when Labour is in government, because its electoral prospects may be bound up with the pursuit of policies opposed by the unions. However, the politicians do face insti-tutional and resource constraints: there must be some payback for the unions, otherwise they are wasting their money and may be tempted either to withdraw it or to create intra-party turmoil. The history of the party-union relationship in Britain is the history of attempts to resolve the tension between PLP office-seeking and union policy-seeking. The party has often been prepared to compromise on policies that were 'popular enough' to be competitive in the electoral arena, while pro-viding some rewards for the unions. In turn, the unions were willing to permit autonomy to the politicians, provided key interests were pro-tected. The latter included progressive industrial relations legislation and the preservation of free collective bargaining – the voluntarist system of employer-union negotiations through which British workers had historically secured significant material improvements. The party conference could then be the public forum where union leaders and politicians struck policy agreements. Since neither side had an in-centive to be embarrassed by public disagreements, they were usually willing to 'fix' votes in advance (facilitated by the concentration of voting resources in a small number of units). This 'deal' at the heart of the Labour Party meant that union leaders left 'politics' to the PLP and used their block votes to keep the left in check. Panebianco (1988: 94) described this system as one of 'crossed oligarchies', capturing the interdependence of the political and industrial elites.

The PLP too has always faced strategic dilemmas. Assuming the politicians prefer policies more moderate than the ones the unions want, at least three strategies exist for the party. One option is to present to the electorate a manifesto that promises pro-union policies, which has the virtue of honesty but it may condemn the party to heavy defeats, as when Labour ran on a leftwing manifesto in 1983. Such an outcome is bad both for the politicians and the union leaders – pro-union policies cannot be implemented from the opposition benches. The favoured strategy of the Labour left is for the party to embark on 'preference shaping', changing the aggregate distribution of voters' preferences so that the median-voter position shifts towards the left. However, it was shown in Chapter 1 that academic critics of 'new Labour' confuse preference shaping with persuasion, and although per-suading the electorate to support leftwing policies is not impossible, it is difficult unless voters' material incentives are changed.

There are two alternative electoral strategies to offering a radical platform. One is to offer a moderate manifesto and implement it in government; the other is to run on the same moderate ticket, but abandon it in government in favour of radicalism. The benefit of a moderate manifesto is that it increases the probability of winning office, but both strategies have major drawbacks. First, offering moderate policies before the election and switching to a more radical course once in office is not impossible. Many policy reversals or new radical announcements go unnoticed by voters. The Blair government approved laws on union recognition ballots and gave workers greater employment rights. In the case of many sectional interests, the costs of special-interest legislation can safely be dispersed across millions of taxpayers, not many of whom will be sufficiently informed to notice the few extra pence per week it costs them in taxes. The decentralised structure of Britain's union movement and the sectional nature of many unions can easily give rise to demands for concessions specific to particular industries. These benefits may be things that firms in the industries agree with, such as subsidies or foreign quotas. The policy can be justified by reference to saving jobs and combating foreign competition. It is precisely in this environment that rent-seeking special interests thrive. Yet many of the things unions want do not fall into this category. The costs of legislation on employment rights, the right to strike, and red tape, fall on domestic businesses rather than taxpayers or foreign competitors. When these costs are concentrated on business, organised opposition emerges, as happened in relation to parts of the Blair government's programme.

The alternative strategy is moderation before and after the election, and for most of Labour's history, this strategy has tended to be the preferred one. The problem is that it can leave the unions cold and destabilise the party. Changes in the postwar economy presented problems for the party-union relationship that the party's institutional structure could not solve. The postwar growth of the unions (in terms of membership and importance) ensured that they assumed a greater role in the nation's political economy. Full employment created the possibility of spiralling wage costs and inflation unless capital and organised labour could agree on how to distribute the national income. The result was the growth of corporatist arrangements between the TUC, the CBI and the government, regardless of whether the latter was Labour or Conservative. All distributional claims by interest groups, including unions, are dependent on a growing economy. When the economy is strong, these claims need not present problems, but in recessions, governments must take measures to restore economic growth, even if they create hardship for their own supporters. Before the Blair government, it was often Labour's misfortune to find itself in

office during times of acute economic crisis. For Labour, crisis management was the 'moderate' response, and was always preferred to the
left's radical anti-capitalist policies. Faced with the economic problems
of the 1960s and 1970s, successive British governments looked to the
unions for wage restraint. For Labour, with its institutional links to the
unions, it meant economic crises could have destabilising effects on
intra-party politics.

Labour's attempts in the 1960s and 1970s to impose wage restraint
violated the longstanding 'agreement' that the party would not intervene in industrial relations without the permission of the unions
(Ludlam, 2000; Minkin, 1992). Moreover, incomes policies met with
limited success in Britain because the unusual extent of decentralisation in British trade unions, compared with that found on the con-
tinent, reinforced the attractiveness of voluntarism. In Scandinavia,
corporatism and incomes policies were viable because the machinery of
moderation existed: governments could bargain with centralised union
movements whose leaders could make deals stick. By contrast, British
union leaders had less control over their members, since considerable
power lay with the shop stewards, whose parochial concern for local
wage rises had no discernible individual effect on inflation, but all such
claims in aggregate had a major impact.[12] Shop steward resistance
bedevilled British incomes policies.

With rising worker discontent, the left finally achieved a critical
mass within the unions in the 1970s, capturing the huge block votes of
the TGWU and the AUEW. For the first time in Labour's history, union
block votes at the party conference were cast consistently against the
preferences of the party leadership. However, rather than bow to the
conference's demands, the Wilson and Callaghan governments simply
ignored the conference defeats, pushing through deflationary policies
and demanding wage restraint. It was at this point that the unions'
own restraint wore thin. They fund the Labour Party to secure the
election of Labour governments that can help them. The unions are
ultimately policy-seeking interest groups, so if the party does not
'deliver' when it is in government, there are fewer incentives to be
loyal. If union leaders do not defend their members' interests, even
under a Labour government, they risk losing them – or their own jobs.
When union leaders wear their interest-group hats, it is rational for
them to oppose the hostile policies of Labour governments. The
Callaghan government's incomes policy caused tensions within the
party. Unofficial strikes proliferated and many union leaders sensed
they were losing control of their organisations to rank-and-file mili-

tants. The result was a serious rupture in the party-union link, culminating in the 'winter of discontent', a wave of strikes that sealed the fate of the government (Coates, 1980; Wickham-Jones, 1996).

The initial response to the demise of the Callaghan government was a two-year-long leftwing assault on the autonomy of the PLP. A number of reforms, inspired by the activist-left but backed by many unions, sought to tighten control over the PLP. Henceforth, all Labour MPs would undergo mandatory reselection contests once every parliament, in which they would need to mobilise the support of their CLPs to survive. Moreover, the party leader would now be elected by an electoral college representing all sections of the party, not just the MPs.[13] These reforms were a reflection of, and response to, the enforcement and commitment problems that characterised the party in government. Yet their effect was to empower radical activists and shift Labour's policies significantly to the left. An even more catastrophic election defeat in 1983 was enough to begin the reversal of the process, marking the start of a new period of PLP autonomy.

The crises of the 1970s created a negative public image for the unions. Party reformers believed that Labour's own reputation among voters was damaged by its association with the unions, and that voters' fears of future party-union conflicts was a major cause of Labour's unpopularity in the 1980s and 1990s. Under Neil Kinnock's leadership (1983–92), Labour distanced itself from the unions, transforming its policies and organisation. The process was given impetus after the defeat of the year-long miners' strike in 1985, and the pace of reform picked up considerably after Labour's election defeat in 1987, with a comprehensive policy review. However, it was with the historic fourth consecutive election defeat in 1992 that the reformers' focus shifted to the unions. Qualitative research by Philip Gould, a key Labour election strategist, suggested that voters distrusted Labour and saw it as a Trojan horse for the unions (Gould, 1999). The party reformed union participation in the selection of parliamentary candidates and reduced the unions' voting strength at the party conference. Block voting was abolished in leadership elections, allowing instead individual union levy-payers to vote by postal ballot (Alderman and Carter, 1994).

After the election of Tony Blair as leader in 1994, Labour seemed to be undergoing more than simply 'reform', but a rebirth. Not only were policies ruthlessly changed and opposition over-ridden; a new ethos and even a new historical narrative for the party were developed. The modernised party was christened 'new Labour', a 'brand name' that was deployed in speeches and party literature. The label was intended to provide a favourable contrast with 'old Labour' from the party's discredited past. The reality was more complex (Smith, 2000; Fielding, 2000), but it reflected an undoubted shift in the party leadership's view of the party and the unions.

The problems that emerged between the party and the unions in the 1970s illustrated the limits to mutual restraint; the experience of both sides in the 1980s demonstrated the costs of this breakdown. Such conflicts robbed the party of credibility and severely damaged its hopes of winning the trust of voters. Party leaders won the upper hand and decided that the best way to restore credibility was to initiate comprehensive reform.

Coalitions for change

One final task before analysing Labour's reforms is to establish the composition of the coalitions for change that assembled in the 1980s and 1990s. Not everyone supported change, and many that did previously had not. It is worth examining the forces that supported organisational change, since reference is made to them throughout this book. The reforms took place in two distinct stages with two different aims. The first, in the mid-1980s, was to undermine the power of the far-left, which was achieved through a 'realignment of the left'. The second, in the 1990s, was to reduce the power of the unions in the party, and created a new cleavage between 'modernisers' and 'traditionalists'.

The realignment of the left

The start of the 1980s was a period of leftwing ascendancy. Labour's parliamentary right had been discredited by the failures of the Callaghan government and the subsequent election defeat in 1979, whereas the left was strengthened. The leftist coalition included not only activist groups in the CLPs, but also a strong bank of support within left-leaning unions. This coalition managed to overhaul Labour's internal power structure during the constitutional revolt of 1979–81. However, Tony Benn's failure to win the deputy leadership of the party from Denis Healey in 1981 indicated that the left's power had reached its peak. Labour's poor showing in the polls in the aftermath of the formation of the Social Democratic Party (SDP) encouraged union leaders to agree an end to the constitutional reforms in the so-called 'peace of Bishop's Stortford' (Taylor, 1987: 142–5). Left unity was dealt a devastating blow by the landslide election defeat of 1983,

Labour's worst since 1935, which destroyed the left's credibility and widened the split that had emerged since 1981.

Between 1983 and 1985, the left fractured. The balance between left and right in the party was delicate, as was evident on the NEC, which remained evenly split despite the right's rollback of leftwingers in 1981 and 1982. The leadership and deputy leadership elections of 1983 resulted in landslide victories for the moderate 'soft left' (centre-left) candidate, Kinnock, and the centre-right Roy Hattersley. The radical 'hard left' (far-left) performed poorly in the contest, as the fissure between it and the soft left widened. It also demonstrated a desire for unity among the soft left and right factions. Table 3.2 offers a simple game-theoretic depiction of these factions' strategic choices.[14]

The soft left had the option of allying with either the hard left or the right, while the right had to decide whether to seek compromise with the soft left. Combinations of these choices produce leftist domination of the party, rightist domination, a centrist compromise or outright factional conflict. At the height of the left's assault on Labour's constitution in 1980, the soft left preferred an alliance with the hard left. At this time, the Labour right was in disarray, with rumours of defections to what later became the SDP. With continued anger at the 'betrayal' of the Labour government, the left unified around a programme of constitutional reforms designed to reduce the autonomy of the PLP. Some centrist and soft left unions, such as the GMWU and the TGWU, sought compromise, but the right fought against all the reforms and the left preferred a fight rather than continued rightwing control. Thus, the soft left's preference ordering at the time was $T_L > R_L > P_L > S_L$. The right wanted nothing to change, but would have preferred compromise with the soft left while excluding the hard left. Hence, its

Table 3.2 Strategic Options for Labour Factions (mid-1980s)

		RIGHT	
		COMPROMISE WITH SOFT LEFT	DON'T COMPROMISE WITH SOFT LEFT
SOFT LEFT	ALLY WITH RIGHT	Centrist compromise: R_L, R_R	Rightist domination: S_L, T_R
	ALLY WITH HARD LEFT	Leftist domination: T_L, S_R	Overt conflict: P_L, P_R

(i_L, j_R) payoffs to soft left and right

preference ordering was also $T_R>R_R>P_R>S_R$. Together, these preference rankings created a prisoner's dilemma between the soft left and the right: the soft left would have preferred compromise with the right to civil war ($R_L>P_L$), but it did not trust the right and so was prepared to ally with the hard left irrespective of whether the right was conciliatory ($T_L>R_L$) or not ($P_L>S_L$). Although the right wanted to detach soft leftists from the left coalition, it was not prepared to offer many concessions on policy and feared that the left would seriously damage Labour's election chances ($T_R>R_R$ and $P_R>S_R$). The result was the civil war that engulfed Labour between 1979 and 1983.

However, this game was not a one off; it was a repeated game[15] in which the contending forces faced similar choices over a period of time, and it was 'nested' (Tsebelis, 1990) in the wider game of electoral competition. Fluctuations in the latter modify the payoffs from intra-party outcomes, something that was apparent for the soft left during the period 1983–86. Not only had Labour's civil war contributed to its defeat in 1983, but the miners' strike of 1984–85 and the fiasco surrounding the activities of the Militant Tendency in Liverpool further damaged the standing of the party and severely eroded the credibility of a leftist stance in general. In terms of the game matrix, the value of T_L fell considerably, such that $T_L<R_L$. The 1983 defeat strengthened the right, and the new leader, Kinnock, was soon pulled away from his soft left roots. For the right, P_R fell, as it accepted that further overt factional conflict would play into the hands of the Conservatives and the SDP. However, even if its preference ranking remained $T_R>R_R>P_R>S_R$, compromise was likelier, because the soft left had few incentives to renege on a deal (thus, a low chance of the right being stuck with S_R), while the gap between R_R and P_R grew. Thus was born the 'realignment of the left' in 1985, by which soft leftists reasoned they could secure more by supporting Kinnock and restricting any rightward drift than by joining the hard left on the road to electoral oblivion. This realignment manifested itself in a solid soft-left–right coalition on the NEC and a steady base of support among the major unions at the annual conference. The price the soft left extracted was a commitment to retain Labour's non-nuclear defence policy, the abandonment of which might have re-ignited the party's civil war.

Critics later complained that far from constraining Labour's shift to the right, the soft left facilitated it (Heffernan and Marqusee, 1992: 62–70). There was some inevitability about this outcome, because once the hard left was reduced to a rump, the soft left was no longer so pivotal (see also Shaw, 2000: 132–3). The hard left attempted to reassemble the left coalition in 1988 when Benn challenged Kinnock for the party leadership, but his 11 percent poll demonstrated that the hard left was a broken reed. Even Labour's median individual member was by now firmly on the soft left.[16] The election defeat of 1987 created a consensus about the need to improve Labour's electoral standing, bearing expression in the policy review, and a series of organisational reforms that sought to centralise power and attack the power-bases of the hard left in the CLPs. For the remainder of the period under review, the Labour leadership would not face another challenge from a strong left. The right increasingly set the policy agenda, and in 1989 Kinnock was able to banish Labour's non-nuclear defence policy. Rather than moving the party into the top-left cell of Table 3.2, the 'realignment of the left' eventually led it into the top-right cell.

Modernisers and traditionalists

The final vanquishing of the hard left coincided with the emergence of a new fissure in the Labour Party in the late-1980s. Attention among Kinnock's allies turned towards the party's relationship with the trade unions, in terms of their constitutional standing and Labour's industrial policies. Immediately, many union leaders became defensive about their role in the party, but the election defeat of 1992 put their power under the spotlight as never before. In place of 'left versus right' came 'modernisers versus traditionalists', the former wanting to reduce union influence or even abandon the union link altogether, the latter seeking to defend it. The modernisers wanted to push Labour in the direction of a 'direct' unitary membership structure, whereas the traditionalists, whose ranks included much of the union movement, wished to retain the existing federal structure. Not everyone slotted easily into these two polar opposites, many occupying an intermediate position seeking compromise, including the new leader, John Smith, and John Prescott, who both made the case for the party-union link while also backing the one-member–one-vote (OMOV) reforms.

The modernisers emerged in the late-1980s, as key Labour figures sensed that the party-union link might be damaging the party's electoral prospects. The chief modernisers at this early stage were Kinnock and his office, joined later by younger MPs such as Tony Blair and Gordon Brown. Each successive election defeat strengthened the modernisers' case and enlarged the size of the coalition for reform of the union link, even if the new converts did not go as far as the ultra-modernisers. By the late-1980s, support for reform was growing in the CLPs, which would benefit from any redistribution of power. Seyd and Whiteley collected data on party members' attitudes to the modernisation strategy, the two main indicators of which were a willingness to let the leader initiate change, and the conflict between principles and electoral pragmatism. They found that, outside the ranks of the hard left, Labour members accepted the necessity of capturing the political centreground, were willing to permit autonomy to the leadership, and sensed that the unions wielded too much power in the party. Thus, there was a constituency of support for reform among Labour members, though it was particularly pronounced among centrist, rightwing and inactive members, with little support among hard-left activists (Seyd and Whiteley, 1992: 162, 164).

The modernisers could expect some backing from members in OMOV ballots (for example, in NEC elections), but they could not rely on much *active* support. A wider base of members, including conference delegates, might be expected to support a redistribution of conference voting power from unions to CLPs. Divisions between modernisers, traditionalists and intermediates cut across left-right divisions, though the left in general preferred more control 'from below' while the right in general wanted greater central direction (see Figure 3.2).

Thus, there was the potential for a coalition in support of 'new deal' institutional reform, encompassing key NEC and PLP figures, together with an important section of the individual membership. However, control of Labour's constitution resides in the annual conference, which was dominated by union block votes. Therefore, any attempt to reduce union power in the party would require the support of the unions themselves, or at least, from enough of them to achieve a majority. The desperation of the unions to remove the incumbent Conservative government provided the modernisers with some leverage, but it would be a slow process. Kinnock's attempts to erode the unions' power achieved limited success. It took the shock of the election defeat of 1992 to change the balance of opinion on reform of the union link. The NEC set up a review group to examine ways of reforming the party-union relationship, but the group was dominated by traditionalists from the big unions, and its initial ideas for change were extremely limited. The new leader, John Smith, accepted that some reform was necessary but wanted party unity above all else. Smith sought compromises with the unions, though it took a knife-edge vote at the 1993 annual conference to secure the passage of OMOV. A substantial union 'no' was narrowly

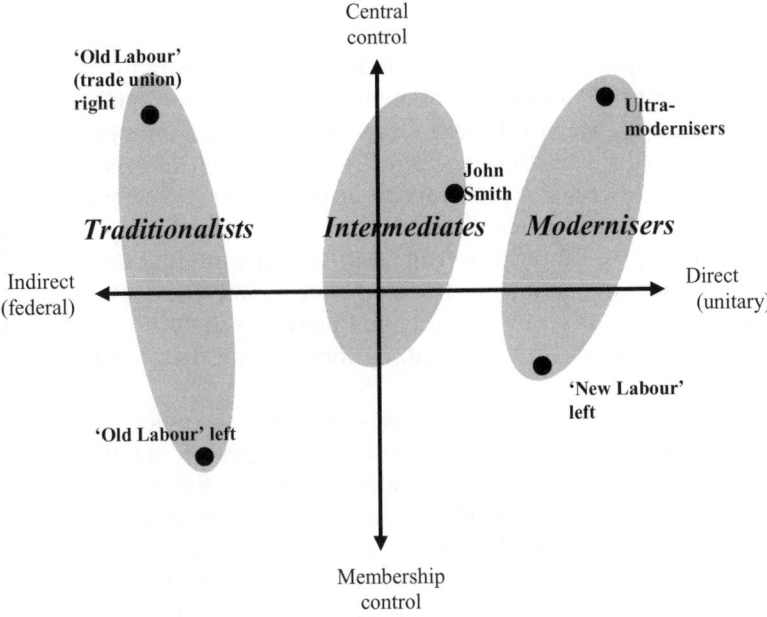

Figure 3.2 Institutional Preferences of Labour Factions
Horizontal plane: Direct (unitary) versus indirect (federal) membership structure
Vertical plane: Distribution of power between centre and party members

defeated by a minority union 'yes', together with a considerable 'yes' vote from the CLPs.

The agreed reforms fell short of what the modernisers wanted, but they would have their chance after Smith's death a year later. Blair's accession to the leadership gave the modernisers an enormous boost and his period in charge has seen considerable change. For a period before the 1997 election, modernisers encouraged talk of a party-union divorce to emphasise that Labour was not run by union barons, though these voices have since fallen quiet. Indeed, calls for divorce nowadays tend to come from leftwing union officials, angered by what they perceive to be the poor return on their 'investment' in the Labour government. Meanwhile, the party membership appears closer to Blair on a range of policies, with CLP delegates to the party conference often backing the leadership even when the unions do not. Nevertheless, Labour's individual membership has fallen considerably (after a brief surge during 1994–98), raising questions about how prepared the members are to continue having little say.

Conclusion

Labour's historic problem has been its frequent inability to overcome the commitment problems inherent in a trade-union-funded vote-seeking party. Moreover, before the election victory of 1997, it has been the party's misfortune normally to find itself in office during recessions, when these problems are at their worst. No internal party institution can solve such difficulties. Yet, given these unpropitious circumstances, we can acknowledge that Labour's internal institutions did alleviate other problems. The block vote was an efficient institution that kept the unions in the party and preserved the supply of union finance for a century. It reduced, but never eradicated, commitment problems.

The significance of the block vote altered once the unions shifted to the left, resulting in the organisational changes of the 1980s and 1990s. The next three chapters examine reforms in the areas of policy-making, candidate selection and electing the party leader. Labour's membership structure has increasingly shifted from an 'indirect' federal structure to a 'direct' unitary one, if not completely then significantly. The institutionalisation of political exchange in block votes was dismantled and a party geared towards individual membership and donations emerged in its place. However, this process was never completed, and serious barriers remain to making Labour a purely unitary party. The next chapter examines the first of these areas of reform, party policy-making.

4
Policy-making

One of the fundamental ways that parties institutionalise political exchange is by allowing their members a role in policy-making. This process includes the research that is conducted to assess the impact of policies, the forums in which decisions are made over which policies to adopt, and the interpretation of those policies. This chapter explores the nature of Labour's policy-making structure and the changes to it since 1983. According to the party's constitution, the annual conference is the sovereign policy-making body. This body was long dominated by the block votes of the trade unions but recent changes have increased the voting power of the CLPs. The chapter begins by considering the policy-making structure until 1983, before assessing the traditional relationship between the PLP and the annual conference. It then examines the reduced role of the unions in policy-making, with the downgrading of the conference and the formation of a national policy forum in the 1990s. The main effects of the changes to the policy-making process have been to increase the autonomy of the PLP leadership and to reduce the role of the unions.

Policy-making in the Labour Party before 1983

Before examining the reform of Labour's policy-making structure after 1983, it is necessary to understand the institutions and rules that existed until then (and in many cases, beyond). The aim of this section is not to provide a detailed description of all features of the policy process (see Minkin, 1980), but to outline the basic elements. The unions' block votes gave them collective control of all the major policy-making organs of the extra-parliamentary party, including the annual conference, the NEC and the Conference Arrangements

Committee (CAC). The 'floor' of the conference consisted of delegates sent by trade unions, socialist societies and CLPs. Each body was entitled to send one delegate per 5000 affiliated members, though not all unions took up their full allocations. Their votes were allotted on the basis of affiliation levels, not numbers of delegates, and as was shown in Chapter 3, these votes were cast as blocks so the unions did not lose out by taking smaller delegations. (It would have been impractical: the TGWU alone was usually entitled to 250 delegates!) Typically there were 1200 delegates at an average Labour Party conference, roughly split evenly between CLPs and affiliated organisations, though until the 1990s the CLPs cast only 10–15 per cent of the votes. In addition to voting delegates, MPs and members of the NEC were (and still are) entitled to attend the conference in an *ex officio*, non-voting capacity.[1]

The NEC is the party's governing body between conferences and was previously the major site of policy formulation. The NEC's members are elected by different sections of the party, though the precise format has changed over the years (see Appendix 2 to Chapter 6). The NEC is formally subject to control by the conference, its major decisions requiring conference approval. Furthermore, the NEC is responsible for implementing conference decisions. The NEC possessed an array of resources that facilitated detailed policy-making, including control of the party's research department and a range of policy study groups and subcommittees. These resources made the NEC the major policy-initiating body in the extra-parliamentary party until the late-1990s. The CAC's role is to organise the conference agenda and together with the NEC, it comprises 'the platform' at the party conference. In the 1980s, the CAC had five members, who were elected by the entire conference, normally ensuring that the major unions could pack it with their allies.[2] The platform was usually associated with the PLP leadership, because the party leader was a member of the NEC, and he and his allies normally controlled it.[3]

The platform enjoyed procedural advantages that enabled it to shape the course of policy-making. Each union, CLP and socialist society could send one resolution and one amendment to the conference, all of which had to be submitted in advance to the CAC, which could direct the agenda through its gate-keeping powers, most notably through compositing. Each year, hundreds of policy proposals were submitted over a range of issues but not all could be discussed in the course of a five-day conference. The CAC had to reduce the number of resolutions by combining some in 'composite' resolutions, which could cover a number of different yet connected issues. For each policy area, two or three resolutions or composites might go forward for debate at the conference, providing delegates with clear choices. The CAC was constrained in that any composite resolutions it produced had to retain the wording of the original resolutions, often resulting in bloated composites. However, it could use this restriction to its advantage when dealing with resolutions hostile to the platform, ensuring that incoherent composites were put to the delegates. Similarly, it could 'tidy up' resolutions that the NEC broadly supported (see Minkin, 1980: 138–46).

Whereas resolutions submitted by voting bodies faced an uncertain passage, the NEC's proposals stood a much greater chance of adoption. Unlike conference delegates, the NEC could put its own resolutions to the conference, and in contrast to the clumsy composites on the agenda, the NEC could devise concise resolutions, which were not subject to compositing. The NEC could tailor its resolutions to be sure of winning majority support at the conference through what Minkin (1980: 46–7, 53; see also 142–3) called 'the "anticipated reactions" effect', whereby the NEC took soundings from the major unions to determine what policies it could secure at the conference.

A further noteworthy feature of the policy-making system was Clause V.1 of Labour's constitution, which stated that '[n]o proposal shall be included in the party programme unless it has been adopted by conference by a majority of not less than two-thirds of the votes recorded on a card vote'. The constitution provided no definition of the term 'party programme'.[4] It was not synonymous with the election manifesto, because Clause V.2 implied the latter would be *drawn* from the party programme. This ambiguity ensured that simple majorities were usually deemed sufficient to affirm a resolution as party policy unless the party leadership and its platform allies used the two-thirds-majority rule to justify ignoring embarrassing conference defeats. However, party leaders did not always seek to use this rule to extricate themselves from defeats, especially when the party's public standing was at stake. After the most famous conference defeat suffered by a Labour leader – the 1960 vote on unilateralism, which failed to secure two-thirds-majority backing – Hugh Gaitskell did not resort to the two-thirds-majority rule, but instead challenged the authority of the conference (Minkin, 1980: 280).

We saw in Chapter 3 that despite Labour's constitution situating sovereignty in the conference, there were no direct means by which the latter could impose its demands on a reluctant PLP. The PLP was not completely free of the extra-parliamentary party, but neither was the conference fully sovereign. However, party leaders knew that shirking on promises could cause damaging intra-party strife. The ties that ultimately bound politicians to activists and unions were the resources that the latter supplied, and which they could withdraw if the politicians did not honour their promises. The PLP-conference relationship was best seen as a bargaining game in which each side brought to bear certain resources. One of the extra-parliamentary party's greatest sources of power was, and still is, its ability to impose voice costs on the PLP. Meanwhile, it was often noted that the PLP in government had more autonomy from the extra-parliamentary party than when it was in opposition (Brand, 1989; Kavanagh, 1985). The reason was that in government, the PLP was not dependent on Labour's own internal policy-making resources, but had the resources of the state at its disposal, with the civil service to implement government policies. By contrast, in opposition the PLP did depend on access to Labour's own policy-making resources. Therefore, the cost to the PLP of ignoring the conference (and now other policy-making institutions – see below) was lower when it was in government than in opposition, *ceteris paribus*.

The relations between the conference and the PLP depended on the interaction of these resource constraints with preferences. Whether in government or opposition, when the PLP was centre-right in Labour Party terms (as it historically has been), it was easier to bargain with the conference when the latter was similarly centre-right. The conference could accept the PLP's policies, and votes could be promised in advance. During the 1950s, a group of large rightwing unions consistently coalesced to deliver the conference to Gaitskell. McKenzie (1964) described these unions as a 'Praetorian Guard': at twelve annual conferences, between 1948 and 1959, the platform suffered only one defeat.

Problems arose when the conference was leftwing because its preferences differed from those of the median voter among the electorate at large. A Labour government that bowed to a leftwing conference would receive adverse comment from the press and the opposition, as well as from its own MPs. The charge against the government would be that it was weak, which would incur further electoral costs, perhaps greater than the costs arising from the disunity that would ensue from an outright rejection of the conference's decision. When Harold Wilson's governments faced wishlists from leftwing conferences, they ignored them. The danger was that this practice could become the norm, because the incentives for the conference (and hence, for the unions) to compromise were reduced when the party was in government, as the unions demanded that the party 'deliver'. The *arena* of bargaining historically shifted from intra-party bodies in opposition to national institutions, such as tripartite bodies, in government. Paradoxically, when Labour was in opposition, the PLP was usually more closely controlled by the conference, but the latter was constrained from imposing policies that were too extreme lest it scupper the party's election hopes. When Labour formed a government, the unions and the conference wanted the PLP to use the opportunity to implement their favoured policies, but the PLP was more independent and could ignore them.

When the PLP was in opposition, ignoring or disowning decisions could carry very high costs in terms of party disunity. Its disinclination towards leftwing policies meant that it was likely to risk more defeats but would usually end up having to accept them, though compromises were possible if the unions did not want to encumber the party with unpopular policies. Prior to the February 1974 general election, Wilson faced demands for a Labour government to nationalise 25 top firms. The big unions were opposed and the proposal was defeated at the 1973 conference after the CAC included it in an extreme composite, though the 1974 manifesto did promise more nationalisation (Wickham-Jones, 1996: 126–9). It was not impossible for the PLP in opposition to reject conference decisions, as Gaitskell's rejection of the vote on unilateralism in 1960 demonstrated, but it was *costly*. Policy bargains in opposition were usually more favourable to the conference, otherwise the PLP would have to accept defeat.

Naturally, numerous other factors were involved, including the proximity of an election (the closer it was, the greater the autonomy of the PLP leadership) and the length of time spent in opposition. The longer the party was out of government, the hungrier it became for office and the greater the freedom of the PLP leaders, something that helps explain the dominance of Kinnock and Blair (see Koelble, 1996). The most notable example was the unions' gradual acceptance during the 1980s that a future Labour government would not repeal the Conservatives' trade union legislation, because the latter was popular with voters.

The relationship between the PLP and the annual conference was thus one of bargaining, with policy preferences and resources shaping the negotiated outcomes. However, the enforcement problems that arose when Labour was in government were the spur for leftwing attempts to change Labour's constitution in the early 1980s. The left's capture of extra-parliamentary policy-making bodies later enabled it to remould Labour's policies – the same policies that were identified by moderates as the cause of the party's crushing election defeat in 1983.

Not surprisingly, on becoming Labour leader in 1983, Kinnock targeted the party's policy-making structure for reform. The remainder of this chapter shows how these and later reforms gave the PLP more autonomy over policy-making than at any previous time in Labour's history.

The PLP and policy-making after 1983

The PLP's autonomy from the party conference enabled party leaders largely to evade direct control by activists and unions. However, the disadvantage of this state of affairs was that the leadership could do little to stop the conference and the NEC sniping from the sidelines when Labour was in government, and controlling valuable decision-making bodies when it was in opposition. Leftwing control of the conference and the NEC posed considerable problems for the rightwing PLP during the Callaghan and Foot years. The institutional and factional separation of the NEC and the PLP created a weak centre in the Labour Party (Kitschelt, 1994: 251). The PLP was always at its strongest when (shadow) ministers sat on the NEC and dominated its policy initiatives. With the CLPs still electing leftwing MPs to the executive in the early 1980s, Kinnock wound up the NEC's subcommittees in 1983 and established a set of joint policy committees consisting of NEC and shadow cabinet members. (Figure 4.1 depicts Labour's policy-making structure in the mid-1980s.) The shadow cabinet did not come under the control of the extra-parliamentary party, because the committees were not formalised in Labour's constitution. Nevertheless, their formation was a step towards strengthening the hold of party leaders over policy-making by increasing their initiating power.

An important aspect of Labour's policy-making structure after 1983 was the shadow cabinet's big increase in resources compared to previous spells in opposition. The NEC was constitutionally in charge of Labour's research department, which possessed administrative and research facilities essential to policy-makers. However, Labour was now eligible for 'Short money', an annual grant paid by the state to opposition *parliamentary* parties amounting to £440,000 in 1983 (see Chapter 7).[5] It meant that 'there were now, for the first time in Party history, resources for a sizeable alternative policy advisory staff available to the PLP leadership' (Minkin, 1992: 400). Kinnock was able to fund an extensive office consisting of advisors and strategists, who devised moderate policies and were answerable solely to the leader. With significant increases in secretarial and research allowances to MPs

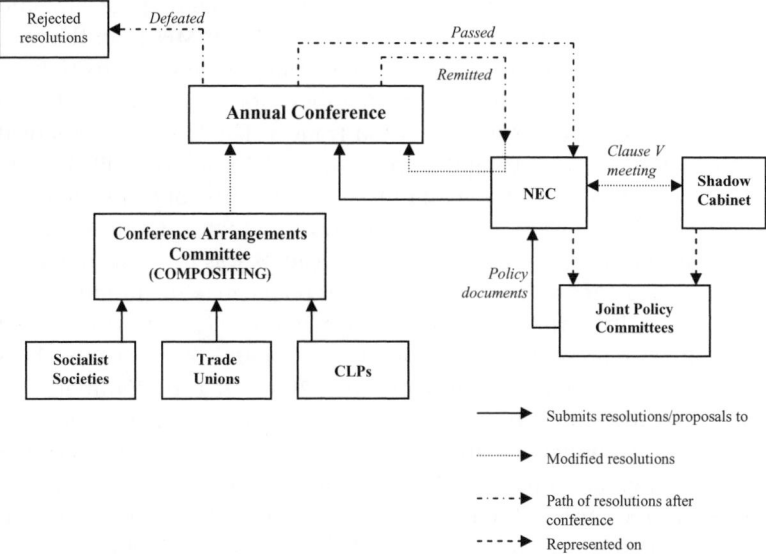

Figure 4.1   Labour's Policy-making Structure (mid-1980s)

during the 1980s, the PLP had more resources beyond the control of the extra-parliamentary party, strengthening its independence.

This trend towards greater PLP autonomy was evident during the major policy review after Labour's election defeat in 1987. The abandonment of leftwing policies, such as unilateral nuclear disarmament and the party's earlier withdrawal of its opposition to Conservative trade union legislation showed that the unions realised new policies were required if Labour were to enter government. However, the process of the policy review was itself noteworthy for the extent to which the PLP leadership had almost completely taken over policy-making. Already in the first four years of Kinnock's leadership, the unions had taken a less visible and non-interventionist role in policy-making, though informal links between PLP and union leaders increased significantly.[6] Rather than the PLP setting policy in line with union preferences, the unions themselves smoothed the way for the PLP to seek vote-winning policies. As Minkin (1992: 408) writes, 'all eggs were now in the basket of a future Labour Government' to deliver them from mass unemployment and the Conservative administration's policies. The PLP's autonomy derived from the unions' desperation for a Labour government. Since the unions were widely seen an electoral liability, they stayed out of sight, with the PLP taking the initiative.

The policy review continued the practice of integrating the NEC and the shadow cabinet in policy-making. With soft left MPs from the NEC prominent, MPs dominated seven new policy review groups (PRGs). Each PRG consisted of about nine members drawn from the NEC and the shadow cabinet, as well as union leaders. The PRGs were charged with looking at ways to update party policy. In only two PRGs were MPs in a minority and trade unionists in a majority, one of which, the People at Work group, dealt with issues in which the unions had a direct interest. The inclusion of union leaders was the first time they had been assigned a direct role in Labour policy-making (union leaders are not usually permitted to sit on the NEC). The CLPs were excluded from direct representation on the PRGs, though MPs from the NEC's constituency section were present. The PRGs were thus dominated by the party and union hierarchies (Taylor, 1997: 47–9). However, the NEC saw its policy-making role contract, as the shadow cabinet assumed a greater presence. Even on the issue of the election manifesto, Kinnock ensured that his own allies wrote the document, which was then confirmed by the NEC and the shadow cabinet (Heffernan and Marqusee, 1992: 81).

Here is not the place to analyse the transformation that Labour's policy programme underwent during the policy review (see Shaw, 1994: 81–107; Wickham-Jones, 1995a). The important point is that party leaders saw the review as a chance to abandon unpopular policies in the wake of Labour's 1987 election defeat and adopt policies that enjoyed broader electoral appeal. They did not achieve everything they wanted and faced resistance on some issues. However, on the most important economic questions, a broad coalition agreed on the need for change, and on issues such as keeping the Conservatives' trade union legislation, the unions were sympathetic to the party's needs. The PRGs were expected to take account of public opinion when framing policies, supplied with information from the shadow communications agency, a loose internal network of strategy advisers close to the leadership (see Chapter 7). They were also free to establish working parties and co-opt specialists (Shaw, 1989). On occasions, aides from the leader's office were on hand to steer the groups in the desired direction, though in only one case (the People At Work group) was intervention necessary (Hughes and Wintour, 1990: 143–52). On the whole, there was a consensus on the PRGs as to the type of policies required (Taylor, 1997: 57).

A significant feature of the policy review was the greatly restricted role of the party conference. The PRGs' final reports were presented to the conference in 1989 as *faits accompli*, which could be accepted or rejected but not amended. In practice, the conference had little alternative but to accept the reports: as Gerald Taylor (1997: 62) notes, '[w]holesale rejection would have left two years of Party strategy in ruins, Party policy in tatters, and the Party itself deeply divided and needing to pick up the pieces with a possible General Election looming in 1991.' The unions still dominated the conference and would not vote against reports agreed by the major union leaders on the PRGs. Electoral considerations meant they were largely content to allow the PLP to establish the parameters of party policy.

Kinnock's reform of Labour's policy-making structures after 1983 was designed to wrest control of party policy from the left. His strategy was to integrate the shadow cabinet into the policy-making process and let it play the major role. The abandonment of the last vestiges of the left's programme during the policy review showed that the new structures had achieved their intended goal. However, it was also becoming evident that union influence in policy-making was being diluted. A major re-examination of the unions' role in policy-making and other areas of intra-party decision-making would soon be under way.

Trade unions and the party conference in the 1990s

Some of Labour's most symbolic reforms concerned the trade unions' role at the party conference. The modernisers' call for reform of the party-union link gathered momentum after Labour's election defeat of 1992, as they claimed the link contributed to voters' distrust of Labour. Even traditionalists accepted that change was necessary. The NEC's trade union links review group, in which traditionalists comprised a majority, suggested some changes to conference policy-making. Most notably, the block voting system should be reformed and there would be further moves to increase the CLPs' share of votes.

The main problem with the conference was that it vividly illustrated the unions' predominance in the party. The problem worsened over the years because of the increasing concentration of votes in a few large unions: by 1990, the four biggest unions collectively controlled over half the conference votes. Given the balance of forces in the party under John Smith's leadership, there was no chance of fundamental change, but there was a realisation that the *status quo* was not an option. The focus centred on proposals to redistribute votes. The 1990 conference had agreed to reduce affiliated organisations' share of conference votes from about 90 per cent to 70 per cent, with the CLPs controlling 30 per cent (the change took effect in 1993). The review group observed that the new distribution of votes 'reflects the relative financial contributions of the trade unions and maintains the stability of Conference' (cited in Alderman and Carter, 1994: 329). This statement was a further illustration of the intertwining of votes and finance, but it also obliquely referred to the potentially destabilising effect of giving too many votes to the CLPs, especially if they were to come under leftwing control.

However, the modernisers were not satisfied. They wanted parity between the CLPs and affiliated organisations, but the NEC recommended that such a move be contingent upon a rise in individual membership to 300,000, which it saw as possible if a scheme such as 'levy-plus' were to be adopted, in which union members were offered cut-price subscriptions to the Labour Party. As well as ensuring that the CLPs shouldered a heavier financial burden, modernisers hoped that a rise in membership would bring an influx of 'moderate' members to outweigh the influence of the hard left. CLP delegates would have greater voting power so the unions would find it harder to play their traditionally protective role towards the PLP leadership. In 1996, parity was achieved, with the CLPs and the affiliated organisations each controlling 50 per cent of the votes. Since the affiliated organisations included the small socialist societies, it meant that the unions controlled marginally fewer than 50 per cent of the votes. However, the national policy forum was also operating (see below), so the CLPs' greater voting power at the party conference arrived at the point when that body was being increasingly sidelined.

In an apparently major change to Labour's structure, the review group recommended, and the 1993 conference agreed, that unions no longer cast their votes as single blocks but should instead divide their votes among their individual delegates, with a maximum of one delegate per 5000 levypayers. This system is not the same type of 'one-delegate–one-vote' (ODOV) discussed in Chapter 3. In that hypothetical example, all conference delegates wielded votes of equal weight, but in the Labour Party after 1993, there was a subtle difference. Unions would possess their entire block of votes, which would be divided equally among however many delegates they brought to the conference. Thus, a union with a million affiliated levypayers would be entitled to a maximum of two hundred delegates, but if it brought 40 delegates, each would have 25,000 votes. It would be misleading to describe this system as 'one-delegate–one-vote': a more accurate description would be 'one-delegate–one-mini-block-vote', with the size of these blocks varying among delegates from different unions.

Nevertheless, any system of ODOV reduces individual unions' 'effective votes', (the net votes of a union's delegates). It was suggested earlier that ODOV could significantly dilute the voices of unions qua organisations and weaken the link between financial donations and voting power, possibly leaving the party vulnerable to financial free-riding by the unions. Given the greatly reduced authority and importance of the party conference, such a development might be expected to be less of a threat nowadays. Yet there remained concerns within the unions about the impact of ODOV, and the PLP leadership understood them. In his speech to the 1993 conference, Smith emphasised that unions would be free to continue mandating their delegates. Individual delegates would still be regarded primarily as delegates of an organisation, even though each would be individually responsible for casting a proportion of that organisation's votes. They would not be seen as representatives of strands of opinion within individual unions, still less as free agents. Indeed, the party's then general secretary, Larry Whitty, assured the NEC that the change was 'largely presentational', designed to avoid television pictures of union leaders casting enormous block votes. He added, 'we will then say we don't have the block vote' (Rentoul, 1995: 323). The very fact of mandating assumes that organisational interests are above individual delegates' preferences. We have seen that mandates entail measurement costs, particularly in the case of composites, though delegation meetings could be used to iron out such problems. Indeed, since the change came into effect in 1994, that has been precisely the pattern, with unions continuing to cast their votes to all intents and purposes as single blocks. It illustrates the continued 'efficiency' of block voting, and not only for the unions. A noteworthy feature of conferences since Blair became leader is that the platform has continued to lobby union leaders for support in vital votes, knowing that individual union delegates are unlikely to break ranks from any agreed position.

Indeed, this development illustrates a feature of conferences of old that the present party leadership has sought to resurrect: the managerial role of the block vote. With 50 per cent of the conference votes, the unions remain extremely important. Four large unions – Amicus, the TGWU, the GMB and Unison – now control 70 per cent of all the unions' votes (see Table 4.1). If the support of three of these unions can be secured, victory for the platform is likely. It is their votes that party leaders invariably try to win first because if they do success is likely. The major conference

Table 4.1   Union Affiliation Levels 2002

Union	Affiliated Membership
Unison	580,000
AEEU*	400,000
GMB	400,000
TGWU	400,000
USDAW	291,587
CWU	240,000
MSF*	135,100
Total†	2,790,923

These figures are affiliation levels on 31 December 2002, and they determined vote allocations at the 2003 party conference.
* MSF merged with AEEU to form Amicus
† Includes socialist societies and smaller unions (not listed in table)
Source: Labour Party Head Office

votes since 1997 have been preceded by intensive negotiations between ministers and leaders of the big unions. This way, the government was able to avoid defeat over such controversial policies as university tuition fees in 1997.

However, as the 1970s demonstrated, when Labour is in government the managerial effectiveness of the block vote can diminish if the unions are antagonised. In its first term of office, the Blair government enjoyed a relatively quiet relationship with the unions but there were setbacks. Most notably, the government was defeated at the 2000 conference on its policy of index-linking pensions to prices rather than wages. CLP delegates backed the government by nearly two-to-one but despite negotiations between union leaders and ministers keen to avoid a defeat, the unions voted five-to-one against, ensuring defeat for the government. After the 2001 election, public sector reform emerged as a divisive issue between the government and the unions. The 2002 conference saw the government lose three votes on the private finance initiative. However, it has paid little notice of the defeats, as it knows its own survival depends on improving service delivery in the public sector.

Policy-making in the 1990s: the national policy forum

From the start of his leadership, Kinnock wanted the party to speak with a single voice and to this end, the joint policy committees and PRGs were attempts to synchronise the shadow cabinet and the NEC.

However, he believed the format of the party conference, with its set-piece debates and public displays of discord, damaged Labour. From 1986, the conference underwent an image makeover, adopting a more professional and corporate look. Conference debates were subject to platform management, and shadow cabinet ministers acquired a prominent role. However, the potential remained for embarrassing showdowns, which would be a problem for a Labour government. Few images are more redolent of the traumas of the Callaghan government than that of the Chancellor, Denis Healey, being given five minutes at the 1976 conference to defend the government's economic policy amid a crescendo of jeers from delegates.

To avoid recurrences of such incidents, thought was given to overhauling party policy-making on a permanent and constitutional basis. However, the PLP leadership faced a dilemma. It wanted to modernise the policy-making process because it was unwieldy, inefficient, and block votes brought Labour into disrepute. One way of establishing greater control would be to integrate the PLP into the extra-parliamentary party's policy-making structures in the expectation that it would play the leading role in policy development, a process that had already begun with the establishment of the joint policy committees and the PRGs. The NEC mooted a proposal for an electoral college at the conference, similar to that for leadership elections, with the PLP taking a 30 per cent stake (Labour Party, 1990: 8). In theory, the conference made policy, and the PLP worked within parliamentary and electoral constraints to implement it. In reality, the PLP had always been closely involved in policy development, something the new proposals would formalise. Yet the integration of the PLP would also ensure, as Minkin (1992: 377) remarked, that 'the stakes of Party democracy would be raised considerably'. There would be no new institutional constraints on the PLP, because there would still be no direct enforcement mechanisms through which the conference could punish a shirking PLP. Instead, it would be an issue of the *legitimacy* of the conference. For this reason, plans to integrate the PLP into the conference were shelved. Instead, the decision was taken to marginalise the conference by creating a new body, in which the PLP and the (shadow) cabinet were not merely represented but played a leading role.

The NEC presented a statement to the 1990 party conference proposing to establish a national policy forum (NPF) to work alongside the existing institutions (Labour Party, 1990). The ostensible aim of this new body was to improve the efficiency of the policy-making process. The statement pointed out the many weaknesses of the existing system

of conference policy-making. Most resolutions submitted to the conference were not debated; most resolutions that were debated were
clumsy, often contradictory composites that made mandates difficult
to follow; and most delegates did not participate in debates. To ensure
greater participation and properly researched and discussed policies,
the proposed NPF, consisting of delegates elected by all sections of the
party, would develop policies in a clearly-defined cycle. Once agreed,
these policies would then pass to the party conference, which would be
required to back them before they officially became party policy.

The NPF was eventually set up in 1993 and met on eight occasions
up to 1997, but its formal status was unclear and its impact limited
(Seyd, 1999: 390). Labour's return to power in 1997 signalled a new
emphasis on the NPF, as Tony Blair demanded his government should
not experience the same conflicts with the extra-parliamentary party as
previous administrations. After a consultation exercise, the NEC wrote
a report, *Partnership in Power* (Labour Party, 1997), which contained
proposals to entrench the NPF in a new policy-making apparatus, in
which the government and the extra-parliamentary party would seek a
consensus over policy. The report was sent to the 1997 party conference, which duly passed it. The remainder of this section analyses the
present functioning of the new structures.

The NPF is the apex of a multi-level policy-making structure, whose
function is to develop over a three-year cycle a rolling policy programme from which Labour's election manifesto will ultimately be
drawn.[7] It consists of 183 delegates (initially 175) representing all
sections of the party, including the government and the PLP (see
Table 4.2). Acting as a steering group for the NPF is a joint policy

Table 4.2 National Policy Forum Membership 2003

Division	Number of Representatives		Method of Election
I. Constituency Labour Parties	55	5 (incl. 1 Young Labour) for each of Scotland, Wales and 9 English regions	Regional groups of CLP delegates at party conference
II. Trade Unions	30	Unions represented approximately by size (5 Amicus, 4 Unison, 4 GMB, 3 TGWU, 2 CWU, 2 USDAW, 1 each 10 others)	Formula agreed by unions on TULO; individual unions nominate their own representatives*

Table 4.2   National Policy Forum Membership 2003 – *continued*

Division	Number of Representatives		Method of Election
III. Regional Labour Parties	22	2 for each of Scotland, Wales and 9 English regions	Regional conference or policy forum
IV. Local Government	9	4 Local Govt Association 1 COSLA 4 Association of Labour Councillors	Labour group on LGA* Labour group on COSLA* ALC members
V. Socialist Societies	3		Affiliated socialist societies
VI. Black Socialist Society	4		Black Socialist Society conference
VII. Parliamentary Labour Party	9		Backbench MPs
VIII. European Parliamentary Labour Party	6		MEPs
IX. Labour Students	1		National Organisation of Labour Students
X. Peers	2		Labour Peers
Other NPF Members	42	8 Government 2 Co-operative Party 32 National Executive Committee	Government* Co-operative Party NEC *Ex officio*
Total	**183**		

* Appointees

Note: Quotas for women operate in most divisions: at least 50 per cent in Divisions II, III, VI, and VIII; at least two of each region's four representatives in Division I, with each region's Young Labour representative being a woman every other election; at least 50 per cent of the LGA and ALC places in Division IV; at least one member of Division V; at least four members of Division VII; and at least three of the eight government members, and one of the two Co-operative Party members must be women. Separate quotas for the NEC ensure that at least 12 of its 32 members are women. Therefore, in any year, at least 78 of the NPF's 183 members are women.

Sources: Labour Party (1997: 12; 2003a: Rule 4C.5)

committee (JPC – not to be confused with the joint policy committees formed in 1983), which is charged with 'strategic oversight of policy development in the party and the rolling programme', shaping the agenda for the whole policy process. The JPC currently consists of 32 members: eight from each of the NEC and the government (the co-convenors of the individual policy commissions), nine from the NPF, and seven other leadership figures, including the Prime Minister (who chairs it), the Deputy Prime Minister, the party chairman, and the leader of the European Parliamentary Labour Party (EPLP). The JPC's domination by the party elite has led to it being described as '[t]he main institutional vehicle for the leadership in the policy-making process' (Webb, 2000: 204). In reality, it has played a rubberstamp role thus far, and its lack of proactivity has been a cause of complaint (Hain, 2004: 26). On the other hand, its non-interventionist stance may simply reflect the fact that it has not often needed to step in, because leadership power is exercised at other points in the policy-making process.

The detailed work on policy formulation is carried out by specialist policy commissions, which have usurped the policy-making powers of the NEC. The commissions' members are drawn from the government, the NEC and the NPF, with the NPF's representatives elected by NPF delegates divided into three sections (see Table 4.3).[8] During the policy cycle of 2002–04, there were eight commissions, three of which had 15 members and the remaining five had ten members.[9] The fifteen-member commissions consisted of seven members elected by the NPF (three by the CLP section and two each by the elected members and affiliates' sections), and four representatives from each of the government and the NEC. The ten-member commissions had four NPF-elected members (two by the CLPs, one each by the elected members and affiliates), and three representatives from each of the government and the NEC. However, the key role is played by the relevant ministers

Table 4.3   Policy Commission Elections

CLP section (77 members)		Elected members' section (26 members)		Affiliates' section (40 members)	
55	CLPs	9	PLP	30	Trade unions
22	Regional parties	2	Peers	3	Socialist societies
		6	EPLP	2	Co-operative Party
		9	Local government	4	Black Socialist Society
				1	Labour students

and their advisers, and policy staff at party HQ, who draft the policy documents that are presented to the policy commissions, the JPC and the NPF. It is here that the power of the party leadership is greatest, since ministers provide the proposals that subsequent debates revolve around. Policy commissions can make some initial alterations to the documents, as can the JPC. The NPF discusses all documents and can make amendments to draft final policy statements (see below).

The new structure ensures that party policy is revamped in two waves over the policy cycle. During the 2002–04 cycle, the party had the task of producing documents from which the election manifesto for 2005/06 would be drawn. The first wave of five policy documents were drafted and sent to the NPF in February 2002, before being approved by the JPC and sent out, as part of a broad consultation exercise, to CLPs, affiliates, local all-member policy forums,[10] and external organisations, such as businesses and interest groups. The policy commissions took note of these stakeholders' submissions, and presented the redrafted second-year documents to the NPF in February 2003. A second phase of consultation then began, more formal than the first and restricted to party members, culminating in the presentation to the NPF of draft final documents in March and July 2004. At these meetings, the NPF can make textual amendments, before the documents are sent to the 2004 annual conference to be debated. The second wave of five policy documents began nine months after the start of the first, and had its own consultation periods and meetings of the NPF. These documents were also due to be sent to the 2004 conference for final approval, after which Labour would have ten final policy statements. Figure 4.2 depicts the new structure.

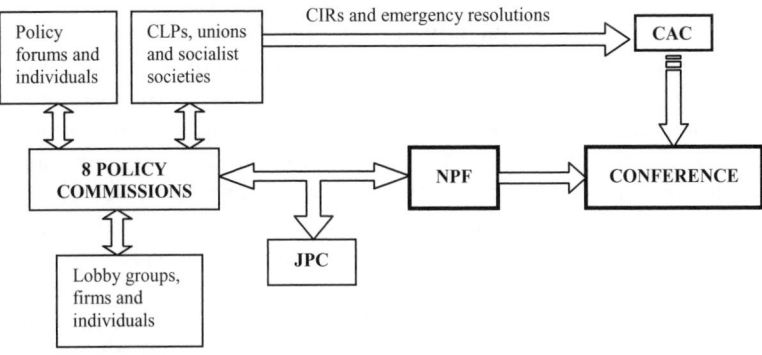

Figure 4.2   Labour's Policy-making Structure (since 1997)

Meetings of the NPF take place over the course of a weekend in private, away from the television cameras, two or three times a year.[11] First- and second-year consultation documents, and draft final statements are considered by NPF delegates in small workshops, which are facilitated by NPF members of the relevant policy commission, with notes taken by party officers. The workshops do not vote on documents, but instead try to reach a consensus. If agreement is not possible, points of significant disagreement are recorded. The views of all the workshops in each area are then combined into a single statement, which is agreed by note-takers and the relevant ministers and facilitators to ensure it is representative of the workshop discussions. The statement, which can also contain points of disagreement, is then discussed at a plenary session of the entire NPF. Each plenary also operates on the basis of consensus, though again, points of disagreement can be recorded in report-backs on consultation documents and draft final policy statements. First- and second-year draft documents are sent to the party conference, where they can be accepted or rejected *in toto*.

NPF delegates can table textual amendments to the draft final documents, but amendments must 'accurately represent the strength of feeling in the two-year consultation, be relevant to the document and have the support of at least two members of the NPF', with the JPC deciding whether these criteria have been met. Of the amendments that navigate these screens, their submitters will be told whether or not they have the support of the JPC. The latter can recommend small changes and/or seek consensus. Compromises tend to be found on most amendments, though ministers have often used these negotiations to remove specific pledges or contentious points.[12] Where agreement is not possible, the submitter's original amendment and an alternatively-worded JPC version are put to NPF workshops for discussion, and to the NPF plenary session for a vote. Amendments are included in the final policy document if they gain majority support at the plenary. Minority positions can also be included if they secure the support of 25 per cent of NPF delegates present and a minimum of 35 members of the entire NPF. Minority positions are sent with the majority documents to the party conference, where they are voted on separately. The 1998–2000 policy cycle saw seven amendments reach the 2000 party conference, though none was ultimately accepted.[13]

The annual conference formally retains its position as the sovereign body of the extra-parliamentary party. However, it now spends much of its time discussing policy documents sent to it by the NPF, rather than debating resolutions submitted by CLPs and affiliates. The two exceptions to this rule are the provisions for contemporary issue resolutions (CIRs) and emergency resolutions. CLPs and affiliates can submit resolutions on important contemporary topics not being considered by the NPF, with four or five being discussed by the annual conference each year (see below). Emergency resolutions are similar, except that they are for issues that arose after the closing date for the receipt of CIRs (usually the Friday before the start of the conference). Nevertheless, the bulk of party policies come through the NPF. As part of the changes, Labour's constitutionally enshrined 'party programme', which hitherto had an ambiguous status, is now officially 'based on the rolling programme presented to conference by the National Policy Forum as approved by conference' (Labour Party, 2003a: Clause V.1).[14]

Reaction to the new policy-making system has been mixed. The emphasis on consensus and the prohibition on television cameras have reduced voice costs arising from the policy-making process. Annual conferences have also tended to be more sedate occasions. Modernisers are relieved that the old cycle of government-activist conflicts appears to have been broken, which was the principal aim of *Partnership in Power*. For their part, activists elected to the NPF have the opportunity to engage with ministers over policy in a way that never happened under the old system. However, the biggest complaint of members has been that the system has enabled the PLP leadership to muzzle dissent, which has left many members feeling they have no influence over policy. At meetings of the NPF, it has been alleged that activists have little real say, despite their considerable representation:

> [I]n the preliminary discussions of policy documents at the national policy forum, the imbalance of power between the well-resourced ministerial team and the others is very apparent. Initial drafts, in which the parameters of policies are being determined, are coming from ministers. (Seyd, 1999: 393–4)

Given the increases in 'Short money' and the consequent range of independent research resources it enables, these advantages are likely to remain when Labour is in opposition. CLP delegates to the NPF are unlikely to overcome such high information costs. There have also been allegations that reports sent to the JPC and the NPF have given a misleading impression of consensus, when differences of opinion in fact existed. The effect has been to breed resentment (Hain, 2004: 24). A survey of party members indicated that many no longer felt a great sense of 'ownership' of party policy (Seyd and Whiteley, 2002: 23). It is possible that a principal cause of this alienation is the ending of adversarial debates on all the great issues at the annual conference; most members do not, and did not in the past, participate in the policy-making process, but the difference now is that they rarely hear about it either. Lines of accountability are weak, though the same was true of Labour's old organisational structure (Kavanagh, 1982). The CLP section's electorate consists of annual conference delegates divided into regional groups, a small body whose personnel change regularly, making mandating difficult (Seyd, 1999: 394). The party leadership is aware of some of these problems. Early on in the life of the new system, local and regional policy forums were established, with Seyd and Whiteley (2002: 24) claiming that, by 1999, between 35,000 and 40,000 members had participated in one. Furthermore, a review of *Partnership in Power* is in progress at the time of writing, with a preliminary report to be presented to the 2004 annual conference, and a final report due the following year.

The response of the trade unions to the new system has been positive. The unions are specifically allocated just 30 places at the NPF, though this figure considerably understates their power. In the first place, the NEC, whose members all belong *ex officio* to the NPF, has 12 places reserved for the unions. Roughly half-a-dozen delegates from the NPF's regional parties' section are also usually union officials who are broadly aligned with the unions. The unions' strength on the NPF is thus closer to 50 delegates. Furthermore, union delegates have tended to operate as a caucus, with access to the resources of their organisations, and capable of mobilising to defend their interests (Shaw, 2002: 164). By acting as a cohesive bloc, the union members have the ability to put minority NPF positions to the annual conference, which in turn encourages the party leadership to seek compromise. By focusing on areas of interest to their members, the unions have managed to extract concessions at the NPF, and in return have not lent their support to leftwing amendments from other delegates.[15] Despite their greater numbers, CLP delegates are more atomised and therefore dependent on ministers.

The most dramatic effect of the new structures is their usurpation of the policy-making powers of other institutions. Although the sovereignty of the annual conference is reaffirmed, in reality the new structure significantly curtails the policy-making role of conference delegates. The change was justified by the efficiency improvements it would herald. The old system concentrated policy-making power in the NEC, with the conference often little more than an occasion for set-piece debates, even though most of the votes had already been decided in advance. Nowadays, conference delegates are greatly constrained in the subjects they can discuss. Policy areas under consideration by any of the policy commissions cannot be debated at the conference, and resolutions on such subjects submitted by CLPs and affiliates are forwarded by the CAC to the relevant policy commission. NPF reports must be ratified at the party conference, but the latter's scope for action is restricted. *Partnership in Power* originally appeared to indicate that conference delegates would be able to vote on separate aspects of policies:

> In the past, policy statements have been presented to Conference on an-all-or-nothing basis. Under the rolling programme Conference would for the first time be able to have separate votes on key sections and proposals in the policy statement. The final statement as agreed by Conference would then become part of the party's rolling policy programme. (Labour Party, 1997: 15)

However, at the 1999 annual conference, the CAC interpreted this passage to mean that the conference could refer back individual reports, not sections within them, because, it argued, the term, 'final statement' referred to the entire policy programme of the NPF (Shaw, 2002: 154). The effect was to give the conference veto power over whole reports but not over elements within reports. This ruling significantly restricted the conference's pre-emptive ability to shape the content of reports. Consider Figure 4.3:

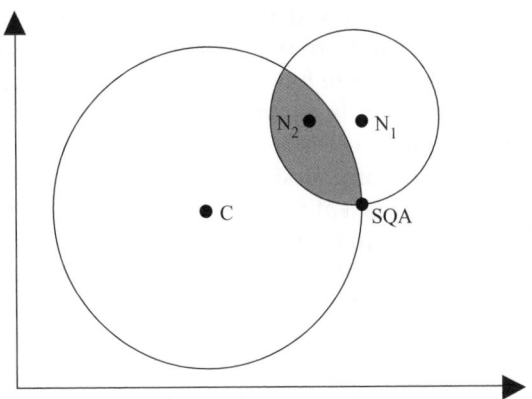

Figure 4.3   Policy Determination: Party Conference and the NPF

In this policy space, SQA represents the *status quo ante*, while points C and N_1 are the ideal points of the dominant coalitions at the conference and the NPF respectively. The shaded area enclosed in the intersection of the two indifference curves contains the set of policies that are preferred by the conference and the NPF to SQA (the winset of SQA). The NPF can formulate a policy report closer to its own ideal point than is SQA, but it cannot choose its ideal point, because the conference prefers SQA to N_1 and would be prepared to refer back the entire report. Instead, the NPF chooses a position within the winset of SQA, such as N_2. The NPF prefers N_2 to SQA, whereas the conference only marginally prefers it but will nevertheless vote for it rather than refer back the entire report. The conference cannot cherry-pick the best parts of the report and refer back or amend the parts it dislikes. If it possessed such a line-by-line veto, incremental amendments would continue until the content of the original report had unravelled, leaving an amended report at point C. The NPF would probably short-circuit this process and present a report at point C from the start.

However, the outcome could be different if a coalition at the NPF mobilised sufficient support to present a minority report to the conference. Given that half of the delegates at the party conference are now sent by CLPs, it might be easier nowadays for the conference to shift to the left. If there were propitious circumstances for a growth in support and recruits for the activist left, such as disillusionment with a Labour government, the mobilisation costs for the left at both the NPF and the conference could be lowered. Alternatively, if the unions mobilised against the PLP leadership in both bodies, they too could inflict a defeat at the conference. (As things stand, opposition appears more likely to come from the unions than CLP delegates.) A majority at the NPF would not be needed. Instead, if a coalition could mobilise 25 per cent of NPF delegates (or 35 in total, whichever is the greater), it could secure a victory for a minority report.

Consider Figure 4.4, which is identical to Figure 4.3 except that it includes the ideal point of a 'sizable minority' in the NPF (point M), defined as a minority sufficiently big to issue a minority report. In this example, M is fairly close to C, so much so that virtually any point the minority prefers to SQA is also preferred by the conference (the light and dark shaded regions). Only a few of these positions are also preferred by the NPF's dominant coalition to SQA (the small dark shaded region only). Thus, the minority could choose its own ideal point and defeat the majority NPF report at the conference. If this situation arose, we should expect to see negotiations between the NPF's dominant

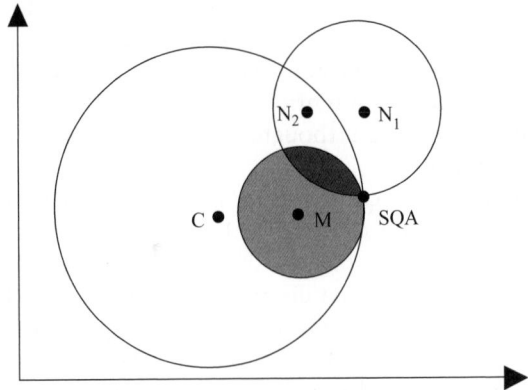

Figure 4.4 NPF Minority Reports and the Party Conference

coalition and the minority to secure agreement on a single report. However, if the minority is not satisfied with what is offered, it can settle for a minority report and go for a conference victory. It would still be possible for a Labour government to ignore the policies demanded by the conference, because the conference and the NPF still do not have the ability to enforce their decisions against ministers. Yet the party would be returned to the type of confrontations the new system was designed to avoid. It is possible that the party leadership might seek in the future to raise the threshold for minority reports or further dilute the power of the annual conference. However, Labour's membership decline and its problems with the unions since 2001 suggest that further centralisation would only exacerbate existing tensions (see Chapter 8).

Much of the conference agenda is thus predetermined, with debates scheduled for policy forum reports and drafts. However, resolutions can be submitted 'on a topic not substantially addressed in the ongoing policy work of the NPF...' (Labour Party, 1997: 16). The CAC judges whether resolutions submitted fall outside these areas, and ones that do may qualify as CIRs. Eligible resolutions go through to a ballot of conference delegates, who, until 2003, could decide which four would be added to the agenda.[16] Thus, the chances of a resolution being debated are fairly small unless it is on a burning issue. Even then, there is no guarantee it will navigate past the CAC, because the latter has discretion in deciding whether a topic is being 'substantially addressed' by the NPF. Shaw observes that 30 resolutions hostile to the government's contentious policy of privatising air traffic control were disallowed by the CAC at the 1999 conference, much to the government's relief (Shaw, 2002: 155). In 2003, the trade unions struck a deal with the government to ensure that all four CIRs were on issues of interest to the unions; contentious motions on the war in Iraq were not debated or voted upon (though Iraq was discussed during a debate on an NPF document).

CIRs have become a controversial part of Labour's policy-making structure, in large part because of weaknesses in the NPF format. Some of the Blair government's greatest difficulties with its own supporters have arisen over policies that did not emerge from the NPF. Plans for semi-autonomous foundation hospitals led to disputes with the unions and a large backbench revolt by Labour MPs. Government legislation was not preceded by any discussion of foundation hospitals at the NPF, which meant that the path for the policy was not prepared and trust broke down (Hain, 2004: 25).

The intention behind the new system was to make policy-making more efficient, yet it is hard to escape the conclusion that a major aim of the exercise was to reduce voice costs for party leaders. Rows at the party conference made Labour look divided, while providing the left with a televised platform from which to denounce the PLP. It also gave credence to the view that block-vote-wielding union barons were running the party. Both images entailed electoral costs. By contrast, the conference is now stage-managed and its agenda is largely predetermined, with less time available for set-piece debates. Policy-making has shifted to the NPF, the JPC and the policy commissions, whose proceedings are not televised and of little interest to outsiders. However, these gains for the leadership have come at the price of growing discontent among the membership at their perceived powerlessness. It is likely that the review of *Partnership in Power* will address these problems; if it does not, the dearth of channels for voice may be expressed in the form of members exiting.

Membership referendums

The ideal of Labour's modernisers was an OMOV-based party in which individual members were valued above union affiliates. However, although OMOV ballots are useful for electing candidates or leaders, their utility in policy-making is less evident. Policy-making involves discussion and negotiation, which is why it is usually decided in committees and voted upon at conferences. In the mid-1990s, however, Labour did engage in two experiments in membership referendums. In

1995, Blair ordered a consultation exercise on reforming Clause IV of Labour's constitution, the party's commitment to public ownership. Blair had hinted at his desire to reform Clause IV in his first leader's speech at the 1994 conference, but it became clear that there was considerable activist and union opposition to the move. A survey of CLPs found that 59 of 61 wanted to keep the old Clause IV, though these were the preferences of the activist-led general committees (Rentoul, 1995: 418). To bypass these activists, all individual members were sent a copy of the proposed new Clause IV and asked, 'Do you agree that this statement should be adopted in the Party rules as Labour's new aims and values?', with a simple yes/no choice. The members overwhelmingly supported the change (over 80 per cent, though less than a third participated) and this ballot was intended to pressurise delegates at the special conference of 1995 called to vote on Clause IV reform. Despite the unions controlling 70 per cent of the votes, the conference voted for reform by 65 per cent to 34 per cent, with a 90–10 per cent majority in the CLP section and a 55–45 per cent majority in the union section (Seyd, 1999: 389–90; Taylor, 1997: 179–85; Harmer, 1999: 27).

A second membership ballot was held in 1996 to gain grassroots support for Labour's draft election manifesto. Members were sent a document setting out six fairly uncontentious policy proposals, which were offered on a take-it-or-leave-it basis, with no alternatives and no amendments permitted. Members were asked to respond 'yes' or 'no' to the statement: 'I support Labour's manifesto, New Labour new life for Britain'. Nearly 95 per cent of members (on a 61 per cent turnout) voted to accept the draft (Seyd, 1999: 390, 402, n.6).

No further all-member ballots have thus far been held, though Labour's constitution was amended in 1995 to make provision for them (Labour Party, 2003a: Clause VIII.3(j)). However, only the NEC can decide the issues on which to call ballots, as well as the question wording. Party members do not have the right to call referendums. Thus, rather than the conference wielding veto power, it is now the members, but the NEC's agenda-control powers enable it to choose a point guaranteed to secure membership backing (especially when the questions are vague). Providing that the NEC has not miscalculated the distribution of members' preferences, membership ballots will prove unthreatening to party leaders; indeed, by generating a wider base of legitimacy for decisions, they can facilitate oligarchal control. However, they are costly to organise and do not involve much membership participation aside from casting a ballot. They are unlikely to become a regular feature of Labour's policy-making structure and it is difficult to disagree with Seyd's (1999: 399) assessment that the manifesto ballot was mainly a public relations exercise.

Conclusion

The main focus of reform of the policy-making structure has been on shifting power away from the old conference-based system of delegate democracy and NEC subcommittees towards structures in which the (shadow) cabinet plays the major role. Under both Kinnock and Blair, policy reviews and the structures that came with them were used to ensure that policy was increasingly made by the leadership rather than the members (Smith, 2000: 152). The progressive diminution of the role of the party conference has greatly reduced the significance of union block votes, while the proceedings are now largely an occasion for speeches by ministers rather than ordinary delegates. Intra-party bargaining over policy now occurs in the NPF, though ministers take most of the important decisions. The integration of the PLP into policy-making is a principal change in this area since 1983 and has facilitated centralisation, rather than PLP accountability to members.

However, as with other centralising measures, the risk remains that ordinary members will feel marginalised in the policy-making process. Party members may have been willing to accept centralisation in the last years of opposition, but leadership attempts to maintain tight control in government will prove counterproductive if members become alienated. A strong case can be made that the new system has rationalised policy-making and given activists' representatives a chance to debate policy with ministers. However, whereas ministers and the unions have their own resources and support-staff, activists do not. One of the complaints about the new system is that it has left members feeling they do not have 'ownership' of party policy. A further aspect of this feeling of distance is the fact that the NPF meets in private, which means that most party members are unaware of its deliberations. There has also been disquiet over the passing of controversial government legislation that did not emerge from the NPF. In short, policy-making structures may have to be opened up to a greater extent than they presently are, if members are to be persuaded that government policies are the end result of grassroots preferences. The alternative may be a continued exodus of those members.

5
The Selection of Parliamentary Candidates

The fiercest battles over institutional change in the Labour Party have concerned the selection of parliamentary candidates. This area is the major interface between the 'party on the ground' and the 'party in office', and often becomes the focus of reform, as politicians attempt to increase their autonomy from activists, and the latter seek to reduce it. Candidate selection rules first became contested in the Labour Party in the mid-1970s, when they were targeted by the activist left as a means of asserting control over the PLP. Labour's modernisers in turn sought to unravel the left's reforms in the 1980s by devolving voting rights downwards from activists to ordinary members, in tandem with a strengthening of central veto powers. They also identified selection rules as a key aspect of the party's relationship with the unions, and subsequently fought to remove union influence, as part of their project to transform Labour's image as a party of sectional interests. However, union resistance to change was determined and persistent. Powers over candidate selection provide access to, and control over, the gateways to parliament. Given that the unions formed the Labour Party precisely to acquire parliamentary representation, it was to be expected that they would mount a rearguard defence of their institutional prerogatives.

This chapter sets out the major reforms to candidate selection since 1983. It begins by describing Labour's local organisational structure, since it is the CLPs that choose parliamentary candidates. It then details the main stages of the selection process and examines the battle to replace the old activist-controlled structures with OMOV. Other changes to the selection procedures are then considered, including the reforms of the nomination and shortlisting stages, and union sponsorship. The chapter concludes that the reforms had the dual effects of diluting Labour's federal structure and centralising power, despite the formal enfranchisement of individual members.

Labour's local organisational structures

Each MP in the UK represents a geographical constituency, and corresponding to each is a constituency Labour party. CLPs have been the principal organisational structures for Labour's individual members, providing the latter with an institutional shell in which to organise their activities. They are hybrid organisations combining features of the branch structure typical of mass parties, and affiliated membership characteristic of indirect parties. CLPs were formed in 1918, as Labour's leaders realised they needed local structures to campaign during elections. Until then local unions had performed this function; the move to a network of CLPs enabled direct membership of the party for the first time. Since 1989, individuals have been able to join the party nationally, after a computerised national membership list was introduced, though all members are assigned to CLPs.

Each CLP consists of a number of ward branches and is run by a general committee (GC), consisting of about 100 people, from which is drawn an executive committee (see Figure 5.1). The branches within the CLP can send delegates to the GC, as can locally affiliated unions and socialist societies. Along with the executive, the GC coordinates local campaigns and possesses a number of important powers, but the most significant of its functions until 1989 was the selection of the CLP's prospective parliamentary candidate (PPC – see Figure 5.2). Local branches and unions could nominate candidates, union nominees being particularly attractive because the sponsoring union provided

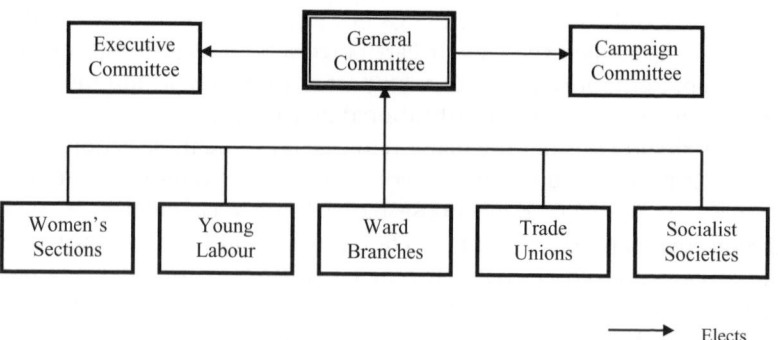

Figure 5.1   Constituency Labour Party Structure

- Select CLP's parliamentary candidate, including deselection of existing MP if desired
- Decide which candidate to support in leadership and deputy leadership elections. Elect a delegate to attend meeting of electoral college and mandate him to vote for given candidate(s)
- Submit a resolution to Labour's annual conference
- Elect a delegate to attend party conference and mandate him to vote for/against given policies
- Decide which candidates to support in NEC elections and mandate CLP's conference delegate to vote for them
- Elect and hold accountable CLP officers
- Hear monthly reports from MP (if Labour)
- Hear monthly reports from local council leader (if Labour)
- Receive national party documents including consultation documents
- Receive and debate correspondence from external organisations

Source: Richards (2000: 35)

Figure 5.2 Powers and Responsibilities of General Committees (pre-1989)

election funds. Sitting MPs could be deselected if the local party so wished, but the process was fraught with difficulty. However, a left-inspired reform ensured that after 1979, all MPs faced mandatory reselection contests between general elections.

The GCs are local oligarchies, consisting mainly of committed activists. They stand above the mass of ordinary members, who play little role in the party other than paying their annual subscriptions (and nowadays, casting postal ballots when invited to do so by the NEC). The inactive members are atomised, whereas the activists are in regular contact at branch or GC meetings and during election campaigns. They enjoy social payoffs from their membership, such as friendship and mixing with like-minded people. GCs provide them with bases from which to organise collective action, though some factional divisions usually exist.

Trade union branches that fall within the geographical reach of a given CLP may affiliate to it. As at the national level, they affiliate for a stated number of levypaying union members, paying a sum of money to the party for each affiliated levypayer. In return, they may send delegates to that local party's GC. Their allocation of delegates depends on their affiliation level: they are usually allowed one delegate for 1–100 affiliated union members, two delegates for 101–200 members, three delegates for 201–300 members, and so on.[1] A union branch can sometimes send delegates to more than one GC. In industrial areas, GCs could be dominated by scores of union delegates representing a variety of unions. CLPs in mining areas were once heavily dominated by delegates from the NUM. Generalist unions such as the TGWU and the GMB send delegates to GCs in constituencies all over the country.

If a single union dominated a CLP or formed a large minority, it could often ensure the selection of one of its own officials as the PPC. This direct gateway to parliament was an important aspect of the party-union link. Securing union candidates as MPs can be more useful for the unions than the uncertain process of trying to persuade Labour governments to accept conference decisions. It was the basis for the prevalent belief that regional union bosses were able to secure parliamentary seats for union candidates by packing selection meetings with delegates instructed how to vote. In theory, delegates benefited from the old informal rule of 'no mandating' in candidate selection contests; moreover, the vote was conducted by secret ballot. However, the low rate of activism in union affairs, let alone party affairs, by ordinary levypayers ensured regional organisers wielded considerable influence in these matters, securing places for their allies on GCs, who functioned to all intents and purposes as a block vote. Andy McSmith (1996: 46) claims, '[t]his practice was so common that it was barely remarked upon…' (see also Ranney, 1965: 175; Rush, 1969: 159). That being so, it is not difficult to see why union leaders would later oppose OMOV.

Reform of parliamentary candidate selection

Candidate selection is a multi-stage process in which a series of screens produces candidates who enjoy the support of their CLPs and the NEC. Different groups or factions may control different stages, and reform of candidate selection may involve procedural changes to any of these screens. The first screen is *eligibility and application* to be a candidate.[2] Labour's most basic requirement is that candidates must have been party members for at least two years. Aspiring PPCs could either apply directly in writing to CLP secretaries or wait to be approached by a nominating body within the CLP (any ward party or affiliated organisation), especially if they were 'big' names or local *notables*. Until 1993, most applicants were streamed into different lists, which were sent on request by the NEC to CLPs. They included nominees the unions were willing to sponsor (list A), candidates nominated by CLPs (list B), and names submitted by the Co-operative Party (list C). From 1988, a list W of women nominees was also available. Names that did not appear on a list could also be nominated.

The second stage in the process is *nomination*, in which ward parties and affiliates nominate candidates to be the PPC. Pippa Norris and Joni Lovenduski (1995: 62) estimate that on average each CLP contains 23 nominating bodies (seven party ward branches, 13 union branches, and other affiliates), each of which could nominate one candidate. Branches typically interview applicants seeking their nomination, and here ideological filters normally come into play. Cultivating local links can build up a large number of nominations for a candidate and improve his chances of progressing through later stages, giving an advantage to local councillors and union officials.

The third stage is the production of a *shortlist* drawn from nominated candidates. Shortlists were formerly drawn up by CLPs' executives, but since 1993 GCs have voted to decide them. Shortlists must include at least four or five candidates (where there was no incumbent Labour MP), but can include more. In reselection contests the sitting MP must be included on the shortlist. The fourth stage of the process – *selection* – has been the focus of the most contested reforms since 1983. Before 1989, GCs chose candidates in secret ballots, but after that, various schemes involving OMOV were used, including local electoral colleges until 1992, a provision for the participation of levypaying trade unionists during 1992–93, and finally straight OMOV from 1993 onwards. The final stage is NEC *endorsement*, which was usually automatic, though the NEC occasionally intervened. Since 1983, Labour has undertaken comprehensive reform of most of these screens. The most important reforms relate to the fourth screen, selection, and are analysed in the remainder of this section. Reforms of the other screens are assessed later.

The selection stage involves voting on the shortlisted candidates and has been the target of the most contested reforms in the Labour Party. The debate concerned the identity of the selectorate choosing the final candidate, with a long leadership attempt to wrest control of selection from the GCs and give all individual members a right to vote in OMOV ballots. This campaign was the response of the PLP leadership to a rule change pushed through by the left in 1980. Before then, sitting Labour MPs were assumed automatically reselected to contest their seats unless they were challenged by rival candidates for the position of PPC. The left achieved a number of high-profile deselections in the 1970s, but it required a lot of effort to mobilise for a selection contest. To reduce these costs, the left fought for mandatory reselection, whereby all sitting Labour MPs had to undergo a reselection contest once per parliament (see Seyd, 1987: 103–16). This rule change significantly eased the hostile pressure applied by the party leadership and the media to those CLP leftists who sought to deselect (usually moderate) MPs. As George Tsebelis writes:

> [Mandatory reselection] makes the reselection of the MP the rule rather than the exception, as it had been before. Before, the [GC] had to mobilize against its MP; now the MP requires the support of the [GC]. Before, the [GC] needed to provide the NEC with reasons for not readopting its MP. No such reasons are required now. Therefore, this formula dramatically reduces the costs of rejecting the MP. (Tsebelis, 1990: 149)

In theory, mandatory reselection would make it much easier for the grassroots left to cull moderate Labour MPs. In practice, it did not produce the dramatic results that the left hoped for and the right feared (see below). However, it was instrumental in persuading Neil Kinnock to tackle the power of the left in its CLP heartland, partly through a policy of expulsions of members of the far-left Militant Tendency and partly through OMOV. Before examining OMOV, it would be useful to have a simple model of the selection process in the pre-OMOV era. One has been provided by Tsebelis (1990: 119–58), who depicts the re/deselection process for Labour MPs as a sequential game between the sitting MP, a leftwing GC and the NEC. In the game, the MP must first choose to be moderate (rightwing) or extreme (leftwing), and the GC then decides whether to reselect or deselect him. Finally, the NEC can affirm or veto the GC's decision. The GC prefers a leftwing MP in the model, and if the final decision were left to it, it would deselect moderates. Anticipating the GC's antipathy to moderates, the MP will adopt a leftwing stance. However, the NEC possesses veto power so everything depends on its own political composition: if it is leftwing, it will not veto the deselection of rightwing MPs, but if it is moderate it will. Similarly, the GC will not deselect rightwing MPs if it knows the NEC will use its veto. For the most part, GCs will deselect rightwing MPs only if the NEC is also leftwing.[3]

This description offers a pared-down account of the selection process but its interest lies in the strategic relationship it posits between MPs, GCs and the NEC. Its focus on ideology leaves out other considerations that affect GCs' decisions during reselection contests, such as the overall performance of the MP (for example, in fulfilling his constituency duties). Nevertheless, this focus on ideology is retained in the following discussion, not least because the original motive for mandatory reselection and OMOV was ideological (the first to make it easier for leftwing activists to control the PLP, the second to make it harder). It might be objected that empirically the model is suspect, because few MPs were deselected and even fewer decisions were vetoed by the NEC. Only eight MPs were deselected before the 1983 general election, though several more might have been had they not defected to the SDP (Seyd, 1987: 129–31). However, it is likely that an even greater number toed the line with their GCs for fear of being deselected: a power need not be exercised to be effective (Tsebelis, 1990: 150; Williams, 1983: 45). In the early-mid 1980s, many Labour MPs took seriously the threat of deselection (McSmith, 1996: 38–9).

However, two points are in order. First, Tsebelis understates the autonomy GCs enjoyed relative to the NEC. He believes the NEC could veto any deselection and reject GCs' preferred candidates if the latter were politically unacceptable. That is indeed the case when a candidate is chosen for a vacant seat, a famous example being the NEC's refusal to endorse the leftist Liz Davies in Leeds North-East in 1995. But insofar as the deselection of sitting MPs is concerned, the adoption of the so-called 'Mikardo doctrine', first as NEC policy from 1974 and then as an official rule from 1978, narrowed the grounds on which the NEC could intervene (Shaw, 1988: 185–94). This rule gave deselected MPs the right to appeal to the NEC only on the grounds of an alleged breach of the rules (Labour Party, 2003a: Rule 5C.5(c)). It appeared to rule out intervention on political grounds and thus enhanced the power of GCs. Deselected MPs could no longer rely on the NEC to save them unless they could demonstrate procedural irregularities.

However, the NEC can decide how seriously it takes claims of procedural errors. Paul McCormick (1980: 385) observes that such errors are bound to occur frequently in voluntary organisations such as parties, where those taking decisions are not paid professionals with a great understanding of legal and constitutional issues. McCormick suggests that if a determined NEC wanted to save an MP from deselection, 'there is never any difficulty in finding an irregularity should one be required'. In 1989, Frank Field was an MP who found himself deselected by his Birkenhead CLP in favour of a leftwing union official. After the vote, Field sent a dossier of allegations to the NEC, most centring on Militant infiltration of his constituency, as well as irregularities in affiliated unions concerning voter eligibility. The NEC launched an inquiry into the regional Wirral Labour Party but despite finding no evidence of irregularities it ordered a re-run ballot, because it accepted that six members of Birkenhead CLP were Militant supporters (they were subsequently expelled). Field narrowly won the re-run ballot in 1991. Counter-allegations of irregularities were made by Field's main opponent but the NEC dismissed them (Heffernan and Marqusee, 1992: 271–7). Thus, despite the adoption of the Mikardo doctrine, there remained scope for the NEC to impose its will. Nevertheless, this rule does impose costs on the NEC because the search for irregularities entails time-consuming investigations. A political veto would circumvent such problems.

Second, Tsebelis's model understates the effect of mandatory reselection on the selection process. Tsebelis argues that it simply modified the reselection game in the middle of the process and did not alter the NEC veto, so the major factor is the political composition of the NEC (Tsebelis 1990: 151). Yet not only does this argument ignore the 'Mikardo doctrine', it fails to consider the totality of NEC-GC conflicts. Even if the NEC were inclined to look for procedural irregularities, it would be overwhelmed by the task if dozens of cases emerged simultaneously; focusing on selection disputes entails high opportunity costs. Mandatory reselection vastly increased the likelihood of numerous deselections. Only if we bear these points in mind can Tsebelis's model provide a useful schematic approximation of the re/deselection process before OMOV.

How serious, then, was the threat posed by leftwing GCs to moderate MPs? For much of Labour's history, relations between GCs and MPs were fairly sedate, shrouded in an air of deference. Until the 1960s, most Labour activists were working class and moderate, posing little threat to MPs (Tanner, 2000). Furthermore, GCs were often dominated by union delegates instructed how to vote, despite the rule of 'no mandating'. Most GCs were concerned to leave the MP to Westminster business while they engaged in local affairs. However, this relationship changed in the 1970s, as a new generation of leftwing activists joined the party. Labour's individual membership had been falling steadily since the war, as party membership generally held fewer social attractions for individuals, but the party haemorrhaged older, working-class members in the 1970s in the wake of the unpopular policies of Labour governments. Membership decline left many CLPs as little more than hollowed-out shells ripe for take-over by newcomers. At the same time, a generation of young, university-educated activists, radicalised by the 1960s and largely working in a public sector wracked by industrial militancy, increasingly saw the Labour Party as a means to further their ideological goals (Seyd, 1987: 44–7). These members were less respectful of Labour's deferential traditions and they assumed greater importance within CLPs.

Labour's federal structure enabled this new left to assume local power. Within a given CLP, each ward branch was entitled to a minimum of three GC delegates, possibly more depending on membership levels. It meant that a number of wards with low memberships could outvote on the GC wards that collectively had higher individual memberships, because what mattered was numbers of delegates, not individual members (see McSmith, 1996: 42–3, for an illustrative example in Liverpool Knowsley North in the 1980s). Given Labour's state of organisational decay at the time, only a small number of leftists was required to capture wards, and after that CLPs. Consequently, many areas became prone to 'entryism' – organised groups of leftists, such as Militant, infiltrating ward branches and CLPs, and capturing them (Seyd, 1987: 50–4). This goal was achieved most clearly in Liverpool, where Militant controlled the local council and a number of CLPs. One way of taking over CLPs, particularly in university towns, was by mobilising small numbers of young people sharing a handful of addresses in a constituency. They would join the local Labour Party and take over ward branches, from where they could elect GC delegates. Once a local party was captured, this 'bed-sit left' could move on to the next constituency.

From the mid-1980s, entryist groups came under fierce attack from Kinnock, with a spate of investigations and expulsions (including two MPs). However, many leftwing activists remained members of the party and continued to dominate its local structures. A survey of Labour members confirmed some correlation between ideology and activism: 32 per cent of hard leftists claimed to be very active compared to a party average of 24 per cent. The proportion of hard leftists admitting to being completely inactive was 10 per cent, compared to an average of 14 per cent (Seyd and Whiteley, 1992: 101). The left was well-represented on the activist-dominated GCs.

Although the left's star waned in the 1980s, mandatory reselection continued to be one of its legacies. If the activists were largely leftwing, then moderate MPs were vulnerable to deselection. Given the shift to the left on the NEC, deselected MPs could not hold out much hope for saviour. After Labour's general election defeat of 1983, Kinnock was besieged by anxious MPs voicing a fear widespread in the PLP that mass deselections of moderate MPs were imminent (McSmith, 1996:

38–9). Many MPs wanted mandatory reselection abolished, but given the continued strength of the left this option was never feasible. Besides, the abandonment of the mandatory element would not in itself end the possibility of deselection, as the experience of the 1970s showed. Strengthening the NEC's veto power was not, at this point, a viable alternative, though it would become so in the following years. In the aftermath of a grassroots insurgency, a brazen act of centralisation would have been divisive. On the other hand, doing nothing was not possible either, given the enormous unease in the PLP.

Kinnock's options were narrowed, but there was an alternative: to undermine the leftwing cliques on the GCs by opening up selection meetings to all local party members, who would vote in OMOV ballots. The assumption was that the largely inactive members comprised a majority of the membership and were ideologically moderate. OMOV would involve the dismantling of the federal structure that had provided such favourable opportunities for the left. At this stage, OMOV was not seen as an attack on the party-union link, but instead a necessary measure to redistribute power away from left-dominated party organs to help improve Labour's electoral performance. However, opposition was already forming.

One-member–one-vote

The modernisers' campaign to introduce OMOV began in 1984, but it would not be achieved until 1993, by which time its main champion, Kinnock had resigned the leadership. The quest for OMOV evoked leftwing opposition early on, but increasingly it was the trade unions that posed the greatest obstacle. An ill-prepared voluntary OMOV scheme was defeated at the 1984 annual conference, after Kinnock failed to secure sufficient union backing in advance. The three-year rule on constitutional amendments prohibited a return to the issue at the party conference until 1987, by which time union hostility had risen, as union leaders realised that OMOV would seriously undermine their own local power. In some industrial localities, unions could effectively determine who the Labour MP would be, and often he would be one of their own officials. OMOV threatened this arrangement by letting individual party members choose the candidate. Self-interest was reinforced by 'a fear that what was being proposed might be the thin end of the wedge of separation', which 'strengthened opposition in some major unions to the breaking of the federal arrangements' (Minkin, 1992: 381).

Consequently, the period until 1993 saw repeated attempts to find a compromise solution. A local electoral college was proposed, giving locally affiliated unions a maximum of 40 per cent of the votes in selection contests, with the remaining votes going to individual members, who would vote on the basis of OMOV.[4] One of the problems that emerged was that candidates could win majorities in the OMOV ballots but not gain sufficient union votes and thereby lose. Alternatively, candidates could be successfully chosen despite failing to win majority support among individual members. Each of these scenarios occurred on a number of occasions and each raised questions over the legitimacy of the adopted candidate. Moreover, OMOV was strictly applied to individual party members but not to the unions, where decision-making procedures were non-uniform and did not guarantee involvement by the mass of levypayers (Minkin, 1992: 247; Alderman and Carter, 1994: 325). In centralised unions such as the GMB and the EETPU, voting rights shifted from branch delegates to central or regional union officials (Shaw, 1994: 235, n.14), with unions' branch-vote allocations effectively wielded as block votes. The unwieldy nature of the system and its susceptibility to fraud[5] led to its abandonment in 1990.

It was replaced by another compromise in which CLPs could choose to use straight OMOV or allow the participation of union levypayers, whose individual votes would be worth only one-third of those of full party members. It was another short-lived compromise that pleased no one, though it ended delegatory union influence in selection. However, only the most active union members would likely use this opportunity, so the possibility of organised cliques influencing contests remained. With the election defeat of 1992 came the formation of the union links review group. Its interim report listed five different options for candidate selection but the preference of the newly-elected leader, John Smith, was for pure OMOV. At the 1993 party conference, Smith put his reputation on the line and asked the conference to support a move to a full OMOV system. Amid much acrimony and some arm-twisting of MSF union delegates,[6] the conference voted by 47.5 per cent to 44.4 per cent to adopt the new system. As a consolation, union levypayers were allowed to join the party at a reduced rate, under a new scheme called 'levy-plus' (see Alderman and Carter, 1994; Rentoul, 1995: 308–49). OMOV ended up being the dividing issue in a new intra-party cleavage between modernisers and traditionalists.

However, the initial purpose of OMOV had been to undermine the left rather than the unions. Only GC delegates had been allowed to vote in selection contests, ensuring that the left remained an important influence in the CLPs. However, the system meant that ordinary party members who did not attend meetings had no say over Labour's PPCs. If the politically moderate inactive members were to be enfranchised, there should be less pressure on moderate Labour MPs from their CLPs. This idea is represented in Figure 5.3, which depicts the ideological difference between the median member overall (B in the bottom panel) and the median activist (A in the middle panel), and their distances from the median voter in the electorate at large (MV in the top panel). (The Conservatives are assumed to capture all votes to the right of MV.) Ordinary members are more moderate than the left-wing activists, but not even the median member is very close to MV, because all members and activists are recruited from one side of MV. Thus, there were limits to the moderating effects of OMOV.

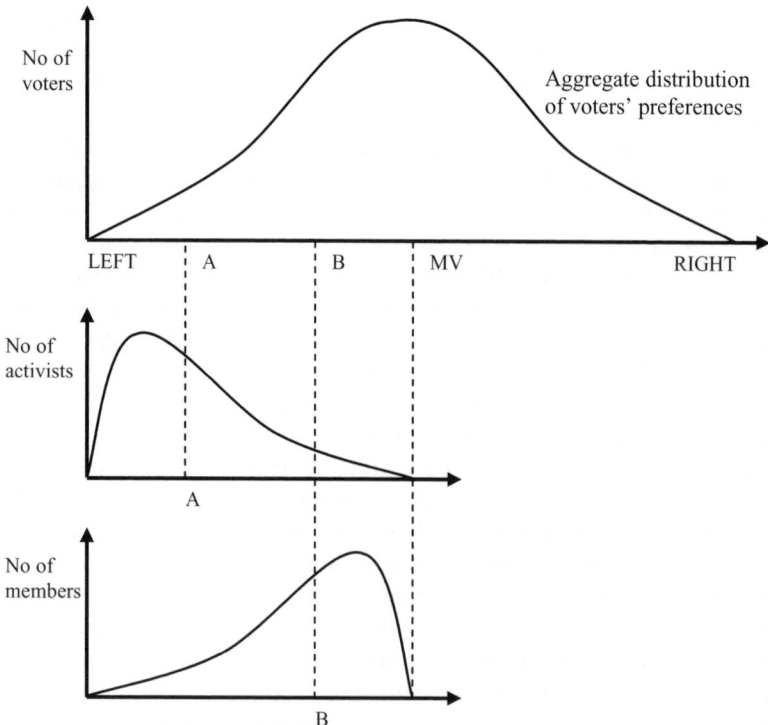

Figure 5.3 Distribution of Preferences of Voters, and Labour Members and Activists

However, OMOV also crucially impacted on the mobilisation costs of the activist left. There are significant differences between active and inactive members. Within each CLP, activists tend to know one another because they are in regular contact, whereas ordinary members, who rarely attend meetings, know few people. Activists can organise collective action, but inactive members are atomised. Participating in an OMOV ballot is qualitatively different from engaging in delegatory decision-making. Delegates can bargain with each other and coordinate tactics. If they have a Labour MP, they can use the resources of the GC to monitor his performance in the House of Commons, which in turn may affect his behaviour. Through the GC they enjoy low communication costs with the MP and can raise important issues. They can also make threats to the MP, holding out the possibility of deselection if they are unhappy with his performance.

These costs are much higher under OMOV, because inactive members do not benefit from the power of collectivity. To see why, consider the distinction between horizontal and vertical 'voice'. Horizontal voice consists of 'the utterance and exchange of opinion, concern, and criticism *among* citizens' and is normally low-cost since everyday grumbling is not subject to the free-rider problem. By contrast, vertical voice is an 'actual communication, complaint, petition, or protest addressed to the authorities by a citizen or, more frequently, an organization representing a group of citizens'. However, '[h]orizontal voice is a necessary precondition for the mobilization of vertical voice' (Hirschman, 1986: 82, emphasis in original), particularly when vertical voice is high-cost and requires the overcoming of a collective action problem.

The contrast between vertical and horizontal voice is relevant when comparing OMOV with the old GC system of candidate selection. Voice among an atomised membership takes longer to make itself heard in the party and may not even be heard at all. Voice generally begins horizontally, as members grumble among themselves about policies or decisions, and once it attains a critical mass it can ascend vertically through the party. However, horizontal voice has few roots in an atomised membership, because members are almost never in contact. *Ipso facto*, vertical voice is less likely, as opposition is dispersed and the position of the politicians becomes safer *vis-à-vis* the members. It explains, *inter alia*, the phenomenon of party democratisation in tandem with centralisation, a phenomenon evident in many contemporary parties (Katz, 2001: 290). This effect of OMOV on politicians' autonomy has been more important than the ideological dilution of the selectorate that it was intended to bring about.

Communication costs are higher, as ordinary members find it difficult to gain access to the Labour MP (if they have one). Monitoring costs are higher, because members obtain information about the MP from the media, which in most cases is unlikely to be sufficient. Carrying out a deselection is problematical because it involves mobilising ordinary members against the MP. Candidate selections undertaken by OMOV ballots involve a special selection meeting, which selectors must attend. Postal ballots can sometimes be arranged if members are unable to attend the meeting. Even at such meetings, members find it difficult to bargain with each other and coordinate their actions. Although they can vote, they are simply giving their preferences on candidates they may know little about. Access to information is constrained, since they are not party functionaries and are hardly ever in contact with those who are. They depend for their information on party literature sent to their homes by the local or national party. When ordinary members are asked to vote for candidates in NEC elections, their information consists of brief statements by candidates sent with ballot papers. In short, ordinary members face high coordination and information costs, leaving MPs facing fewer constraints under OMOV than previously.

Some observers regard OMOV as being almost purely about centralisation (Shaw, 2002), yet there must be more to it than that; after all, the left has enjoyed some success in the CLP section of NEC elections in recent years. For centralising party leaders the problem with giving party members votes is that they may take their voting rights seriously and choose candidates not favoured by the centre. Enfranchising inactive members may have different consequences to allowing local elites to take decisions. In the pre-OMOV candidate selection game (see above), activists seeking to deselect MPs had to weigh up the risk of facing sanctions, perhaps on spurious procedural grounds. Given that the selectors were GC delegates in close communication with each other, they would be easy to identify by an NEC 'hit squad'. It could thus be rational for the NEC to develop a reputation for toughness, as Kinnock's NEC did in the 1980s, to signal to local elites that deselection would invite punishment.

Under OMOV things are different. Although inactive members face informational and coordination problems, giving them voting rights *eases* some mobilisation problems by providing them with the means to remove MPs without the need for low-level horizontal voice. If there is more than one name on the ballot, the result is uncertain. Passive members are unlikely to be dissuaded from deselecting an MP out of fear of an NEC 'hit squad' descending on the area, because they are either unaware of the NEC's powers or feel they have little to fear. NEC signalling games are less likely to be effective when the voters are inactive members. Mandatory reselection is crucial. Selection contests involving members who are unafraid or unaware of NEC intervention might lead to numerous deselections. Thus, it is little surprise that OMOV was accompanied by a tightening of other selection screens, including the *de facto* abandonment of mandatory reselection. The next section examines some of the changes made to the rules on application, nomination, shortlisting and endorsement.

Other changes to candidate selection

Eligibility and application: Candidate lists

The debate in the Labour Party concerning the first screen, application, has focussed on candidate lists and rules on union sponsorship. List A candidates were sponsored by trade unions and enjoyed a distinct advantage because they brought with them union money (see below). List B contained candidates of varying quality who brought no promises of financial or personnel assistance to CLPs. There was little preliminary screening, ensuring that list B was a catch-all list for candidates hoping to secure selection. A candidate's inclusion on list B was no guarantee of NEC endorsement. Typically, about 180 individuals appeared on list A and 650 on list B (Norris and Lovenduski, 1995: 57). List C contained individuals sponsored by the Co-operative Party. About 100 party members were on it and inclusion required the negotiation of Co-operative Party screening procedures. List W contained all women candidates who appeared on lists A, B and C.

These lists were abolished in 1993 and combined into a single list of approved candidates, now known as the national parliamentary panel (NPP). Where a union has a suitably rigorous selection procedure for its own list of approved candidates, the latter are added to the NPP. CLPs are free to choose candidates not on the approved list, but if they do, these candidates must undergo an interview with the NEC before being endorsed (Labour Party, 2003a: Rule 5C.8(a)). Every candidate for the NPP must attend a training and assessment weekend, submit a standardised CV, and be interviewed. It enables the centre to screen out poor quality candidates and narrow the ideological range of new recruits to the PLP. A party official quoted by Byron Criddle (2002: 186) admitted that the purpose of the NPP was 'to remove the need for the NEC to refuse endorsement', which may simply create resentment. The existence of a veto power so early in the selection process ensures the centre has little to fear from OMOV and saves it from needing to exercise its veto later in the glare of publicity. The NPP will likely lead to standardised candidates who will gradually replace the PLP's last remaining hard leftists and mavericks as the latter retire or are defeated.[7]

As ever in the Labour Party, greatest controversy surrounded the unions. The practice of union sponsorship of parliamentary candidates involved unions agreeing to bankroll the election campaign of pre-ferred candidates, together with further payments to the relevant CLP and the candidate if he were elected to parliament. It dated back to the nineteenth century when unions sponsored Lib-Lab candidates, and became an essential feature of the early Labour Party because MPs were not paid by the state until 1911. Even after that change, MPs' salaries were fairly low. In the 1920s, the miners' union paid its MPs £300 a year on top of a parliamentary salary of £400. From the 1970s, allowances to MPs were phased out or frozen at low levels in response to worries about the perception of MPs being financially supported by unions at a time when questions were being raised about union power in the country generally. By the 1990s, sponsorship involved fairly trivial sums, typically a few hundred pounds a year to MPs,[8] though of more importance was the approximate sum of £750 a year paid to a sponsored candidate's CLP and the covering of most of his election expenses (Norris and Lovenduski, 1995: 57). Sponsorship was an in-centive to cash-starved CLPs to adopt union nominees. CLPs knew that choosing a union-sponsored candidate would make them eligible for financial assistance from the nominee's union. Such financial help has long been attractive: Austin Ranney (1965: 223) claimed that in the 1930s, 'contests for adoptions increasingly resembled auctions in which CLPs bid for the support of wealthy trade unions'. This develop-ment resulted in the Hastings agreement of 1933, whereby unions could contribute no more than 80 per cent of a candidate's election expenses, after fears that some unions were 'buying seats'. With this ceiling, CLPs also need to raise funds for the candidate (Norris and Lovenduski, 1995: 66).

Unions targeted sponsorship on safe Labour seats to maximise their chances of sponsoring an MP and not just a defeated PPC. Only about a quarter of PPCs were sponsored by unions at any given election, compared to about 70 per cent by CLPs, yet the proportion of union-sponsored Labour MPs was always over a third, and after 1979 it was over a half. The proportion of union-sponsored candidates who successfully entered parliament as MPs never fell below 70 per cent in the postwar period and was usually above 80 per cent, whereas in the 1980s less than 20 per cent of those with just CLP backing entered parliament (see Figure 5.4). For their part, the major unions always liked to have a batch of sponsored MPs on whom they could call in parliament to defend union interests from the backbenches. (Access to frontbenchers was also useful.) Union officials with many years of experience in their organisations were often sponsored and became MPs. The NUM had over thirty sponsored MPs in the 1950s but this figure fell as the mining industry declined. The TGWU increased its sponsored group from 14 in 1959 to 38 in 1992, while the GMB, the AEEU and NUPE also had sizable contingents of sponsored MPs.[9]

There would be no incentive for unions to sponsor candidates unless they expected to receive something in return, but the latter was generally understood to be an effort by the sponsored MP to raise issues of importance to the union in parliament. Most of these issues related to trade and industrial matters; for example, if the union were involved in a strike, it might expect the MP to make a speech in the House or lobby for legislation. However, the effectiveness of sponsorship as a means of

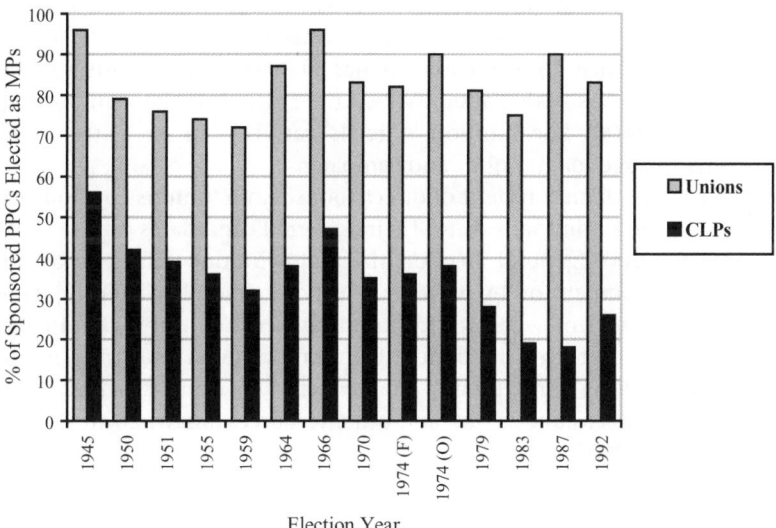

Figure 5.4   Sponsored MPs as a Proportion of Sponsored PPCs
Sources: Derived from Craig (1989: 91–2, Tables 7.03 and 7.04) and Norris and Lovenduski (1995: 57, 59).

control was blunted, not only by the fact that it involved small sums of money, but also by a ruling of the Parliamentary Privileges Committee in the 1940s. While recognising the legitimacy of sponsorship, the committee prohibited unions and other outside bodies from using it 'as an instrument by which it controls or seeks to control the conduct of a Member or to punish him for what he has done as a Member' (cited in Minkin, 1992: 260). Unions retained the right to withdraw sponsorship if they no longer thought it in their interests to continue with it, but they had to be careful about attempting to influence MPs.[10] Unions have occasionally sought to pressurise MPs and then quickly backed down amid public concern – though some MPs opted for a quiet life by voting in line with union policy on important industrial issues (Minkin, 1992: 266).

The rules on sponsorship came under scrutiny in the 1990s after a series of financial scandals involving the Conservative government. John Major set up a commission headed by Lord Nolan to examine standards in public life, and in response to the Nolan report, Labour announced an end to the direct sponsorship of MPs by unions in 1995. However, many of the bigger unions continue to make payments to CLPs through new constituency development plans, whereby a union pays a grant to a CLP to develop party-union links at the local level. Many agreements were concentrated in key marginal seats that Labour won in 1997 to build up its organisational strength (Criddle, 1997: 206). For instance, Unison currently has 53 development plans, not all in constituencies with Labour MPs, under which it pays an annual grant of £1500. Local union officials can coordinate with CLPs, shaping the agenda in policy and campaigns.

Despite the abandonment of direct sponsorship, unions continue to work to secure nominations for their preferred candidates on the NPP. Before the 2001 general election the major unions agreed to avoid destructive competition by putting up just one union-backed candidate in winnable vacant seats. It did not always ensure union candidates were selected but they did benefit from union help in securing nominations, making constituency contacts, and covering expenses, and they had access to union staff and other resources (Shaw, 2001: 47; see also Criddle, 2002: 192).

Nomination

Labour implemented one reform of fundamental importance to the nomination screen. It was argued earlier that OMOV combined with mandatory reselection could produce significant problems for the leadership because local selectors might use ballots to deselect MPs. Consequently, mandatory reselection was effectively abandoned when the 1990 party conference decided to introduce a 'trigger mechanism' into the procedure. From 1993 a sitting MP who received two-thirds of all nominations was deemed automatically reselected without the need for balloting. In 1999, the life of the incumbent was made easier still when the proportion of nominations required for automatic re-selection was reduced to 50 per cent, with the system now called 'affirmative nomination' (Criddle, 2002: 187). To surmount this hurdle still requires broad support in the CLP, but the mechanism may enable the MP's allies to pressurise nominating bodies to offer their support, whereas in its absence there would be no compelling need to do so. Relations between MPs and CLPs are more sedate than in the 1970s and 1980s, and the NEC would examine closely attempts to deselect MPs. Affirmative nomination may serve as a means by which the NEC signals to activists that anything other than automatic reselection will invite NEC scrutiny of the CLP. The mobilisation costs of the MP's opponents are significantly increased, since not only must they fight to win a deselection vote, they must struggle to hold a ballot at all. MPs are now as safe in their positions as they generally were before mandatory reselection.[11]

Shortlisting

Rules on shortlisting were never detailed but a number of changes were introduced. First, the right to draw up shortlists was thrown open to GCs, whereas previously executives had carried out the task. This change widened the local selectorate and was designed to prevent small cliques on executives manipulating the shortlisting process. Second, a minimum of four candidates must be on shortlists in seats where there is no Labour MP (or where an incumbent Labour MP is standing down). There must be equal numbers of men and women on each shortlist (chosen in separate ballots of GC delegates) unless the CLP in question has agreed to have an all-women shortlist. Pressure had mounted throughout the 1980s for a greater representation of women at all levels of the party, particularly in the number of women MPs, which stood at just 37 in 1992. The leadership was won round to the idea of having all-women shortlists for some CLPs as a way of increasing representation, and the party conference agreed the measure in 1993. It stipulated that half of all inherited seats (safe Labour seats where the sitting MP retired) and half of all Labour's targeted Tory marginals should have a woman candidate in the following general election. To achieve this target, many CLPs would have all-women shortlists so that they could choose from a number of women candidates. From its inception the policy was controversial and aroused resentment in CLPs. Two defeated male candidates successfully appealed to an industrial tribunal that the policy contravened sex discrimination laws. However, by then many candidates had already been chosen from all-women shortlists and the policy was largely responsible for the record intake of 102 women Labour MPs in 1997. The policy was then abandoned, but after the 2001 general election, the government introduced legislation to permit all-women shortlists. In the round of selections for the general election expected in 2005/06, half of all vacant Labour-held seats will have all-women shortlists. All non-Labour seats have open shortlists.[12]

There are no similar shortlist rules for ethnic minority candidates. However, if any Black/Asian members of the NPP express an interest in being selected for the constituency, the executive must nominate one name to go forward to the shortlisting meeting. These circumstances are the only ones in which an executive can nominate a candidate.

The period under review also saw the adoption of special powers for the centre in the realm of shortlisting, the most important being the formation of a special NEC by-election panel, which short-circuited the selection procedure. By-elections can become national events because they provide snapshots of the state of the parties. Shortly before the 1987 general election, a by-election was called in the safe Labour seat of Greenwich after the death of the incumbent MP. The CLP selected as its candidate, Deirdre Wood, a leftwing official for the Inner London Education Authority. The campaign was dominated by tabloid smears on Wood, and hysteria about the 'loony left'. Relentless media interest in Wood's private life eventually took its toll and the SDP won the seat, leaving Labour's general election preparations in turmoil (McSmith, 1996: 56–60; Heffernan and Marqusee, 1992: 72–4). A year later in another safe Labour seat, in Glasgow Govan, the locally adopted leftwing candidate, Bob Gillespie, was defeated by the Scottish National Party after a rancorous by-election in which, contrary to party policy, Gillespie expressed sympathy with a campaign of non-payment of the poll tax.

The disastrous consequences of choosing unsuitable candidates for by-elections prompted Kinnock to institute a central by-election panel, run by the NEC, which would interview candidates and, if need be, impose them on CLPs. This new mechanism would be used a number of times in the following years but the most famous case was the first to arise after the rule was approved. Vauxhall CLP chose a black activist, Martha Osamor, to fight the by-election in Labour-held Vauxhall in 1989. The NEC objected and drew up a shortlist of five, from which the only black candidate later withdrew. It was put to the CLP, which rejected it and demanded the right to choose a black candidate. The by-election panel refused and imposed a white candidate who subsequently won the seat (see Heffernan and Marqusee, 1992: 265–70). Central control over by-elections has since become the norm.

Prior to a general election, a number of MPs usually announce their decision to step down. A spate of such announcements before the 1997 and 2001 general elections left the respective CLPs with no time to organise shortlists so the NEC was able to impose its own. Suspicion arose that the exercise was a ruse to avoid unacceptable candidates being chosen and to parachute in Blair loyalists (Seyd, 1998: 68). Included among them was Alan Howarth, the former Conservative minister who joined Labour as late as 1995 and for whom the leadership was desperate to find a seat in time for the 1997 general election. He eventually secured a safe Labour seat in South Wales. Even more controversial was the case of Shaun Woodward, a former Conservative propagandist who defected to Labour in 1999 and became Labour MP for the safe seat of St Helens South in 2001, after the NEC imposed on the CLP a shortlist that excluded strong local candidates (Criddle, 2002: 191–2).

Endorsement

The NEC is a major player in the selection process and under Kinnock and Blair it has adopted an interventionist stance. One of the most important NEC interventions was the decision to veto the selection of Liz Davies, a leftwing London councillor, in 1995. What made this decision unusual was that Davies was not fighting a by-election but was chosen as the Labour PPC for Leeds North-East in the 1997 general election. Davies was accused of having been a member of Trotskyite organisations and of failing to tell the CLP about committal proceedings she had faced for refusing to pay the poll tax. Both charges were disputed but the NEC barred her from standing as a candidate, and the 1995 party conference reaffirmed this decision, with Clare Short telling delegates, 'On the basis of her views and record, it is impossible for the NEC to endorse Liz Davies' (*The Times*, 4 October 1995). An interventionist NEC was the corollary of OMOV, because all-member ballots increase uncertainty in selection contests. When, as in this case, party members made the 'wrong' choice, the NEC could step in and order a new ballot without Davies' participation.

Conclusion

The Labour leadership's long battle to reform selection procedures (see Table 5.1) involved the pursuit of two organisational goals. OMOV was initially envisaged as a distributional reform that would undermine the activist left in the CLPs and smooth relations with MPs that had been strained in the 1970s. It is true that deselections occur less frequently than they did in the early-1980s; but in explaining this turnaround, it is difficult to estimate the relative importance of OMOV, the fear of NEC intervention, and genuine contentment with MPs. However, there have been some acrimonious incidents in OMOV ballots: rules have been bent and allegations made of vote fixing. Moreover, the left has on occasion succeeded under OMOV (Liz Davies was elected in an all-member ballot). Many ballots involve low turnouts of party members, giving the committed activists a proportionately greater say, though not nearly as much as under the old GC system. It is because OMOV has not proved a panacea for the modernisers that central control had to be strengthened. The NEC under Kinnock and Blair intervened in OMOV ballots if they produced the 'wrong' results. Recent reforms have continued this centralising impulse, with the compilation of the NPP, which enables the NEC to neutralise most potential selection problems at the earliest stage of the process. This new centralisation, together with 'affirmative nomination', vastly increases the mobilisation costs of opposition factions. Since selection procedures help determine the composition of the PLP, a centralising leadership will inevitably continue to exert control. Central control is nowadays so strong that the greatest threat to MPs' security of tenure comes not from plotting activists, but from the party leadership itself. As central control has extended to the PLP, rebellious backbench MPs must beware of falling foul of the whips lest the NEC pressurises their CLPs to deselect them.

As the 1980s drew to a close, it was apparent that party modernisers were pursuing a second goal: weakening the union-link and imposing a unitary membership structure. It was this symbolically important aim that created much consternation among the unions. Many feared OMOV was the thin end of a wedge leading to eventual separation, that it was an attempt fundamentally to alter the entire basis of political exchange in the Labour Party. Unions cannot sew-up local selections to the extent they once could in unionised areas. Nomination rights remain, as do seats on the GCs, but voting rights have gone and historically it has been the ability to cast concentrated blocks of

Table 5.1 Candidate Selection Changes, 1983–2003

Stage	Procedures in 1983	Changes by 2003

Eligibility & Application	• Mandatory reselection of MPs once per parliament
	• Vacancies: CLPs await individual applications or seek applicants from national lists:
	  – List A: union-sponsored candidates
	  – List B: CLP-sponsored candidates
	  – List C: Co-operative Party-sponsored candidates
	  – List W (from 1988): All women candidates from lists A, B and C
		Lists merged into single NEC-approved national parliamentary panel
		• All selected candidates not on NPP must be interviewed by NEC
		• Direct sponsorship of MPs and candidates ended (but constituency 'development plans' permitted)

Nomination	• Party branches and locally affiliated unions, socialist societies, Co-operative Party, women's sections and Young Socialists each entitled to one nomination • Reselection contests: sitting MP eligible for nomination	• Branches and affiliates entitled to two nominations (one male, one female) unless all-women shortlist • 'Affirmative nomination': if sitting MP receives 50% of nominations, s/he is deemed automatically reselected

Shortlisting	• CLP executive draws up shortlist, which must include sitting MP in reselection contests and (from 1988) at least one woman
	• Shortlist presented to GC for confirmation and to NEC for ratification
		• GC draws up shortlist, which must include:
		  – at least four names if no Labour MP
		  – sitting MP (if not automatically reselected)
		  – equal numbers of men and women, unless all-women shortlists (from 1993–96 and since 2001)
		• By-elections: NEC can impose shortlist

Selection	• Secret ballot of GC members	• Where MP has not been automatically reselected, and in contests for vacancies, OMOV ballot at selection meeting
Endorsement	• NEC endorses/rejects candidate	• NEC endorses/rejects candidate

votes that has underpinned the unions' domination of Labour's extra-parliamentary organs. OMOV has ended that. Local trade unionists can still participate in selection ballots but only in their capacity as individual party members. Sponsorship has been reformed and no longer exerts the same pull on CLPs.

Labour expanded participation rights while strengthening the powers of the centre. The effect has been to prevent party activists from effectively using local institutions to pressurise MPs. Although such stability has obvious benefits for the party, the question remains whether selection institutions are still an adequate 'selective incentive' for party members. If institutions do not provide means of control and fail even to enable adequate internal 'voice', then the outcome may be membership exit. This issue is addressed in Chapter 8.

6
Electing the Party Leader

Since 1981, Labour has elected its leader and deputy leader through a tripartite electoral college that gives votes to the party's three principal stakeholders: MPs, local activists and trade unions.* The formation of the college was the culmination of a leftwing campaign to bring the party elite under greater grassroots control after the perceived failures of the Callaghan government. Previously, the leader was elected by Labour MPs, and since the latter were traditionally more moderate than party activists, the Labour leader usually came from the centre-right of the party. The day after the college was established, a group of high-profile social democrats effectively abandoned the party and issued the famous Limehouse Declaration, which began: 'A handful of trade union leaders can now dictate the choice of a future Prime Minister' (cited in Minkin, 1992: 220). Labour moderates feared that the new system would rob the leader of effective control.

Yet, years later the consensus was that the college had *entrenched* leaders' security of tenure. As Margaret Beckett remarked, the system 'has had, in a sense, almost the reverse effect of what some of its proponents intended' (cited in Stark, 1996: 66). This chapter explores the reasons for this unintended consequence. It begins by sketching a principal-agent model of party leadership, before examining the functioning of Labour's electoral college as it was originally constituted, identifying the nomination and selection stages as the most important. Next, it considers the reform of the college in 1993, showing that the shift from block voting to individual voting transformed the nature of leadership contests.

---

* Much of the material in this chapter first appeared, in a slightly different form, in *The British Journal of Politics and International Relations*, 6 (3), August 2004 (© 2004 Political Studies Association and Blackwell Publishing).

Finally, some conclusions are drawn about the effectiveness of the college as a means of controlling party leaders. Two appendices offer reflections on the use of electoral colleges to choose Labour candidates for devolved administrations, and on the reform of elections to the NEC.

Party leaders as agents

Most parties have formal institutional means by which to select leaders, such as ballots of MPs, membership votes and electoral colleges. In each case, the identity of the selectorate may differ, but whichever system is deployed, those intra-party actors entitled to participate generally choose leaders they believe will benefit them, whether that means improving the party's election prospects and/or adopting a given policy platform. In this sense, the relationship between leader and selectors is a principal-agent one.[1] Principals are actors who wish to achieve some goal and recruit agents to help them, the agent receiving compensatory benefits for his efforts. Principals face problems monitoring agents to make sure they do what they have been contracted to do, as agents may have incentives to substitute their own goals for those of principals.

Leaders help followers overcome their collective action problems by monitoring principals, enforcing decisions (for example, through 'whipping'), offering selective incentives (such as patronage) and punishing free-riders (Strøm, 1993: 318–9). A leader is also the public face of a party when it appeals to voters. Leaders are recruited for their valuable skills – 'to reason, persuade, bully, inspire, rally, intimidate, mediate, and so on' (Shepsle and Bonchek, 1997: 383). However, these skills can also enable leaders to dominate principals. Principals face four problems when recruiting a political leader (Laver, 1997: 72–80). (1) How is the mandate awarded (and who awards it)? (2) What sanctions does the politician have at his disposal, and can his use of them be controlled? (3) Does the politician have incentives to renege on deals made with intra-party principals? (4) What mechanisms exist to evict a politician who outstays his welcome? Principals want to recruit a high-quality politician who will not renege on his promises. Politicians want to win elections while keeping the principals happy – or escaping their control. As we saw in Chapter 2, if intra-party principals have more radical policy preferences than the median voter, leaders face a dilemma: appease the party but risk losing elections, or accommodate the median voter and alienate the party, whose activists could exit, hampering its ability to campaign. Leaders need some autonomy, but too much of it leads to agency losses. Institutions are needed that permit autonomy while preserving ultimate control for the principals.

Principals can attempt to constrain leaders with *ex ante*, *ex post* and on-going control mechanisms. There are four ways of reducing agency loss: (1) contract design, by which the terms of the agent's remit are established; (2) screening and selection, that is, *ex ante* mechanisms to filter out unsuitable candidates; (3) monitoring, whereby agents' activities are formally observed by principals, with procedures for reporting back to committees; (4) institutional checks, such as committee veto powers (Kiewiet and McCubbins, 1991; Strøm, 1993: 318–9). Screening and selection have assumed an important place in the debate about party leaders, relating to how the leader is recruited and how he can be removed.

Labour's electoral college, 1981–93

The position of Labour Party leader is an important one, carrying intra-party powers of patronage over (shadow) cabinet portfolios, an *ex officio* seat on the NEC, and enormous power over policy when Labour is in government. The British system of government confers great power on the prime minister, whereas extra-parliamentary actors have no direct influence. Unlike other European socialist parties, but like other British parties, Labour did not have separate parliamentary and organisational leaders.[2] This fact was largely a consequence of the UK's Westminster model of government (Lijphart, 1999) and as such, it was not surprising that British parties generally left leadership selection to party elites. Until 1981, Labour's leader was elected by his fellow Labour MPs in a secret ballot. However, the lack of direct links between leaders and followers has often resulted in Labour prime ministers presiding over policies opposed by party members, and after the conflicts between leaders and activists in the 1970s, it was no surprise that the ascendant left would seek to bring the leadership under grass-roots control. This goal was unattainable as long as MPs chose the leader. By changing the leader's intra-party constituency, the activists wanted to alter his incentives for reneging on policy deals and replace him if need be.

At a special conference in 1981, Labour formed an electoral college and spread responsibility for choosing the leader (and deputy leader) between MPs, CLPs and unions. The debate was over the precise pro-portions of votes allocated to each section. Moderates wanted to max-imise the PLP's share, but tactical blunders by the Labour right and tactical ingenuity by the left (together with sheer luck) ensured that just 30 per cent of the votes in leadership contests were allocated to the PLP. The CLPs also received 30 per cent, while the unions and other affiliated bodies took the remaining 40 per cent[3] (see Kogan and Kogan, 1982; Seyd, 1987). Both left and right reasoned that the CLPs were dominated by leftists (confirmed by the deputy leadership contest of 1981) and that the unions were likely to contain a higher leftist contingent than the PLP. Hence, the median voter in the electoral college would be to the left of the median Labour MP.

The electoral college contained a series of stages, or screens. The first was an eligibility requirement, and as before 1981, only MPs could become leader – largely a matter of practicality in the British political system. The second screen concerned nomination, and here any MP, CLP or affiliate could nominate a candidate. However, each nominee needed to receive the support of a minimum of 5 per cent of Labour MPs. A third screen, which would operate only when Labour was in government, would be the necessity to receive majority support at the party conference for the principle of a contest. This rule was intended to offer a Labour prime minister protection from frivolous challenges that could undermine his authority. Finally, there would be a ballot at a meeting of the electoral college.

Three other features of the system are important. First, leadership contests in opposition would be held annually, provided that a challenger put himself forward. Leftists wanted this provision because annual contests would lower the costs of challenging the incumbent, making it easier to control him (Kogan and Kogan, 1982: 96). Second, candidates would need to join ballots from the beginning of a contest (as under the old system of MP selection) rather than being permitted to join in later rounds of balloting. The latter rule characterised Conservative leadership elections until 1998 and contributed to the ease with which Conservative MPs could eject unpopular leaders. Challenging an incumbent is risky and may deter serious challengers, but if they can join in later ballots, incumbents may face 'stalking-horse' candidates in early rounds, and if they suffer irreparable damage, stronger contenders can step in. Labour's system increased the security of tenure of the incumbent. Third, both the leader and the deputy leader are elected in the college, creating the potential for rival politicians with different preferences to claim separate mandates.

In the remainder of this section, two features of the electoral college in its old format are assessed. The distribution and concentration of votes at the selection stage had major consequences for contests and were the focus of reform in the 1990s. These questions are examined shortly. Before that, it is necessary to analyse the nomination screen.

PLP nomination rights and gate-keeping powers

Delegates to the electoral college voted on candidates who had secured sufficient PLP nominations. The special conference of 1981 set this threshold at 5 per cent of Labour MPs, but after an unsuccessful left-wing leadership challenge in 1988, Kinnock persuaded the NEC to raise it to 20 per cent. The reasoning was that small leftwing parliamentary cliques could easily surmount the 5 per cent hurdle but would struggle with a higher threshold. Consider Figure 6.1, which plots the ideal policy preferences of various intra-party coalitions along a simple uni-dimensional leftwing-rightwing scale. The most leftwing 5 per cent coalition of MPs will adopt the bliss point of the MP positioned at the first twentieth of the PLP distribution from the left ('5%'). Similarly, the most leftwing 20 per cent coalition adopts the bliss point of the MP positioned at the first quintile of the distribution ('20%'). For simplicity, we can assume that the incumbent leader is the median Labour MP ('50%'), though in reality he is likely to be further to the right (assuming that the median voter in the electorate at large is towards the rightwing end of this intra-Labour scale). Two potential bliss points for the electoral college are indicated: EC1, which is a very leftwing college, and EC2, which is slightly more rightwing. The bliss point of the college is assumed always to be more leftwing than the median MP, because the college contains radical activists even though they control only a share of the votes.

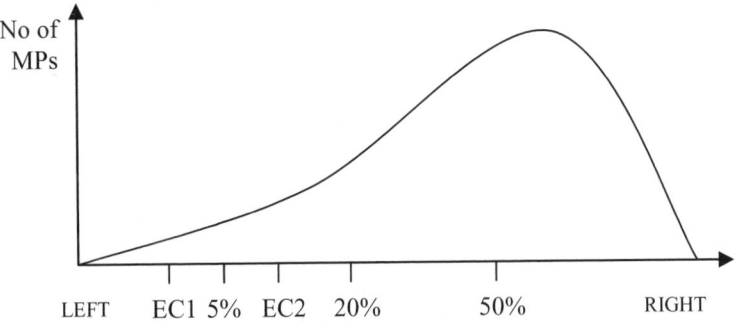

Figure 6.1   PLP Nomination Thresholds in Leadership Contests

Given the nomination rules, a leftwing PLP coalition that can secure sufficient nominations can impose a leader at its bliss point if the electoral college is even more leftwing. Thus, if the college is at EC1 (as leftists hoped and moderates feared in 1981), a leftwing PLP coalition can choose a leader at '5%' or '20%', depending on the nomination threshold specified in the rules. These positions are the most leftwing from which candidates can gain nomination, and the college will support them against the incumbent. Clearly, if the nomination threshold is 20 per cent, candidates are more rightwing than when the rule is 5 per cent. However, if the college's bliss point is EC2, it will be offered its ideal candidate if the threshold is 5 per cent but not if it is 20 per cent. However, it is worth noting that even under a 5 per cent threshold, the college may not adopt a candidate at its bliss point, even if offered one. The reason is that the college worked on the principle of exhaustive ballots until 1993 and the alternative vote (AV) system after 1993, both of which entail candidates being eliminated until one passes the winning 50 per cent threshold. A candidate at EC2 would be a Condorcet winner (that is, be able to defeat all other alternatives in pair-wise ballots), but neither AV nor exhaustive ballots necessarily ensure the victory of Condorcet winners in contests of three or more candidates. The candidate at EC2 might attract insufficient first-preference or first-ballot votes, and find himself eliminated early on.

Nevertheless, this discussion would appear to suggest that the incumbent leader is at the mercy of parliamentary leftwing cliques. The emphasis on specifically PLP factions is particularly important when the threshold is 20 per cent. The 5 per cent barrier was much easier to surmount by leftist challengers. The question, then, is why the leader's security of tenure appears, contrary to expectations, to have *increased* under the electoral college system. The general answer is that although coalitions of MPs may be in a position to launch a challenge, the *costs* of doing so are usually prohibitively high. These costs figure much more prominently for coalitions whose bliss point is close to the incumbent, because here the net benefits of a leadership challenge are lower than the payoffs at the *status quo ante*. The further a coalition's bliss point is from the *status quo ante*, the greater the net benefits of change will be. Hence, other things equal, the net benefits of a challenge to a moderate incumbent will be greater for coalitions under a 5 per cent than a 20 per cent threshold, because such coalitions are more likely to be leftwing.[4] (The issue of costs is discussed later.)

The '20 per cent rule' confers gate-keeping powers on the PLP when the pressure for leadership change comes mainly from outside the PLP.

If, in opposition, the party had 250 MPs, a challenger would need the nominations of 50 MPs to start a contest. However, given that up to a hundred MPs have frontbench positions (the 'payroll vote'), and many more are hopeful of obtaining future preferment, the hurdle seriously impedes challenges. In government, where the party currently has over 400 MPs, the signatures of 80 are required for each challenger. Even then, the further hurdle of a vote at the annual conference needs to be surmounted. The conference is an additional veto player when Labour is in government.

However, vacancies sometimes arise because of the resignation or death of the incumbent. Of the four leadership contests to have taken place since the college was formed, two arose from a resignation (1983 and 1992), one followed a death (1994) and only one was a challenge (1988). Of the five contests for the deputy leadership, three followed resignations (1983, 1992 and 1994) and two were challenges (1981 and 1988). All challenges to the leader and deputy leader were from the left against moderates (reflecting the greater net benefits of leadership change for leftists). Contests for vacancies also require candidates to pass nomination thresholds but here there were differences. The 5 per cent threshold from 1981 and the 20 per cent threshold from 1988 both applied to challenges and contests for vacancies. However, problems arose during the 1992 leadership contest when Bryan Gould, the only opponent of the front-runner, John Smith, struggled to obtain sufficient nominations. Eventually, he passed the threshold, ensuring that a contest would take place, but to forestall similar embarrassment in the future, the rule was changed in 1993 so that in contests for vacancies, candidates would require the nominations of 12.5 per cent of the PLP (see Alderman and Carter, 1993: 55–6). The 20 per cent threshold remained for challenges and implied a maximum of five candidates in a contest, though in reality there would probably be no more than two or three. The 12.5 per cent threshold enabled more candidates to enter contests for vacancies.

Selection in the electoral college

Once a contest was under way, the PLP played a subordinate role. Not only was its vote share reduced to 30 per cent of the college, MPs now had their votes publicly declared – a change from the secret balloting of the old system of MP selection. By contrast, from having no votes previously, the college gave the roughly 600 CLPs a 30 per cent share. GCs decided by a majority vote which candidate to support in leadership contests and cast their votes as undivided blocks so that minority opinion within each CLP was not expressed in the final vote. This rule suited the left because leftwing activists were disproportionately represented on the GCs in the 1980s.

Since GCs took the decisions, leadership candidates could profitably embark on rounds of party meetings to procure votes. Tony Benn performed a punishing round of such meetings in his bid for the deputy leadership in 1981, and he ultimately secured the support of four out of five CLPs. His rightwing opponent, Denis Healey, was much less active in this way, reflecting the reality that his support within the CLPs was limited. However, it was believed that if the CLPs were to conduct membership ballots, the left might be undermined as moderate members were enfranchised. In 1983, a minority of CLPs conducted some form of membership ballot and 90 per cent of these backed the rightwing candidate in the deputy leadership race, Roy Hattersley. Of the CLPs that did not conduct any ballot, two-thirds voted for the leftwing candidate, Michael Meacher. Similarly, in 1988, 337 CLPs conducted branch or postal ballots of their members and only a quarter supported Benn in the leadership contest, though overall, only one in five CLPs supported Benn. But 23 CLPs that had nominated Benn subsequently voted for Kinnock after their consultation ballots (Drucker, 1984; Punnett, 1990, 187–8). A rule change obliged CLPs to hold OMOV ballots in subsequent contests. The first was in 1992, but in that contest, the electoral college votes were still cast on a winner-takes-all basis. Thus, each CLP's entire block vote went to the candidate topping its OMOV ballot.

The most controversial feature of the college as initially configured was the part played in it by the unions. Their 40 per cent share of the votes meant they could not arithmetically determine the winner but they could substantially decide the trajectory of contests. This agenda-setting power owed not just to their share of votes but to the *concentration* of their votes, in the form of block votes. A few big unions dominated the union section of the electoral college and had a substantial say in any contest. Thus, in the 1988 leadership contest, five big unions collectively controlled 62.5 per cent of the union section – a quarter of the entire college. The TGWU alone wielded 8.8 per cent of the college votes. Given that the PLP section consisted of 229 MPs and the CLP section contained about 600 CLPs, it meant the TGWU's block vote was equivalent to 67 MPs or 176 CLPs. The big five unions were collectively worth the votes of 191 MPs or

500 CLPs. Given the time and resources needed to campaign for the votes of such large numbers of MPs and CLPs, the importance of the big unions is apparent.

If a candidate could get an early commitment of support from some big unions, he could quickly find himself home and dry. The construction of coalitions can be greatly assisted by an early build-up of support as the momentum may create an unstoppable bandwagon. David Lax and James Sebenius (1991) argue that 'strategic sequencing' is an important tactic commonly used to construct coalitions. It involves approaching potential allies in a certain order so that gaining one party's support makes it easier to win the support of others later on. As they put it, 'the *prior commitments* of other parties may be used as resources in obtaining the acquiescence of other subsequent parties' (1991: 180, emphasis in original). In the electoral college, if a candidate could secure early backing from some big unions, he could increase the credibility of his campaign and thereby encourage other parties to support him. The huge block votes wielded by the unions could firmly establish a candidate as a frontrunner. Since the unions were unique in their high concentration of college votes, they were in a better position to provide candidates with an early boost, thus increasing the bargaining power of union leaders and leading to claims that they were 'kingmakers'.

It may be objected that the decision as to which candidate to support was not up to union leaders but was made after internal consultation. Nevertheless, union leaders had significant influence because their organisations enjoyed nominating rights. Nominating could be almost as good as voting for a candidate. The importance of nomination was that, unlike the casting of votes, it could be done very early on in the campaign, setting in motion the bandwagon effect described above. Thus, Kinnock's leadership quest in 1983 was settled long before the casting of electoral college votes. Shortly after Labour's election defeat in June 1983, Foot stood down as leader. A succession of union leaders immediately nominated Kinnock as his successor, leading rival candidates to complain of a 'stitch-up' (Heffernan and Marqusee, 1992: 36). By the time the vote took place, no one doubted the result. Many MPs subsequently voted for Kinnock in the open ballot of the PLP section because they did not want to damage their chances of patronage (Stark, 1996: 140). The story was similar in 1992 when union support meant John Smith's bandwagon became as unstoppable as Kinnock's in 1983, with Smith eventually claiming 91 per cent of the votes.

The importance of winning union votes created distinctive styles of leadership campaigns. Canvassing within the unions took two forms. The most obvious way was to seek the backing of the union leader. The second consisted of appealing for support among union personnel below the position of leader – members of the executive committee, regional organisers, delegates at the union's conference, and so on. The favoured strategy of centre-right candidates was to utilise personal links with union leaders and where necessary to call for membership ballots. There were no uniform decision-making procedures inside the unions before 1993. Some left the decision to their executives, others to their annual conferences, many allowed their Labour Party conference delegates to choose, while others held various forms of consultation ballots, whether at meetings or by post. The left was more likely to win votes from unions whose middle-level officers and activists took decisions, reflecting curvilinear disparity. Centre-right candidates such as Healey (1981), Hattersley (1983) and Kinnock (1988) did better in membership ballots or when leaders took the decision (see Minkin, 1992: 334–57; Punnett, 1990, 1992; Drucker, 1984).

Candidates lacking the support of union leaders faced difficulties. The block voting system imposed high mobilisation costs on minority factions. In the absence of leadership backing, candidates needed to seek out intermediate-level supporters in the union. To do so in one union was difficult enough; to do it in many unions was a monumental task, requiring a well-run organisation to mobilise support. The only occasion on which it fully happened was in 1981 during the first ever contest in the electoral college, when Benn challenged Healey for the deputy leadership. Virtually the entire Labour and union establishment (as well as the media) was opposed to Benn. Benn targeted middle-level union officials by utilising the Rank and File Mobilising Committee (RFMC), an umbrella organisation for existing leftwing groups, and exploiting links already established with union officials during the left's 1979–81 campaign for institutional reform in the Labour Party. RFMC activists were able to reduce their mobilisation costs, though in only one medium-sized union did delegates ignore their leadership's wishes and support Benn.

Given the unpropitious circumstances, it is not surprising Benn lost, though only by a tiny margin (see Table 6.1). Nevertheless, Benn's defeat at a time when the left was at its zenith illustrated the difficulty of mobilising block votes against Labour's elite. Ultimately the costs of mobilisation were too great because too many separate unions had to be won over. The aggregate percentages of the ballot conceal the politics of

Table 6.1   Contests Conducted in the Electoral College

	PLP 30%	CLPs 30%	Affiliates 40%	Total
1981 (deputy leader)				
First Ballot				
Tony Benn	22.4	78.3	16.0	**36.6**
Denis Healey*	51.0	17.9	61.7	**45.4**
John Silkin	26.5	3.8	22.2	**18.0**
Second ballot				
Tony Benn	34.1	81.1	37.5	**49.6**
Denis Healey*	65.9	18.9	62.5	**50.4**
1983 (leader)				
Roy Hattersley	26.1	1.9	27.2	**19.3**
Eric Heffer	14.3	6.6	0.1	**6.3**
Neil Kinnock	49.3	91.5	72.6	**71.3**
Peter Shore	10.3	0.0	0.1	**3.1**
1983 (deputy leader)				
Denzil Davies	10.9	0.8	0.0	**3.5**
Gwyneth Dunwoody	4.0	0.3	0.1	**1.3**
Roy Hattersley	55.7	51.0	88.1	**67.3**
Michael Meacher	29.4	47.8	11.8	**27.9**
1988 (leader)				
Tony Benn	17.2	19.6	0.9	**11.4**
Neil Kinnock*	82.8	80.4	99.2	**88.6**
1988 (deputy leader)				
Roy Hattersley*	57.9	60.4	78.3	**66.8**
Eric Heffer	18.1	13.5	0.2	**9.5**
John Prescott	24.0	26.2	21.6	**23.7**
1992 (leader)				
Bryan Gould	22.7	2.3	3.7	**9.0**
John Smith	77.3	97.7	96.3	**91.0**
1992 (deputy leader)				
Margaret Beckett	42.9	63.5	63.5	**57.3**
Bryan Gould	25.7	12.9	7.4	**14.6**
John Prescott	31.4	23.7	29.1	**28.1**

Table 6.1   Contests Conducted in the Electoral College – *continued*

	PLP 1/3	CLPs 1/3	Affiliates 1/3	Total
1994[a] (leader)				
Margaret Beckett	19.9	17.4	19.3	**18.9**
Tony Blair	60.5	58.2	52.3	**57.0**
John Prescott	19.6	24.4	28.4	**24.1**
1994[a] (deputy leader)				
Margaret Beckett[b]	46.3	40.6	43.4	**43.5**
John Prescott	53.7	59.4	56.6	**56.5**

Figures are percentages of votes in each section. Figures in final column are percentages of votes in whole college (weighted summation of the three sections).
* incumbent
[a] affiliates' section – votes cast by individual affiliated members; block vote abolished in CLP section; PLP section includes MEPs. The 1994 leadership election saw votes cast by 329 MPs/MEPs, 172,356 individual members and 779,426 affiliated members.
[b] Beckett was incumbent deputy leader but resigned her position so that she could also contest the leadership.

mobilisation within the unions. The concentration of voting power meant it needed only a handful of delegates to change their minds to transform the result. Had the TGWU voted for Healey, he would have won by a margin of 17 per cent rather than 0.8 per cent. Equally, had NUPE voted the preferences of its leftwing executive rather than holding branch ballots (which went to Healey), Benn would have won by 7 per cent. Block voting introduced an element of arbitrariness.

In conclusion, both the nomination and selection components were crucial factors in determining the distribution of power in the electoral college in its original form. The 20 per cent nomination threshold offered considerable protection to incumbents from both the extra-parliamentary party and from leftwing cliques in the PLP. The best way to secure the leader's position was to stop challenges from occurring in the first place. However, once a contest was underway, it was the unions (and usually their leaders) that held most power. They secured the leaders they wanted in 1983 and 1992, and although Kinnock won a plurality of votes in the PLP section in 1983, it is questionable whether he would have won under the old system of PLP ballots (his performance in the PLP's shadow cabinet elections was never spectacular). Moreover, as is shown later, the selection rules of the college were instrumental in a negative sense: their cumbersome nature made party *notables* wary of leadership contests. A PLP ballot, even with a high nomination hurdle, would not give the leader the same security as the electoral college.

The electoral college after 1993

From 1992, the entire Labour leadership wanted to reform the college because it was seen as unacceptably dominated by the unions, particularly after Smith's election. Labour's dominant coalition had historically been between the PLP and union leaders. The leaders of the major unions accepted the need to reduce their share of the electoral college but were looking for an equal tripartite college in which the PLP, CLPs and unions each controlled one-third of the votes. They wanted a consolidating institution, in which the old dominant coalition was preserved, as a more legitimate college was established. By contrast, modernisers wanted a 'new deal' institution from which the unions were removed entirely, a position Smith sympathised with. The problem for modernisers was that any changes would need to get through the union-dominated party conference, which meant compromise was inevitable.

Reform of the electoral college fell within the remit of the trade union links review group, which was charged with examining all areas of the party-union relationship. It contained representatives from the four biggest unions, ensuring the dominance of traditionalists. The group's most heated debates concerned candidate selection, with the electoral college a long way behind in importance. An interim report (Labour Party, 1993a) listed options but no recommendations, yet it was clear the group favoured only small shifts from the *status quo ante*. Smith would have ideally preferred a different type of college in which parliamentarians and individual party members would each take 50 per cent of the votes. However, his priority was OMOV in candidate selection, so to soften union opposition on this issue, he offered the unions a continued role in the electoral college. However, in the new college, the unions' vote share would be reduced to one-third and block voting would be abolished, replaced by a one-levypayer–one-vote (OLOV) postal ballot. In the CLP section, all individual party members would also participate in a postal ballot, with the votes aggregated for a national total (unlike the old system, candidates would secure the votes of all those individuals who voted for them). Voting procedures remained the same in the PLP section, though now Labour MEPs would also participate, with an individual MEP's vote worth the same as an individual MP's. These reforms broke the power of union leaders, but modernisers and traditionalists failed to realise it at the time. Each side saw only the fact that union involvement was maintained, which is why traditionalists accepted the reform while modernisers such as

Blair and Brown were aghast (Rentoul, 1995: 328–9; Gould, 1999: 189–91). Traditionalists still opposed OMOV, but thanks to the compromise Smith persuaded the review group to recommend straight OMOV in its final report (Labour Party, 1993b). At the 1993 party conference, the reform of the college was passed easily but OMOV adopted only narrowly (see Chapter 5).

The reform of the electoral college dramatically reduced the role of union leaders and officials. Union influence would henceforth be administered through the agency of individuals and would be mediated by turnout rates. Under block voting, if a union had 500,000 levypayers affiliated, it would cast 500,000 votes in the union section, regardless of how many (if any) participated in consultation ballots. Under the new system, by contrast, if only 5000 levypayers cast their postal ballots, only 5000 would be counted in the sectional vote. Furthermore, votes would be aggregated for each candidate: if, out of these 5000 votes cast, 3000 were for candidate A and 2000 were for candidate B, the two candidates would receive precisely these amounts. Under block voting, candidate B would have a minority of the votes so he would get no votes at all from that union, whereas candidate A would take all the votes.

Since each candidate's votes are aggregated, a union qua organisation will have no net influence at all if its members divide evenly between the candidates. A given union will maximise its relative impact on the result of the election by maximising the proportion of its levypayers voting, though this impact will be greater if the members are predominantly uniform in their preferences. Interestingly, union executives are free to print their vote recommendation on ballot papers, but only six unions did so in the first leadership contest to be held under the new rules in 1994. Since voting figures are produced for each individual union, many union leaders feared their authority would be undermined by making a recommendation that went unheeded by the levypayers. It appears these recommendations may have had a marginal impact (Alderman and Carter, 1995: 449–50), but it is clear that the unions qua organisations play a greatly diminished role under OLOV.[5] The union leaders are deprived of their old 'king-making' role, as well as their ability to extract concessions from candidates, because they no longer have it in their power to promise hundreds of thousands of votes (Punnett, 1990: 190). Bandwagons of support are thus less likely to be set in motion by union leaders. The emphasis would now be on candidates making direct appeals to party and union members but not formally bargaining with them as they did with union leaders.

Instead, the need to win the votes of party members and levypayers meant inevitably that the media, especially television, would play an important role in the contests. Although the media could not cast any votes, its control and transmission of information could influence the votes of others. The media could not play this role unless MPs themselves were involved in briefings. During the 1994 contest, Peter Mandelson allegedly worked clandestinely to promote Blair among journalists and denigrate the chances of Gordon Brown. The best way to start a bandwagon is to enlist the support of a large group of MPs, including as many (shadow) ministers as possible. The media has a more important function than it did when only MPs chose the leader, because it transmits information to party members and levypayers (Stark, 1996). It would not be enough simply to do deals with MPs, though the latter would be important. In a reversal of the old college, the vote of one MP would now be worth that of 800 party members or several thousand levypayers (Alderman and Carter, 1995: 445), though these figures were nothing compared to the old block votes. Now, even if a candidate trailed behind another in terms of backing from MPs, he could still triumph once the members' votes were counted. The reform of the college returned to the PLP primary (but not sole) importance in leadership contests, both in its gate-keeping powers over nomination and in its ability to shape the contest as a whole.

The reform of the college related to *who* should award the leadership mandate (Table 6.2 sets out the main differences). By allowing levypayers rather than delegates to vote, the college marked a further step in the defederalisation of the Labour Party. By altering the identity of the voting principals, the OMOV–OLOV college was expected to produce a more moderate electorate, especially in the CLP section. The Labour right supported membership ballots because it believed inactive party and union members were less radical than activists. In terms of Figure 6.1, the bliss point of the college shifts to the right. Another effect of the OMOV–OLOV reforms has been on the types of *politicians* who can succeed in the college. It is questionable whether a candidate as centrist as Tony Blair could have won majorities in every section of the party at any other point in Labour's history. That he did so in 1994 reflected the desperation at all levels for electoral success, but it must be borne in mind that Blair did not need to win union block votes. Union leaders quickly installed frontrunners in the two previous electoral college contests for vacancies in 1983 and 1992, opting for people they thought (wrongly, as it turned out) they could trust on union interests. Had they retained their block votes in 1994, they may have reverted to type, looking for a

Table 6.2   Procedures for Challenging a Labour Leader

Electoral college in 1983	Electoral college in 2003
• Each candidate secures nominations of 5% of PLP	• Each candidate secures nominations of 20% of PLP for challenges (12.5% for vacancies)
• Principle of contest approved by majority at annual conference (only when Labour is in government)	• Principle of contest approved by majority at annual conference (only when Labour is in government)
• College meets at annual/special conference to cast votes. Section vote weights: – PLP: 30% (non-secret ballot) – CLPs: 30% (block voting) – Affiliates: 40% (block voting)	• College meets at annual/special conference to count/cast votes. Section vote weights: – PLP/EPLP: 33.33% (non-secret ballot) – CLPs: 33.33% (national OMOV ballot) – Affiliates: 33.33% (national OLOV ballot)

labourist candidate they thought they could trust. It is doubtful whether that candidate would have been Blair, given his perceived hostility to union interests as shadow employment spokesman in 1989. They may have chosen Gordon Brown instead – in which case Brown's hopes were scuppered by OLOV.

Leadership accountability and contest costs

The aim of the left in arguing for an electoral college in 1980–81 was to make the leader accountable to the entire party. If that meant the leader being subject to control from below over the direction of party policy, the reformers have been frustrated. The 1980s and 1990s saw an unprecedented degree of freedom for Labour leaders over policy and party affairs. Institutional checks on the leader are weak. The NEC possesses veto powers over extra-parliamentary issues, though since the mid-1980s Labour leaders have enjoyed solid majorities on the NEC and recent reforms have taken policy-making powers away from the executive (see Chapter 4).

The only viable institutional check on the incumbent is regular leadership contests. Only the threat of replacement can keep leaders from shirking, yet despite the provision for annual contests, challenges to incumbents have been rare. Without annual contests the college has led to the inauguration of victors with little subsequent accountability. Evidence of what can happen with regular contests was provided by the deputy leadership contest of 1994 when the incumbent, Margaret Beckett, ran again just two years after being elected. The occasion was the death of Smith. Beckett wished to run in the leadership contest making it proper for her to resign her old post first, though she also ran for the deputy leadership in case she lost in the leadership race. However, the gamble did not pay off and Beckett was defeated in both contests. It is difficult to compare the figures for 1992 and 1994 owing to the 1993 reforms, but even the latter could probably not explain why her support in both the CLP and union sections fell by more than 20 per cent compared to 1992. One explanation for the haemorrhaging of her support was the ambivalence of her backing for Smith at the fraught 1993 party conference over the principle of extending OMOV in the Labour Party. John Prescott made a last-minute speech in favour of OMOV and the leadership narrowly won the vote, but afterwards, modernisers accused Beckett of disloyalty, suggesting she was making a play for the support of union leaders in the event of a Smith resignation (Rentoul, 1995: 341). Prescott was possibly being rewarded and Beckett punished for the OMOV dispute of 1993. If so, the 1994 contests were a way of holding Beckett accountable for her actions and rejecting her on that basis. If the college had been used more frequently, this type of occurrence could have happened more often.

The reason that the college has been seldom used to hold leaders in check, despite the provision for annual contests, is that the costs of challenging incumbents are too high. There are numerous costs associated with leadership contests but the most important are *collective costs* borne by all party members and *entry costs* facing individual candidates. A further type of cost that can sometimes be important is *legitimacy costs*, which can arise if a winning candidate's victory is in some way tainted by the manner of his election. Systems that create multiple segmented intra-party constituencies can create legitimacy problems if different candidates win majorities in different constituencies.

Leadership contests can harm a party as a whole, and to the extent that they thereby also harm leadership candidates, such collective costs must be internalised in candidates' cost-benefit analyses. The three main types of collective costs are: (1) the *decision costs* to the party of engaging in a leadership contest, such as lost chances to devise policies and attack the opposing party; (2) the *financial costs* to the party of running the contest; (3) '*disunity costs*' arising from rival candidates publicly attacking each other.

Entry costs entail the effort of trying to instigate a contest against an incumbent or join a contest for a vacancy. It is necessary to distinguish entry costs from entry *rules*. The latter stipulate the formal requirements that need to be satisfied before a contest can take place, such as a nomination threshold. Entry costs refer to the difficulty in mobilising allies to satisfy entry rules. The same entry rules can exist for contests for vacancies and challenges to incumbents, such as passing a parliamentary nomination threshold, but entry costs are higher for challenges: it is much harder mobilising MPs for a challenge than in a contest for a vacancy. The former entails challenging an existing distribution of policy and patronage benefits under the *status quo ante*. Even if MPs do not enjoy front bench positions, they may nevertheless worry about being deselected by their constituency parties if they associate themselves with a failed leadership challenge. Disgruntled MPs are thus confronted by a collective action problem. Entry costs are the first line of defence for incumbents. The political risks of challenging an incumbent are vastly greater than those involved in running for a vacant post. If a challenger loses badly in a challenge or cannot surmount pre-contest hurdles such as nomination thresholds, his reputation and career could be badly damaged. Candidates are less likely to encounter these pitfalls in contests for vacancies because there are no arguments about the legitimacy or wisdom of holding the contest, whereas such arguments are ubiquitous in the case of challenges.

How does the electoral college measure on this scale of costs? Collective costs are fairly high in the college in both its present and old forms. First, the decision costs of leadership challenges include lost chances to devise policies and attack other parties. Leonard Stark (1996: 121) found the average length of campaigns in the electoral college was nearly four months, reflecting the long period of consultation required in the unions and the CLPs (as opposed to about three weeks in parliamentary ballots). The lengthy and bitter deputy leadership contest of 1981 put Labour out of action as a campaigning force. It was at a time when the Thatcher government was in trouble, as unemployment soared to three million, while the newly formed SDP was siphoning votes off both main parties. The unions also faced opportunity costs because their focus on industrial concerns was diverted by party leadership elections. Union officials who could have been campaigning against government policy were instead embroiled in internal politicking. Minkin (1992: 344) claims the 'protracted and unpredictable upheavals of the Electoral College' were vital in dissuading union leaders from seeking to replace Michael Foot before the 1983 general election. The shift to OMOV–OLOV also entails long campaigns; the 1994 contest lasted ten weeks.

The shift to balloting marks a considerable increase in the financial costs to the party of leadership contests.[6] The party must send ballot papers and return postage to about 300,000 party members. The unions also face large financial bills, since they pay for the ballots they send to their own levypayers, which in total can run into millions of pounds. Most unions did not hold ballots in 1992, not even the AEEU, which had a tradition of doing so. Given that the outcome of the 1992 contest was already clear, most unions reasoned that the contest did not justify the expense of a postal ballot. The AEEU held a ballot in the 1988 contest but only 25 per cent of members voted and it cost the union £100,000.

The lengthy nature of campaigns also increases the potential for party divisions to be aired publicly and detrimentally. Naturally, disunity costs are also a function of other factors, such as ideological divisions, though the one leadership challenge and two deputy leadership challenges thus far in the college have both been from the left against a moderate incumbent, resulting in bitter campaigns. The 1988 leadership and deputy leadership contests harmed the party's poll rating, and it was to avoid a repetition that the nomination threshold was raised to 20 per cent.

The collective costs alone make many in the Labour Party extremely unwilling to set in motion the cumbersome machinery of the electoral college. These costs cannot be avoided in contests for vacancies but they will be dissuasive factors in the case of challenges to incumbents. These costs are usually sufficiently high to ensure that only the most serious of challenges are contemplated. They rule out the type of step-by-step approach that Conservative MPs used to dislodge Mrs Thatcher, beginning with a stalking-horse challenge in 1989 and a serious challenge a year later. In the Labour Party, annual leftwing challenges against a moderate incumbent present too many costs to the party and the unions, with few if any benefits.

Labour's electoral college is marked by high entry costs, which protect the incumbent from anything but the most serious of challenges (and will usually protect him from those too). There are three key rules: (a) the '20 per cent rule'; (b) all challengers must join contests in the first round of voting; (c) MPs' nominating and voting records are made public.

High nomination thresholds increase entry costs, first, because there are more MPs to mobilise, and second, the more moderate MPs are, the harder it is to persuade them that it is in their interests to join a chal-lenge against a moderate incumbent. The costs to challengers and selectors alike are made much higher by the rule decreeing that the names of MPs nominating and voting for candidates are made public. It ensures that patronage under the incumbent is a major considera-tion, because in the event of the incumbent retaining power, those individuals associated with the challenge will usually be punished. A further source of entry costs whenever Labour is in government is the requirement for any contest to be approved by a majority vote at the party conference. Any challenge to an incumbent will almost certainly require the blessing of the leaders of the big unions. The latter have often been a stabilising force in intra-party politics over the years, though it is conceivable they could back a challenge if they were sufficiently disenchanted with the government, as they have tended to be of Labour governments. Nevertheless, the fact that the annual con-ference is an additional veto player adds to the obstacles that chal-lengers must overcome whenever Labour is in office.

Entry costs are also raised by the requirement that all candidates must join a contest in the first round of voting. This provision reduces the ability of would-be challengers to free-ride on the efforts of others to instigate a contest. Given the need for all challengers to pass the 20 per cent threshold, a maximum of five candidates could enter the race but it is likely to be no more than two or three. If there were a block of MPs willing to nominate a challenger, they would probably back the first challenger, making it harder for others to join the race later. Two challengers would collectively need at least 40 per cent of the PLP, though if they managed to secure the support of such a high proportion of the PLP, it is probable that the incumbent would resign, clearing the way for allies to stand (who would now require the nom-inations of only 12.5 per cent of the PLP). The zero-sum game for nom-inations makes it less likely that ideologically similar candidates will stand in the same contest (thus, Brown stood aside for Blair in 1994), since they could prevent each other passing the threshold, especially in a challenge.

Entry costs for challengers are very high in the electoral college but they are also fairly high in contests for vacancies because all candidates must secure the nominations of 12.5 per cent of the PLP. This rule is a serious impediment to far-left challengers, even if they have consider-able support within the unions and CLPs. Indeed, if there were a clear front-runner in a contest, it could be difficult for other candidates to secure sufficient nominations, partly because MPs would want to maximise their chances of patronage from the new leader by nominating and voting for him, as in 1992 when Smith secured 162 nominations from the 271-strong PLP. Thus, the lack of anonymity again raises entry costs for many candidates.

Finally, the electoral college can, depending on the breakdown of the results, bring legitimacy benefits or costs, both for the party as a whole and for individual candidates. A political actor can utilise the legitimacy underpinning his position as a power resource (Dowding, 1996: 64). The fact that Labour leaders were, after 1980, elected by sections representing the entire party, and not just by MPs, gave them greater authority (Garner and Kelly, 1998: 146). After Kinnock beat Benn in 1988, he claimed the result gave him a mandate to lead the party as he chose (Heffernan and Marqusee, 1992: 103). However, the three-way division of the college can also create legitimacy costs. Every victorious leadership candidate in the college won a majority in at least two sections and a plurality in the third (see Table 6.1). In the deputy leadership election of 1981, however, Healey won majorities in the PLP and union sections but only a fifth of CLP votes, calling into question his legitimacy among ordinary members. Benn narrowly lost that contest but if four more MPs had supported him he would have won. Benn could have become deputy leader despite Healey winning big majorities in the PLP and union sections. In such circumstances, it is hard to see how Benn could have claimed legitimacy. A further serious source of legitimacy costs was the controversial use of block votes, especially by the unions from 1981 to 1993. The consultation procedures in the TGWU brought the entire party into disrepute in 1981 (largely because the TGWU cast its entire block of 1.25 million votes for Benn). Claims of a union 'stitch-up' also marred Smith's victory in 1992 and partly in response to this controversy, block voting was abolished in 1993, so that in the 1994 contests, all votes were cast by individuals, increasing Blair's legitimacy.

One other issue that may impact on legitimacy and authority is the potential for rival mandates for the leader and deputy leader. Labour leaders do not get to choose their deputies, since the latter too are elected through the electoral college. It is unlikely that Tony Blair would have chosen John Prescott as his running mate in 1994 and similar questions could be raised of the Kinnock-Hattersley 'dream ticket' of 1983. To date, there have been no serious problems between the leader and deputy leader, though things would probably have been different if Benn had defeated Healey in 1981. The incumbent leader, Michael Foot, had urged Benn to challenge Foot himself rather than

Healey – the dual legitimacies of the two posts offers the challenger a choice. Some on the left hoped that if Benn won, Foot might resign then Benn could run for the leadership without directly challenging Foot. Similar problems could emerge if the incumbent deputy resigned or died in office, necessitating an election that could lead to an opponent of the leader being elected.

Considering the sum total of costs is vitally important in the case of leadership challenges because even if selectors are agreed that they would be better off with a new leader, the costs of change may inhibit them from replacing the incumbent. It is likely that these costs prevented challenges to Foot in 1982, Kinnock in 1987 and possibly Blair in 2003.[7] The electoral college shields leaders from all but the most serious of challenges, particularly with the shift to OMOV–OLOV. The party must bear considerable costs, which ensures pressure is applied to rivals contemplating a challenge, making it extremely difficult for them to mobilise their allies.

Conclusion

The electoral college is a good illustration of the importance of unintended consequences in politics. Its designers hoped the college would hold Labour leaders in check, preventing them from straying from the preferences of party and union members. Yet the present Labour government, like its predecessors, has found itself in conflict with sections of the party, particularly the unions. Contrary to expectations the college has left Labour leaders autonomous of the extra-parliamentary party from the moment the votes are counted. Unwieldy, time-consuming and expensive, the college fails to permit on-going control over leaders. The nomination rules ensure that if MPs believe the incumbent could win them the next election, it will not matter what the extra-parliamentary party thinks, while the expense of balloting rules out speculative challenges. The college confirms the view that intra-party democratisation can paradoxically increase the autonomy of leaders. In an age of electoral volatility and with the desire of party elites to increase their autonomy, the college cuts with the grain of general developments in party organisation.

Appendix 1 to Chapter 6: Electoral Colleges and Devolution

A comprehensive analysis of the structures Labour introduced in response to devolution is beyond the scope of the present book. Nevertheless, a few reflections are in order on the selection of Labour candidates for the top posts in devolved administrations because the party has used electoral colleges – with extremely controversial results. The positions of first minister in the Scottish parliament, first secretary in the Welsh assembly, and mayor of London were all posts that Labour was expected to secure in the first devolved elections (1999 in Scotland and Wales, 2000 in London). The national leadership therefore considered it of great importance that selection systems were chosen that guaranteed candidates acceptable to the government. As we have seen, the trend from the late-1980s has been towards OMOV ballots wherever possible. However, in NEC elections, members elected in the CLP section comprised a small minority of the entire executive; in leadership contests, individual members cast one-third of the votes and by the time they did vote, elections had already been decisively shaped by MPs. There were no precedents for important leadership posts being chosen solely by individual members. One reason is that it is risky allowing the members to choose: if they are leftwing, the result is likely to be a leftwing candidate. Party members in Scotland and Wales were seen as being probably leftwing and London members definitely so. On the other hand, it was politically impossible to prevent members from voting and either allowing assembly nominees in Scotland, Wales and London to choose the regional leadership candidate or leaving the decision to the national party HQ. Splitting votes between assembly nominees and individual party members also had no precedent and would arouse union opposition.

The NEC's preferred solution was to adopt regional electoral colleges. These colleges would divide votes between assembly nominees and regional MPs/MEPs (one-third), individual members (one-third) and affiliated organisations (one-third). These proportions replicated those in the electoral college for leadership elections but there was a crucial difference. Although the party members' section would be conducted under OMOV, the affiliates' section would not use OLOV. Instead, affiliates would be free to decide whether or not to ballot their members; each affiliate would have a pre-determined share of the college votes (based on affiliation levels); and each would be entitled to cast their votes as undifferentiated blocks. In other words, whereas the members' section was organised along post-1993 rules for the electoral college for leadership elections, the affiliates' section used pre-1993 rules. A panicky national leadership chose this peculiar hybrid because it was seen as the best way of ensuring that the top prizes went to leadership loyalists.

In Scotland, the most important and powerful of the three posts, there was no controversy, because Donald Dewar was elected unopposed and subsequently became Scotland's first minister. By contrast, in Wales and London the consequence was that the candidates overwhelmingly favoured by individual party members were controversially defeated under the college rules by government-favoured candidates. In Wales, the party initially chose Ron Davies, who had defeated Rhodri Morgan, but a month later Davies resigned after a personal scandal, leaving the post vacant. Morgan announced his intention to run again but the Blair government was worried that he was too close to 'old Labour' and persuaded the home office minister, Alun Michael, to stand against him. After a bitter campaign, Michael narrowly secured the nomination, winning 53 per cent of the college to Morgan's 47 per cent. However, Morgan won 65 per cent of the votes of the 25,000 individual party members to Michael's 35 per cent, while Michael won by 58 per cent to 42 per cent among the assembly nominees, MPs and MEPs. In the latter section, Michael's support had been swollen by the decision to give votes to the twenty candidates who were fighting to be elected to the Welsh assembly as 'list' Assembly Members, even though Labour was expected to win very few 'top-up' seats.[8] Morgan's allies alleged that the party machine had deliberately ensured that these candidates were overwhelmingly supportive of Michael (Flynn, 1999: 107–8). However, it was the affiliates' section that was decisive, with Michael winning comfortably by 65 per cent to 35 per cent. A number of union leaders cast their block votes for Michael without holding membership ballots (which in many cases were likely to go to Morgan), including the TGWU, the GMB and the AEEU, which together accounted for 17.5 per cent of the entire electoral college, or over half of the affiliates' section. If one of these unions had voted for Morgan, he would have won the contest. Every affiliate that held a ballot chose Morgan.

A similar process unfolded in London, where Ken Livingstone was the strong favourite among party members to be Labour's mayoral candidate. However, Livingstone was even more strongly opposed by the party leadership, which again devised a tripartite electoral college that delivered a narrow (51.5 per cent to 48.5 per cent) victory to the leadership's preferred candidate, Frank Dobson. Livingstone won convincingly in the members' section by 60 per cent to 40 per cent, but Dobson won among MPs, MEPs and candidates for the Greater London assembly by 86.5 per cent to 13.5 per cent. In the latter section, there were only 75 voters, each casting an identifiable numbered ballot that was worth the votes of almost 1000 individual party members (Shaw, 2001: 45). In the affiliates' section, Livingstone won by 72 per cent to 28 per cent but crucially, Dobson won the support of two organisations that failed to hold ballots. The AEEU and the South London Co-operative Party together accounted for 8 per cent of the college, and their votes were enough to deprive Livingstone of the nomination, despite his overwhelming victories in two of the three sections.[9]

Ultimately, these fixes backfired. Livingstone ran as an independent candidate and won the mayoralty, leaving a humiliated Dobson fighting for third place with the Liberal Democrats. To avoid a likely fourth place in the 2004 election, Labour let Livingstone re-join the party and contest (and win) the election as its candidate. In Wales, Michael became the Welsh assembly's first secretary in 1999 but resigned a year later after a vote of no confidence – to be replaced by Morgan. The Blair government's first term was notable on the one hand for its policy of devolution and on the other, for its desire to maintain strong control from the centre. This contradiction was resolved with the government being forced to accept the two candidates that it had so strenuously opposed. What is equally interesting for the present discussion is that Labour modernisers reintroduced union block votes to defeat their opponents, emphasising that distributional questions are at the centre of institutional choice in parties. However, the ruse was too transparent and it deprived Michael and Dobson, not to mention the electoral college process itself, of legitimacy. It also dealt a serious blow to popular trust in the Blair government, from which it has arguably never fully recovered. These episodes are cautionary tales about the limits of institutional manipulation. Although the party HQ was able to devise mechanisms that delivered the leadership's preferred candidates, the process was widely seen as 'tainted', as Livingstone described it. Consequently, *pace* Antonio Gramsci, the counting of votes was not the final ceremony of a long process, but the cue for rows, resentment, enduring suspicion and ultimately humiliation for the government. (Anecdotal evidence suggests that a large number of London Labour Party activists effectively went on 'strike' during the mayoral election of 2000.) Not surprisingly, the rules have since been changed, with balloting now compulsory in the affiliates' section of electoral colleges. In London, the elected representatives' section was removed completely for the 2004 mayoral candidate selection, with a new college divided equally between party members and affiliates. The college initially chose Nicky Gavron to contest the mayoralty but she later stood aside for Livingstone, who in turn was confirmed as Labour's candidate by the college.

Appendix 2 to Chapter 6: Electing the NEC and the NCC

Internal elections are held for Labour's ruling NEC, which is the party's extra-parliamentary leadership. The NEC's structure has always been a compromise reflecting Labour's different stakeholders, but from its earliest years the unions dominated its election. By the 1980s, the NEC had 29 members, of which 12 were trade unionists and seven were elected by the CLPs, but with the unions, through the party conference, controlling the election of 18 places (see Table 6.3). The unions usually played a supportive role to the PLP, intervening only when their interests were at stake. Although the CLP section was smaller, its members played leading roles on the NEC because they were usually MPs. (The PLP was not represented on the NEC, reflecting its institutional detachment from the extra-parliamentary party.) Since leftists often dominated the CLPs, MPs elected to the CLP section were also often leftists, and because moderates dominated Labour (shadow) cabinets, the NEC sometimes hosted what was virtually a 'shadow' leadership. The provision for annual elections was a means of maintaining accountability among these MPs.[10]

Since NEC elections offered the left an annual rallying cry, they quickly became a target for modernisers. Kinnock made OMOV ballots to the CLP section compulsory in 1990, replacing ballots of CLP delegates to the party conference, and precipitating a clear-out of the left (Shaw, 1994: 118–20). Newly enfranchised individual members were reliant on the media for information about the candidates, ensuring that members of the shadow cabinet benefited from their higher profiles. However, as Ken Livingstone's victory over Peter Mandelson in 1997 demonstrated, the left could also occasionally win under OMOV.

After Labour entered government in 1997, Tony Blair made reform of the NEC a priority to avoid a return to the open warfare of the 1970s. The *Partnership in Power* reforms of 1997 set out a new relationship between the NEC and the government, in which governing was left to the latter. The NEC's role was 'to provide a strategic direction for the party as a whole and to maintain and develop an active party in the country, working in partnership with the party's representatives in Parliament, the European Parliament, devolved administrations and local government to secure the party's objectives' (Labour Party, 2003a: Clause VIII.2). The NEC's policy-making powers were usurped by the NPF (see Chapter 4), consigning the NEC to managerial functions and neutering it as a channel for intra-party 'voice'.[11]

The NEC's structure was also reformed, with its membership expanded from 29 to 32.[12] The union section was frozen at 12 members and the CLP section was reduced to six. The women's section was abolished altogether, replaced by a provision setting out minimum quotas for the number of women elected to each section (six by the unions, three in the CLP section and a minimum of 12 on the NEC as a whole). MPs are no longer eligible to stand for election in the CLP section, which is reserved for ordinary activists.[13] Instead, MPs have their own section, which elects three members, and there are also three places for members of the government. CLPs are thus prevented from voting high-

Table 6.3   Electing the NEC

Section	NEC 1983		NEC 2003	
	No	Method of Election	No	Method of Election
Leader	1	*ex officio*	1	*ex officio*
Deputy leader	1	*ex officio*	1	*ex officio*
EPLP leader	–		1	*ex officio*
Treasurer[1]	1	*ex officio*	1	*ex officio*
Trade unions	12	ballot of unions at party conference	12[†]	ballot of unions at party conference
Socialist societies	1	ballot of socialist societies at party conference	1	ballot of socialist societies at party conference
CLPs	7	ballot of CLP delegates at party conference[2]	6[†]	OMOV ballot
Local government	–		2[†]	OMOV ballot among members of Association of Labour Councillors
PLP/EPLP	–		3[†]	PLP/EPLP ballot
Women	5	ballot of all delegates at party conference	–	
Young Labour	1	Young Labour conference	1	Young Labour conference
Government	–		3[†]	Appointed by government
TOTAL	**29**		**32**	

Notes
1. The post of party treasurer is elected, but the incumbent sits *ex officio* on the NEC. The treasurer was formerly elected by the party conference at the same time that NEC elections were held. The effect was to hand the position to the unions, who dominated the conference, and they usually ensured it was held by a trade unionist. This practice largely continues, even though the unions control only half the conference votes. The CLPs' votes for the treasurer are now cast by individual members in an OMOV ballot at the same time as NEC elections; as with the latter, elections for treasurer are now held every two years.
2. Compulsory OMOV ballots in CLP section from 1990.
† Government, PLP and local government sections must each include at least one woman. Union and CLP sections must allocate at least half of all places to women.

profile leftwing MPs onto the NEC to cause trouble for the leadership. MPs selected from the PLP and government sections would (it was expected) reflect the traditional dominance of moderates in these bodies. Members elected on the CLP section would be lesser-known figures with few contacts and resources, lacking the confidence to tackle the government. However, the first elections under the new rules in 1998 saw the formation of a leftist slate called 'the grass-roots alliance'. A number of members on the slate had some profile among Labour members and received exposure in the national media. The slate won four of six seats available in the CLP section. Moreover, a leftwing MP, Dennis Skinner, was elected in the PLP section.

The unions' 12 seats now represent a smaller proportion of the NEC, though they also largely determine the election of the treasurer (see note 1 to Table 6.3). Thus, until the mid-1990s the unions could determine 18 out of the 29 NEC seats (62 per cent), but that is now down to 13 out of 32 (41 per cent). This move was in keeping with reforms in other areas of the party. Even so, modernisers had set their sights on removing the union section completely but the unions successfully fought off this proposal (Alderman and Carter, 1994: 332–3). The experience of the electoral college is that a 40 per cent share of the votes is extremely useful and will enable the unions to protect their interests.

The national constitutional committee

The national constitutional committee (NCC) was formed after Kinnock's battle with Militant and met for the first time in 1987. The need for it arose after a legal ruling that the NEC had violated natural justice by acting as prosecutor, judge and jury against party members who were accused of belonging to Militant and who thereby faced expulsion from the party. The NCC was intended to take over the judicial function, while the NEC would retain its role as 'prosecutor'. Despite its title, the NCC did not have control over the interpretation of Labour's constitution, which remained with the NEC. Instead, it plays a narrow role in disciplinary matters, relating mainly to individuals, and has the power to reprimand or suspend miscreants. The NEC retained control over disciplining affiliates and CLPs, which was considered essential for party management, and it also kept its powers over parliamentary candidate endorsement (see Shaw, 1988: 280–5). Initially, the 11 members of the NCC were divided into a union section (five members), a CLP section (three), a women's section (two) and a representative from the socialist societies. The union, CLP and socialist society sections were elected by, respectively, union, CLP and socialist society delegates at the party conference, while the women's section was elected by the whole conference (which effectively meant the unions controlled it). As with other elected bodies, it is susceptible to factional divisions, and Shaw (1988: 284) reports that political considerations were evident in its earliest decisions, over the expulsion of Militant supporters. The individuals elected in the CLP section were on the left, whereas the union members were more rightwing. Nowadays, the NCC is still elected by card vote at the party conference by the respective organisations' delegates, but the women's section has been abolished and in its place are female quotas in the remaining three sections: unions (six members, at least three of whom must be women), CLPs (four members, of whom at least two must be women) and socialist societies (one member, with no gender quota).

7
Resources and Political Communications

The basis of the exchange model is that parties demand resources to campaign for election, and that individuals and organisations supply resources in return for policy promises and other benefits. This chapter looks at both sides of this supply-and-demand problem in the Labour Party. Issues of funding and campaigning are often neglected in studies of the distribution of power in parties, yet they impact on exchange relations. The intention is not to provide a comprehensive account of Labour's finances and campaigning methods, but rather, to offer a brief description of these areas to gain further insight into Labour's modernisation. The first part of this chapter examines the supply side, describing the main resources exchanged in the Labour Party. The discussion is empirical, charting changes in the supply of members and funds. The second part explores Labour's shift from labour- to capital-intensive campaign technologies, and provides a theoretical framework for analysing political communications. The techniques of Labour's communications revolution are briefly recounted, and the intra-party consequences assessed.

Part I Resources

Funding

All major parties need a steady supply of funds. In the UK there has been an upward trend in the costs of elections over the last decade, which is reflected in the growth of Labour's income and expenditure. Head office income rose from £13.2 million in 1992 to £24.1 million in 1997, and £36.4 million in 2001; expenditure in the same years was, respectively, £19 million, £31.5 million and £45.4 million.[1] As its demand for funds rose, Labour broadened its funding base. This section looks at three sources: unions, individuals and the state.

Affiliation fees and donations

Most of Labour's funds have historically come from the unions, mainly through affiliation fees and special donations to election campaigns. Affiliation fees come out of the political levy that individual trade unionists pay, though most unions do not hand over all of the levy to the party, keeping some for union campaigns. Each year, unions pay into Labour's general fund a uniform affiliation fee for each affiliated levypayer. In 1980, union affiliation rates were 32 pence per member per year, as were CLP rates per individual member. Since then, CLP rates have risen far above union rates, as the unions resisted big increases in affiliation rates and the party sought to extract more from individual members. In 2003, the union rate was £2.50 per member per year, but CLPs had to pay £16 per member per year to the central party, after a big rise in membership subscriptions to £24 per year. However, the unions make additional payments to Labour's general election fund. In the 1980s, they contributed £2–3 million during each election campaign; in 2001, this figure stood at £6 million.

The early-mid 1980s saw a marked increase in Labour's dependence on the unions, as its individual membership fell. Affiliation fees increased by 80 per cent in real terms between 1979 and 1987, and although Labour's affiliated membership fell by 11 per cent between 1979 and 1988, the real decline in levypaying members within the unions was 29 per cent (due largely to rising unemployment). Thus, the unions softened the blow of their own falling memberships by affiliating to the party at 105 per cent of their real level (Webb, 1992a: 24). The vigour with which the unions mobilised support to retain their political funds (which finance the Labour Party) in 1985–86 underlined their commitment to the financial well-being of the party. The Thatcher government's Trade Union Act 1984 stipulated that union members must vote every ten years to decide whether their organisations should have political funds. All the ballots held in the 1985–86 period produced comfortable 'yes' votes (as did those in the mid-1990s), though most unions played down their links to Labour (see Minkin, 1992: 562–82; Taylor, 1987: 205–34). These ballots marked the start of an emphasis on individual levypayers that would produce innovations such as the 'levy-plus' scheme to recruit union members into the party as individuals, as well as the provision of levy-payers with voting rights in Labour leadership contests. Levypayer participation diluted Labour's federal structure by moving the emphasis from corporate bodies to individuals.

The formation of pan-union organisations such as Trade Unions for a Labour Victory (TULV) in 1978 and Trade Unionists for Labour (TUFL) in 1986 confirmed the unions' pre-eminent position in the party. TULV encompassed the main unions and helped coordinate Labour's election strategy on the ground by mobilising union staff to work for the party and encouraging union members to vote for Labour. It provided staff to regional Labour bodies and raised money for the party, for example by establishing a levy of 10 pence per affiliated member to contribute towards Labour's election fund in 1983 (Webb, 1992a: 47). TUFL was a similar type of body, established after the first political fund ballots to build on their success. TUFL's task was to reactivate party-union relations at the grassroots level. During the 1987 general election, it provided union staff, resources and transport to aid Labour in targeted constituencies, though it had little long-term impact in recruiting union members as individual party members (Minkin, 1992: 579). In 1994, the party established the Trade Union and Labour Party Liaison Organisation (TULO), a successor to TULV and TUFL. All affiliated unions belong to the national TULO and union leaders sit on the national TULO committee. There are also regional TULO committees in Scotland, Wales and the nine English regions. The national TULO is formally specified in Labour's constitution (Labour Party, 2003a: Clause II.2(i)) and is charged with coordinating union support for the party at election times, and of acting as a communication channel between the party and the unions.[2]

If the 1980s saw the unions increase their financial burden, the opposite happened in the 1990s. As Labour's modernisation increased apace, the unions provided a declining proportion of its income, as individual donors contributed more. The party told the Neill committee's investigation into party funding that during the period 1992–97, affiliation fees and donations each accounted for about 40 per cent of its cumulative income of £100 million, with membership subscriptions providing another 12 per cent. Most donations were classified as small (less than £5000), though about a third were large (over £5000). The 40 per cent contribution from the unions was a steep drop from the 66 per cent of total net income they provided in 1992 (Neill, 1998: 30, 231).[3] Even this figure marked a decline from previous years: Minkin reports that the unions provided 89 per cent of Labour's general funds in 1978. They also provided 95 per cent of its general election fund in the early-1980s, a proportion that has fallen considerably since, though their donations nevertheless covered 55 per cent of Labour's campaign expenditure in 2001 (Minkin, 1992: 509; Ludlam, 2004: 75).

However, the resources made available to Labour by the unions are more than simply financial. Until 1918, Labour's local campaign network consisted entirely of local union branches and they continued to play an important role long after that, supplying personnel to the party during election campaigns and permitting the use of union buildings and offices. In 1997, affiliated unions seconded full-time officials to work in Labour's 93 targeted seats, and again in 2001, they focused resources on key battleground seats (Ludlam, 2004: 75–6). It is difficult to quantify these 'gifts in kind'. Labour can also benefit from independent union campaigns. In the election year of 1997, Unison ran a public campaign for a national minimum wage, a policy supported by Labour and the Liberal Democrats but opposed by the Conservatives. (The Blair government has also been the *target* of campaigns by unions concerning government policy on the public sector.) In their evidence to the Neill committee, union leaders defended their right to campaign during general election campaigns. The subsequent Political Parties, Elections and Referendums Act 2000 permits individual unions to spend up to £1.5 million during general election campaigns.

State funding

There is no generalised state funding of parties' organisations in the UK; for the most part, parties have relied on individual subscriptions and donations, and donations by business and unions. However, since 1975 there have been limited state funds available for opposition parliamentary parties to enable them to engage in research and thus shadow the government. This 'Short money' (see Chapter 4, note 5) is calculated on the basis of seats and votes won, and initially was capped at an upper limit, though this cap was removed in 1987. In 1998, the Neill committee recommended a tripling of Short money, but by then Labour was in government and no longer eligible for it. Short money was a valuable source of funds to Labour under Kinnock: the party received about £400,000 a year from 1983–87 and double that each year from 1987–92. Kinnock used it to fund the leader's office and provide research support for frontbenchers. An attempt by the left-dominated NEC in the early 1980s to place the money under NEC control was defeated by the shadow cabinet. Under Smith and Blair, Labour received nearly £1.5 million a year through to 1997.

State funding is highlighted in recent discussions of 'cartel' parties (Katz and Mair, 1995). It is a crucial development because it involves the provision of valuable resources without the requirement for party leaders to provide policy concessions or other benefits to the donor. For this reason, a more comprehensive system of state funding became an attractive long-term goal for some Labour modernisers, and was floated by Labour's general secretary in the light of membership loss and allegations of undue influence by wealthy donors. The major constraint on its introduction has been that the public may not tolerate it. The UK possesses an entrenched political culture that encourages scrutiny of public expenditure and outcries over perceived waste. The public might tolerate parties 'wasting' their own money on extravagant campaigns but not that of taxpayers. Nevertheless, Short money was a useful addition to PLP finances, enabling it to begin overhauling Labour's policies in the 1980s. The recent increases will prove useful to the next Labour opposition leader, though it would not be sufficient to reduce Labour's reliance on individual and organisational donors.

Conclusion

At the start of the 1980s, Labour was a largely trade union-based party, financially and organisationally. In the early-1980s, most party funds came from the unions, but by 2003, only about a third did. Even Labour's election funding is no longer reliant on the unions to the extent it once was. The Electoral Commission reported that Labour received donations from three wealthy individuals[4] totalling £6.1 million prior to the 2001 general election (as well as other large donations from individuals in business and the arts); the unions donated £6 million. Large and small donations have provided a sorely-needed boost to party income. Furthermore, Labour's status as the governing party makes it attractive to corporate donors, who have been increasingly prepared to sponsor Labour's annual conference and other party events, all presumably in the hope of obtaining access to, and a sympathetic ear from, ministers. Although ministers are sensitive to charges that wealthy donors and big business can 'buy' policy outcomes, there would appear to be no reason to make such donations unless favourable outcomes are the intention. A donation of £1 million from the head of Formula One, Bernie Ecclestone, was followed by an exemption for Formula One from the government's ban on tobacco advertising in sport (though the ensuing controversy led to the donation being returned). Similarly, the steel magnate Lakshmi Mittal, who donated £125,000 to Labour, was later the beneficiary of prime ministerial lobbying of the Romanian government for British access to the Romanian steel market, though the government denied any impropriety.

However, union funds are not surplus to requirements. Donations from individuals and business donors may dry up as the Labour government loses popularity or moves into opposition. The benefit of union funds is that they have been reliably secured for a century. The party's fair-weather friends may desert it when the going gets tough, but the unions have always been there. It perhaps explains why demands by modernisers for a party-union divorce have died down, though dissatisfaction with government policies has led a number of unions to call into question the money they give. In 2001, the GMB decided to cut its funding to the Labour Party by £1 million over four years (*Labour Research Department Fact Sheet*, 19 July 2001) to pay for an advertising campaign against the privatisation of public services.

However, the demand for funds may not grow as quickly as in the past, given the recent legal cap on campaign spending set out in the Political Parties, Elections and Referendums Act 2000. The new legislation prevents the main parties from spending more than £20 million on general election campaigns, which should dampen the growth in demand for finance. This change in the law has the potential to level the playing field between Labour and the Conservatives. It could also reduce the need for Labour to rely on union money, provided that alternative funds are available; without state funding, there is no guarantee that they will be.

Members and activists

Individual members are a vital resource to parties, providing money, in the form of subscription fees and donations; voluntary labour (in quantities that would be prohibitively expensive in labour markets); and links to ordinary voters, to whom they can communicate party policy. The members keep local party organisations running and provide parties with a pool of potential candidates for elective office (see Scarrow, 1996: 40–6). However, like many parties in both the UK and Europe, Labour has experienced membership decline in the postwar era. There are a number of reasons for the general decline in party membership in Western Europe. Among the most important include a long-term trend towards partisan and class dealignment, as the old social class boundaries break down and individuals no longer feel bound by a sense of identity to individual parties, whether as voters or members.[5] Furthermore, there are fewer solidary incentives to join parties, as the increasing privatisation of people's leisure activities means individuals no longer rely on parties for access to cultural resources or clubs. Such supply-side explanations account for membership decline in terms of the supply of recruits drying up (Scarrow, 1996). There are also demand-side explanations, in which membership decline follows the reluctance of party leaders to recruit members, particularly if they are deemed too 'extreme'. However, in the UK, leaders of all parties have sought to recruit members (Webb, 2000: 225–6), though Labour has attempted to reduce its *reliance* on members in campaigns. State funding could in future also ease the need to recruit members for financial reasons (unless the supply of state funds was linked to party membership levels, in which case they could provide an incentive for recruitment).

The general pattern of decline has been particularly evident in the UK, and especially so in the Labour Party. In Labour's case, it is important to be clear what is meant by 'party members'. Labour has traditionally counted among its members not only those individuals who join CLPs, but also the much larger number of people affiliated through unions and socialist societies. Even when Labour's individual membership was at its peak in the 1950s, its affiliated membership was five times greater. The affiliated membership peaked in 1979, after which unemployment reduced union membership and thereby Labour's affiliated membership. Individual membership continued to fall through to the early-1990s, though the extent to which it had fallen earlier was masked by the requirement that all CLPs affiliate a minimum of 1000 individual members. When this rule was changed in 1980, a truer picture of membership levels emerged.

Labour's affiliated membership provided the party with the consoling myth of a mass membership. Some union activists work for the party but they are also usually individual party members. The bulk of the affiliated membership is not active in any way in the party: even in the leadership election of 1994, when individual levypayers could cast postal votes, barely a fifth did so. Nevertheless, affiliated members brought the party money and obviated the need for serious membership drives. It is one reason why little was done to stem individual membership decline in the 1960s and 1970s, leaving many CLPs vulnerable to take-over by the 'bed-sit left' (see Chapter 5).

However, the picture began to change in the 1980s. As part of the attack on the activist left, Kinnock wanted to recruit a mass of moderate members, who would impose fewer electoral costs in terms of policy, and who could help solve Labour's financial problems. A membership drive was undertaken in 1989 and reduced fees were introduced for members of affiliated unions. Kinnock rashly stated that his aim was to increase membership to one million but despite briefly passing the 300,000 mark, there was little prospect of reaching such an ambitious target. Given the postwar trend of membership decline, it would have been surprising had Labour's drive resulted in a long-term reversal of fortunes. Moreover, the membership drive, although intended to increase numbers, was not meant to increase grassroots control of the leadership, but to reduce the influence of the activists and later to dilute Labour's links with the unions.

After Labour's defeat in 1992 and the formation of the NEC's union-links review group, the new leader, John Smith, sought to increase the CLPs' votes at the party conference. However, given that union block votes reflected affiliation levels, union leaders demanded that before any more increases in the CLPs' share of votes could take place, the CLPs would have to carry a greater financial burden, which implied an increase in individual membership. It was agreed that the CLPs could have 50 per cent of the votes only when individual membership reached 300,000. A 'levy-plus' scheme was also introduced to enable affiliated levypayers to join the party for just £3, compared to the normal £15 (Alderman and Carter, 1994).[6] These schemes had some initial success but they were not responsible for the remarkable surge that took place in Labour's membership level in the mid-1990s. From a trough of 266,000 in 1994, membership soared to 405,000 just four years later (see Figure 7.1). This increase coincided with Tony Blair's first years as leader. Blair enjoyed a favourable media image and broad

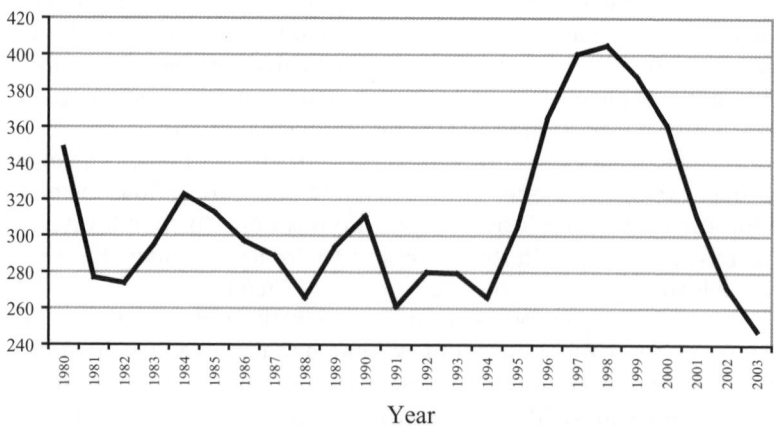

Figure 7.1   Labour Party Individual Membership 1980–2003 (Thousands)
Sources: 1980–99: Tanner et al. (2000: 396–7); 2000–03: Labour Party Head Office.

electoral appeal (reinforced by an intensive recruitment campaign in press advertisements and party political broadcasts). Labour seemed to have bucked the historical trend.

However, this dramatic rise was followed by an equally startling slump. By January 2003, membership stood at 248,294 – the lowest since 1943. There has been some debate about whether those members choosing to exit are disgruntled activists angry with the Blair government or fair-weather supporters who failed to renew their subscriptions (probably a combination of both). The members recruited since 1994 are considerably less active than longer standing members (Whiteley and Seyd, 1998: 200–4), and thereby obtain few social benefits from their membership. A party membership recruited mainly for purposive reasons tends to have a high turnover rate, as issues and personalities lose their salience. Individuals who joined Labour because they liked its leader or wanted to see it replace an unpopular Conservative government had less reason to stay once Labour was elected, and particularly when it had to take tough decisions in government.

A large individual membership seemed to be a prerequisite for turning Labour into a direct-membership unitary party. At first, a large membership was thought necessary because there had to be a way of providing an alternative financial base if the unions were to be edged out. It was eventually realised that Labour would never likely be in a position where it could depend principally upon individual members for finance. Richard Katz and Peter Mair (1995) suggest that large memberships today are valuable to party leaders mainly as legitimising devices, to demonstrate to voters that a party has a large following and that its decisions are backed by party members. However, are the members still valued as a labour resource, as activists who can campaign for the party and mobilise voters? This question is addressed shortly.

Conclusion

It is important to know where a party's resources come from, because these supply lines affect the nature of internal exchange relations and the shape of institutions. The fact that the unions affiliated to Labour principally on a national basis was important in directing resources to the centre and thus strengthening it (Fisher, 1995: 191).[7] The provision for individual members to join the party nationally, together with fundraising exercises that specifically target them (such as mailshots), also increases central control, as money flows nationally rather than locally (Seyd, 1999: 401–2). More generally, however, the new financial relationships emerging in the party will affect institutions, because the considerable reduction in Labour's dependence on union money calls into question their institutional rights in the party. The relative decline in the importance of union donations has tracked the decline in their organisational power in the party. Even the affiliation fees paid by the unions no longer possess the significance they once did. Whereas in the past, each individual affiliation payment bought one vote at the party conference, nowadays these votes are weighted by the unions' overall share of the conference vote (currently just below 50 per cent). Union affiliation fees are less than those paid by the CLPs, but the latter now have 50 per cent of the conference votes, while not contributing anywhere near 50 per cent of party revenue. It reflects a dual trend over the past decade: the shift of power from the unions to individual members and to the party HQ and the PLP leadership.

Parties deploy their resources throughout the electoral cycle, paying for staff, buildings and intermittent campaigns. However, the most crucial use of parties' resources is during election campaigns. The remainder of this chapter examines Labour's demand for resources, in relation to its communication with the voters.

Part II Political Communications

Party resources and political communications

Historically, the benefit to parties of activists was that they provided a means of communication between party leaders and voters, organising local campaigns, delivering leaflets and performing other party work for no financial reward. Such campaigning was decentralised and labour-intensive in that it was usually local rather than national in scope, and depended on the exertions of the activists. However, relying on activists to undertake political communication is not costless, because activists require the inducement of social and purposive benefits to perform these tasks. Giving them influence over policy and candidates might keep them active but it could alienate the voters if unpopular policies are chosen. Yet if not enough concessions are made, activists will exit, and there may not be enough left to run an effective campaign. Figure 7.2 illustrates this dilemma for party leaders.[8]

Policy preferences are plotted from left to right along the horizontal axis, with the median voter at MV, while the number of activists in the party is plotted along the vertical axis. The problem facing party

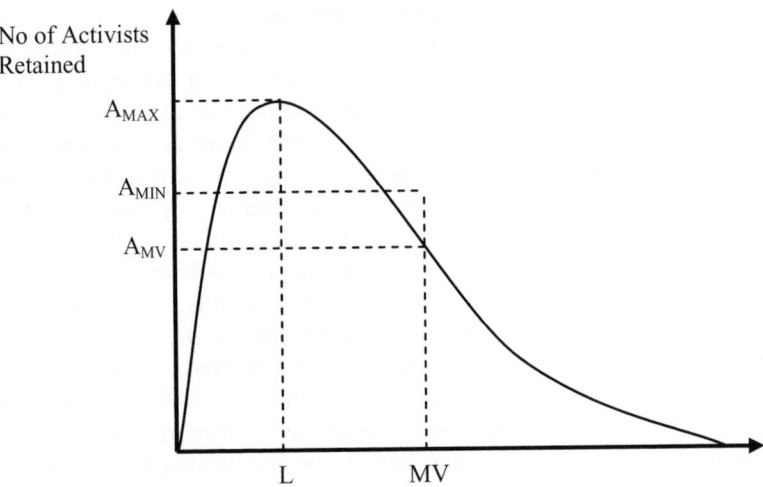

Figure 7.2 Trade-off between Activist Retention and Electoral Support

leaders is that unilaterally shifting party policy to MV risks provoking activist exit (and voice, though for simplicity the latter is ignored here). The maximum number of activists (A_{MAX}) is retained at policy position L, but this point is some distance from MV and may result in electoral defeat. If policy were set at MV, disgruntled activists would exit until only A_{MV} activists were left. Now assume that for a party to win an election, it requires a minimum of A_{MIN} activists. Here, $A_{MV} < A_{MIN}$ so the party will fail to mobilise sufficient support despite having competitive policies. One way out of this dilemma is for parties to 'becloud their policies in a fog of ambiguity', making vague promises to convince voters they are moderate, while holding out the hope of radical measures for activists. This strategy works best when the distance between L and MV is fairly small, but the greater the gulf between activists' and voters' preferences, the harder it is to bridge it through ambiguity, and the possibility of a credibility gap emerges.

However, politician-activist exchange is not static. Politicians can change the technology of political communications to minimise activist-induced costs while maintaining an effective level of campaigning. If politicians can develop communication techniques that are less dependent on activist labour, the activists' bargaining power declines, which alters the distribution of power. Capital-intensive communication involves centralised campaigns conducted through the electronic mass media, including broadcasts and political advertising, and increasingly IT. Television broadcasts can reach millions of voters more regularly and efficiently than an army of activists. The party may still require some activists but not to the extent that damaging policy trade-offs need to be made, depending on how great the reliance is on media campaigning. In principle, various combinations of capital and labour can be forged to give different communication technologies. Figure 7.3 depicts four different technologies employed at MV. Technologies A_1 and A_2 are fairly labour-intensive, but with its policy at MV, the party would not be able to retain sufficient activists to mobilise voters. Technology A_3 needs fewer activists, and the party could possibly withstand activist exit to capture the median voter. Technology A_4 is capital-intensive and could be used to communicate to enough voters to win at MV. Indeed, with this technology, the party would have a 'surplus' of activists in the sense of more activists than the minimum level it requires, both to be able to mobilise sufficient voters and have vote-winning policies. Other things equal, parties may prefer the most capital-intensive technology to avoid policy dilution.

However, other things are not always equal. Capital-intensive techniques may facilitate office-seeking but they are financially costly. Before they allow their activist base to run down, politicians must consider activists' financial contributions. If activists are the major source of party funds, leaders must either continue to offer benefits to activists or seek new sources of funding. In fact, the latter is likely to happen

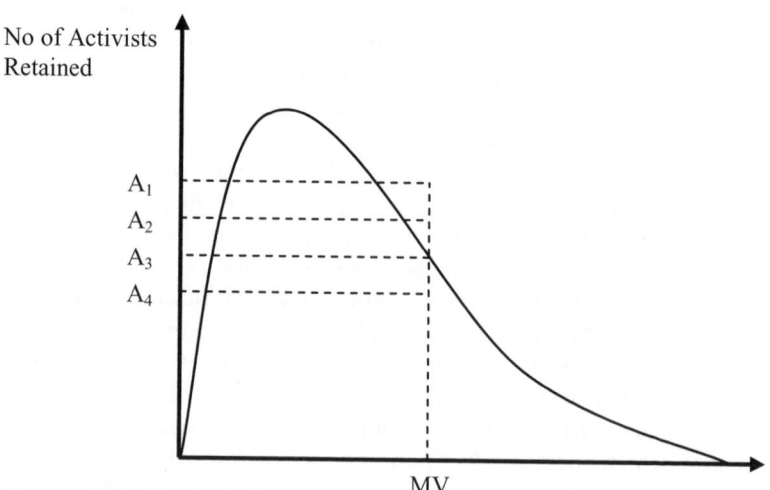

Figure 7.3   Communication Technologies

regardless, because capital-intensive communications and media-based campaigns push up election costs. Labour's election expenditure treb-led in real terms between 1979 and 1997, reflecting greater reliance on advertising and the services of pollsters and focus-group organisers. The necessity to raise ever more funds can influence intra-party exchange relationships, and as we have seen, Labour has diversified its funding sources.

The use of sophisticated techniques for gathering information about voters' preferences and relaying information about policies requires a corps of professionals rather than amateur volunteers. The rise of 'electoral-professional' parties less reliant on bureaucrats and act-ivists, and more dependent on specialists, is a general phenomenon (Panebianco, 1988). Professionals are responsible for specialised tasks rather than administrative or overtly political tasks. Such parties require spin doctors, press officers, pollsters, media consultants, adver-tising agents, marketing experts, designers, image consultants, and a host of other specialists. Many of these areas of expertise involve pre-sentation and the control of information about the party.

The model sketched above illustrates the benefits to politicians of capital-intensive and professionally-run communications. The poten-tial pitfall is that the financial costs are high. The remainder of this chapter offers a brief overview of the transformation of Labour's com-munications structure. The intention is not to provide an exhaustive analysis of modern communications techniques, but to assess the extent to which Labour's new campaigning methods have eased its dependence on activists.

Modernising Labour's political communications

In the mid-1990s, Labour gained a reputation for being the most fear-some election-fighting machine in Europe. The party's former Millbank HQ was a byword for political machinations and ruthless efficiency. It was not always thus. Labour's landslide defeat in 1983 followed what was widely recognised as one of its most unprofessional campaigns ever (see Butler and Kavanagh, 1985). Its spokesmen made too many mistakes, there was a lack of coordination and the party leader, Michael Foot was more at home making stirring speeches to the party faithful than he was communicating over the airwaves to the watching voters. The entire communications edifice needed reforming.

The weakest aspect of Labour's campaign was its use of the media, a fact recognised by the new leader Kinnock, who appreciated the growing importance of the media in modern electioneering. Kinnock wanted a structure that utilised communications professionals, and emphasised marketing and advertising. A capital-intensive communications system would also mean less dependence on activists and thus fewer policy concessions to them. There was certainly wide receptivity to an overhaul of Labour's communications in the light of the 1983 defeat. The existing structure was ramshackle, with responsibility divided between different departments and committees. Lines of control and authority were unclear and there was a lack of coordination between the old head office at Walworth Road, the NEC and the shadow cabinet (Shaw, 1994: 55). Kinnock's response was to establish a campaign strategy committee (CSC), consisting of NEC and shadow cabinet members, PLP representatives and union leaders in TULV. It was charged with overseeing all campaigns-related activities, including party political broadcasts and polling. Although formally answerable to the NEC, the CSC in reality circumvented the leftwing executive and took the important campaign decisions (Butler and Kavanagh, 1988: 50).

A reorganisation of the party's HQ saw a myriad of departments reformed into the policy, organisation, and campaigns and communications directorates (CCD). Peter Mandelson, a television producer at London Weekend Television, was appointed the first director of the CCD in 1985. One of his first acts was to commission an advertising executive, Philip Gould, to prepare an audit on the state of Labour's communications. The report, presented to the NEC in December 1985, argued for 'a shift in campaigning emphasis from "grassroots"/opinion forming to influencing electoral opinion through the mass media' (cited in Gould, 1999: 56). Gould suggested the establishment of a shadow communications agency (SCA), which would tap the professional and technical expertise of Labour supporters in marketing, the media and advertising, who were willing to volunteer their services to the party. The SCA was structured round personnel from the BMP advertising agency, particularly its managing director, Chris Powell. Only Gould and his business partner, Deborah Mattinson, were paid for their services. Gould estimated that two hundred people, including writers, broadcasters, art directors, and other professionals, worked for the party free of charge during the 1987 election campaign, saving it £500,000 (Webb, 1992b: 270).

Officially, the SCA had an advisory role and was answerable to the NEC, but in practice its quantitative and qualitative research had policy implications and it answered to Mandelson. Communicators require autonomy to be effective; their functions are not conducive to anything but the most general forms of NEC control, particularly with the shift to 24-hour news and the 'permanent campaign' (Kavanagh, 1995: 108). It explains why Labour's communications were dominated by a few trusted figures loyal to the leader, notably Mandelson and later, Alastair Campbell. Kinnock could not oversee everything so he built up a sizable[9] staff in his own leader's office, including media advisors, fixers and policy specialists, who could liaise with the CCD and the SCA. Successive leaders have used officials in their office to develop policy and strategy, as well as gathering and disseminating information. The fact that the leader's office is not subject to constitutional controls in the Labour Party gives leaders greater autonomy.

Under Kinnock, Labour transformed its communications. Party campaigns were largely divorced from campaigns run by the unions, such as mass demonstrations against the Conservative government, especially after the defeat of the miners' strike in 1985. Henceforth, media campaigns assumed new significance and became entangled with policy-making and intra-party power relations. Some changes were purely presentational, intended to project a professional image of the party. Image consultants advised MPs on their appearance; the party acquired a corporate image with the adoption of the red rose as its symbol in 1986, replacing the red flag; art designers improved the backdrop at the conference; party documents became glossier. These changes did not affect the functioning of the party, though the left complained that style was being elevated above substance.

Other changes did affect intra-party relations. The rise of spin doctors (together with other electoral-professionals and special advisors) is one of the most noted features of the modernised Labour Party.[10] Spin doctors are commonly regarded as media advisors acting on behalf of certain politicians but their remit is much more political. They are 'courtiers who serve leaders rather than the party' (Heffernan and Stanyer, 1997: 177) and their job is to provide journalists with a favourable interpretation of events before they have been reported to the public. It has also been a persistent claim that spin doctors are often used in intra-party battles, against not only factions but also individual (shadow) cabinet members. The acrimonious pre-contest to succeed Smith as leader in 1994 is only the most famous occasion, when Mandelson was accused of working to promote the candidacy of Blair and to denigrate the chances of Gordon Brown. The episode left a bitter aftertaste and was one of the tensions underlying the internecine warfare between Blairites and 'Brownites' that would explode in

December 1998, resulting in the resignation from the government of Mandelson (who by now was Secretary of State for Trade and Industry), and Geoffrey Robinson, a friend of both Brown and Mandelson, as well as Brown's spin doctor, Charlie Whelan.

Spin doctors are important political operators and their close links with journalists are the source of their power. The manipulation of news content is a skill that requires an eye for what journalists look for when they write their stories and knowledge of decision-making structures inside media companies so that pressure can be applied at the right level. It requires a cool head to deal with crises and the necessary temperament in turn to bully and flatter journalists. Good spin doctors are a valuable asset for politicians. However, it is a mistake to view them as 'running' parties, because they remain dependent on the politicians they serve. They possess no constitutional position in parties and instead rise and fall with their political sponsors, unless they move on to serve new masters. Despite being elected to parliament in 1992, Mandelson's career stagnated after Kinnock resigned and Smith became leader, because Smith distrusted spin doctors and the SCA (Gould, 1999: 161–82). Mandelson returned to the fray with the accession of Blair to the leadership. However, while they are *in situ*, spin doctors exercise considerable influence and their rise brings further centralising tendencies in parties in general.

A further important feature of Labour's communications revolution was the new emphasis it placed on polling. The Labour left was always suspicious of polling but under Kinnock it assumed a central role in the policy-making process and party strategy. Private polls contain information for parties that helps influence important decisions, including timing an election, defining a party's image, testing old and new policies, tracking voters' preferences, targeting voters and ultimately, changing the party (Kavanagh, 1995: 135–9). It is easier for leaders to persuade activists to abandon cherished policies if they can present convincing evidence that those policies are unpopular with voters. Polling data was important in convincing many activists and unions to back Kinnock's repositioning of Labour during the policy review of 1987–89. However, crucially important is the question of who dominates decision-making over polling. In the Labour Party, it was traditionally the NEC that allocated funds and commissioned polls. If the leader and his allies did not control the NEC, they could find themselves in trouble: in 1978, the leftwing NEC denied the prime minister, James Callaghan, funds for polling (Kavanagh, 1995: 134), perhaps worried that it would reveal the left's unpopularity.

Kinnock wrested control of polling from the NEC and assigned it to the SCA.

The biggest change to take place in Labour's communications was the rise of qualitative research, in particular, focus groups. The guru of focus groups, Philip Gould, was a key strategy adviser to Labour during this period, and he used them extensively to gauge the attitudes of floating voters. Focus groups consist of about eight people talking in a room about issues of interest to the convenor. Most of Gould's focus groups consisted of swing voters who had supported the Conservatives but who might switch to Labour. People are able to talk at length and their under-lying feelings can be ascertained. 'In a [focus] group it is possible to test out the strength and depth of feeling around an issue, which can be more difficult, although not impossible, in a conventional poll' (Gould, 1999: 328). Focus group findings first systematically informed Labour's general election campaign in 1987 and reached their apogee in 1997 by which time it was clear that the data affected campaign decisions.

Even more than conventional polling, the interpretation of data from focus groups is subjective: whoever has the task of organising and interpreting it controls an important power resource (Shaw, 1994: 148). Just how important was evident in the aftermath of the 1992 general election, when Gould conducted a number of focus groups to ascertain the reasons for Labour's defeat. He argued that voters did not fully trust Labour and were worried about the possibility of trade union tyranny under a Labour government. He claimed that floating voters revealed in these groups lurking fears about the party, that it had not changed sufficiently: 'The polling was clear: Labour lost because it was still the party of the winter of discontent; union influence; strikes and inflation; disarmament; Benn and Scargill' (Gould, 1999: 158). This finding contradicted conventional polling results, which suggested that Labour lost for other reasons, such as tax, with the unions low down the list. Clare Short (1992: 14) asserted: 'There is no serious political commentator who believes that Labour's link with the trade unions explains our appalling electoral performance'. However, Gould insisted the existence of the link contributed towards voters' general unease about Labour and what was lacking was trust: in other words, union influence imposed commitment costs on political exchange between Labour and the voters. It was difficult for Gould's opponents to chal-lenge his findings because they did not have access to them, seeing only his own interpretations (Webb, 1995: 7–10). Gould would claim subsequent events proved him right and his findings underlay Blair's assault on 'old Labour'.

Communication technology and general election campaigns

The revolution in Labour's communications was reflected in the election campaigns conducted by Kinnock and Blair. Labour's campaign of 1987 marked its coming of age as an exponent of modern electioneering. Although Labour lost the election, it was acknowledged to have run the most competent and professional campaign of the main parties. The campaign was geared towards television, which required a centralised command structure and partly explained the decision to focus on the perceived strengths of Kinnock. The epitome of this near presidential campaign was an election broadcast on Kinnock that presented a more human image of the leader and produced a surge in his approval ratings. Overall, Labour ran its most professional campaign ever, though there were murmurs from internal opponents that too much emphasis had been placed on image and not enough on policy. Similarly, in 1992 there were complaints after Labour's eventual defeat that the 'admen' had taken over from the politicians and sacrificed substance for glitz. The so-called 'War of Jennifer's Ear' – an emotive Labour election broadcast on health that badly backfired – called into question the role of the SCA and the wisdom of handing over communications to non-political professionals.

However, it is Blair's leadership that is most closely associated with the new era in communications. It marked a further professionalisation of campaigning, influenced by techniques developed by the American Democrats in Bill Clinton's presidential campaign in 1992. Many of these techniques addressed problems and opportunities arising from media-centred elections. The most obvious difference with the past was the trend towards the 'permanent campaign'. Although campaigning before the official election campaign gets under way is nothing new, Labour took a quantitative and qualitative step forward after 1994 (Kavanagh, 1997: 540). The theory is that elections are not won or lost in the four weeks of the official campaign but over the months and years prior to the election. With the omnipresence and diversity of the electronic media, it is possible for parties to spend considerable time between elections campaigning for the next election, especially if they are in opposition and unencumbered with the burden of governing. The emergence of satellite and digital television, 24-hour news, and the internet, has accelerated the news cycle, making it imperative that parties respond quickly to attacks from opponents and adapt to (and try to set) the news agenda (Norris, 1998: 126; Gould, 1999: 295).

These developments increase the importance of spin doctors because it is essential to have experts who understand decision-making structures within the electronic news media, and who can attempt to manipulate news for their party's advantage. It also led to innovations such as Labour's rapid-rebuttal unit, an idea borrowed from Clinton's Democrats, which was used to offer detailed responses to Conservative attacks within the same 'news cycle' and neutralise anti-Labour stories. Rapid rebuttal relied on 'Excalibur', a computerised database of facts and figures, providing further evidence of the shift towards capital-intensive technologies (Butler and Kavanagh, 1997: 59).

Labour's 1997 campaign was coordinated by a core of planners and advisors at Millbank Tower. Labour's 'inner core elite' (Heffernan and Stanyer, 1997) of leader, spin doctors, strategists, pollsters and advisors, formed a 'war room' at Millbank from where, with the help of 200 staffers, they coordinated the national campaign, maintaining contact with candidates and campaigners on the ground by telephone, fax, email and pager (Gould, 1999: 298–309; Norris, 1998: 126–7). During the 2001 general election, Labour's communications structure was flatter and more fluid than in the 1980s and 1990s. Most operational tasks during the campaign were carried out by eleven taskforces at party HQ.[11] General election planning and strategy groups, consisting of leading politicians, were responsible for planning and running the campaign. The taskforce structure remains in place, with their leaders meeting every week to coordinate activity, while the general election planning group meets every month to discuss strategy.

Intensive polling and qualitative research have become crucial elements of campaigns for Labour. Polling in 1997 was conducted by NOP, which regularly surveyed throughout the parliament and twice-weekly during the election campaign. The results were reported to Gould, whose agency was hired by Labour to undertake qualitative research. The latter consisted of focus groups of floating voters; Gould met about 70 such groups during the official campaign of 1997, having conducted 300 in the pre-election months (Butler and Kavanagh, 1997: 129–30; Gould, 1999: *passim*). Gould used quantitative polling evidence to test themes in the focus groups. In total, Labour spent £500,000 on NOP surveys from 1993, and £180,000 on focus groups conducted by Philip Gould Associates (Butler and Kavanagh, 1997: 242). In 2001, Gould was again instrumental in organising focus groups, and NOP carried out polling (Butler and Kavanagh, 2002: 127–8).

The election campaigns of 1997 and 2001 saw a return to constituency campaigning, though in a more centrally controlled form.

There were two key differences with the past, one strategic and one technological, though the latter underlay the former. Strategically, Labour adopted an aggressive system of targeting, not only key seats but also key voters. Prior to the 1997 election, party HQ officials drew up a list of 90 key marginal seats, which became the focus of campaigning 18 months before the election. Activists undertook voter identification by telephone, ascertaining voters' party identity, current party preference and other pertinent information. The data was used to identify voters by category, for example, 'reliable Labour', 'weak Labour', 'switchers', 'first time voters', and so on. The aim was to contact 80 per cent of voters within these constituencies and use the information to target direct mail to voters depending on their category. Although the Conservatives and the Liberal Democrats also targeted seats and voters, the process was carried furthest by Labour (Denver, Hands and Henig, 1998: 176–80). The same techniques were used in 2001, but now Labour targeted its resources on 148 priority seats, almost all of them won in 1997, where many voters had supported the party for the first time. Activists were encouraged to work in these constituencies, and the central party made available full-time staffing support.

This new focus on the constituencies depended on technological advances. Cheaper telephone calls enabled telephone canvassing to begin supplanting doorstep canvassing, much of it conducted outside the constituencies. Telephone canvassing was particularly important in target seats in 1997 (Denver, Hands and Henig, 1998: 183) and 2001, when up to 60 per cent of voters canvassed by Labour in target seats were approached by telephone. The party's new national telephone bank in Tyneside was crucial, with its 250 telephone operators making 1.5 million contacts in the six months before the 2001 election (Ballinger, 2002: 216, 212).

Meanwhile, email enabled instant communication between the centre and candidates, and the transmission from the centre of party literature (Butler and Kavanagh, 1997: 211–13). Mobile telephones also enabled candidates and canvassers to coordinate more easily, and Labour experimented in sending text-messages to voters (Ballinger, 2002: 219, 231). The biggest impact was made by the increased use of IT. Not only could PCs be used for printing address labels; they were essential for the targeting strategy, as they could sort information quickly. PCs were common in 1992 but became near ubiquitous in 1997 and 2001, with Labour concentrating them in its target seats (Denver and Hands, 1998: 82–3). Finally, 2001 saw Labour (and the other parties) start using the internet to campaign, and the party relaunched its website. The latter is now an important source of information from the centre for party members and activists, and includes access to policy documents.

There is a clear shift to capital-intensive technologies in the constituencies, yet telephones need people to dial them and PCs require operators. In short, there is still a need for local activists, though these more efficient technologies require fewer workers to operate them. In a survey of local campaigning in the 1997 election, David Denver and Gordon Hands (1998: 79) found Labour had a daily average of 56 campaign workers in each constituency, though there was some concentration in marginal seats. This figure implies Labour had 35,000 campaign workers nationally per day, representing less than 10 per cent of its total membership, though there was probably some turnover of workers throughout the weeks.

Since parties still require activists, it raises the problem of incentives for activists to participate. Since 1983, decision-making power has been centralised to such an extent that the influence of activists has been greatly curtailed. Institutions that over-centralise power alienate activists, encouraging them to reduce their activism and eventually leading to membership decline. Seyd and Whiteley's membership surveys have consistently found that members are becoming less active. At the height of Kinnock's modernisation in 1990, they reported that 43 per cent of members said they were less active than five years earlier, while only 20 per cent said they were more active – a ratio of two-to-one. The following decade saw things get worse and by 1999, 48 per cent said they were less active than five years earlier compared to 9 per cent who said they were more active – a ratio of five-to-one. They also found that half of members in 1990 said they devoted no time to party activities, but by 1999 that proportion had risen to nearly two-thirds (Seyd and Whiteley, 2002: 88). By 1997, Labour had been out of office for 18 years and there was desperation at all levels of the party for an election victory. Activists swallowed their disagreements with the leadership and continued campaigning. However, with Labour in government the danger is that adopting policies opposed by party members will cause further declines in local political activity, which may harm Labour's strategy of targeting individual constituencies.[12] The effect will be compounded if union officials, who traditionally offer local support during election campaigns, reduce their efforts in response to government policies. Labour will suffer in the future if it does not replenish its stock of volunteers, though the age of media campaigning ensures it will never be as beholden to activists as it once was.

Conclusion

Labour's communications revolution since 1983 was an essential part of the party's modernisation. It entailed the adoption of capital-intensive techniques in preference to older forms of campaigning based on meetings and marches. Although media-based campaigns were well established at election time, Labour has been at the forefront of innovations in political communications. Much of this development can be put down to changes in the organisation of the news media, but it has had the further consequence of downgrading to some extent the importance of constituency activists. Since the latter demand policy concessions and institutional rights in return for their resources, media-based campaigns enable the party leadership to maintain tight central control and moderate policies. Electoral-professionals recruited by the party do not impose policy costs on party leaders. However, Labour's new constituency-based campaigning requires a core of activists, and although more effective use can now be made of fewer activists, recent years have seen a plummeting individual membership and reduced levels of activism. The general elections of 1997 and 2001 delivered landslide victories to Labour, but future elections will be closer and the party may depend on its activists in the constituencies to make the difference.

The greater reliance on media-based communications, the growing importance of polling and focus groups, and the employment of specialists is reflected in the rising cost of electioneering. It means that fundraising will not go away as a problem, though legislative spending caps will have some effect in controlling costs. Nevertheless, Labour modernisers' early calls to end the party-union link have died down, as they realise such a project would leave the party in a precarious financial position in the absence of alternative arrangements. Corporate funders cannot be relied upon when Labour goes into opposition, and problems confront any attempt to introduce state funding. However, the trend has been towards a reduced union presence in Labour's organisation foreshadowing the financial change. The final chapter examines the constraints on a party-union divorce and the extent to which Labour has changed.

8
Conclusion: Labour's Modernisation

The Labour Party was a trade-union-funded party that transformed its power structure to the extent that the paymasters' own prerogatives were diluted. The unions could not ignore the electoral imperatives facing the party and, grudgingly they permitted a series of reforms that cumulatively transformed Labour. The unions were moderately conservative, providing a brake on the speed and extent of reform – more would have changed faster had it not been for their opposition – but they realised all-out opposition to every reform would have greatly harmed the party. Modernising politicians provided the initiative while the unions scrutinised, criticised, opposed but eventually acquiesced in many reforms. This final chapter gauges the extent of the reforms as a whole, identifying two principal stages. It concludes with reflections on what the changes mean for Labour today, in particular the incentives for members – individual and corporate – to remain in the party.

Explaining organisational change in the Labour Party

The purpose of developing the exchange model was to understand parties' internal dynamics and the forces that promote change. In Chapter 2, a number of precipitants and aims of change were identified. We have seen that the two principal types of change in the Labour Party were the successive waves of centralisation to increase leaders' autonomy from members, and the loosening of the party-union link to increase the party's legitimacy in the eyes of voters. Thus, on the one hand, political exchange between leaders and members was rebalanced in favour of the former. On the other hand, the predominant type of institutionalised exchange relations progressively shifted from PLP-union exchange to PLP-individual member exchange. The leadership's ultimate motive for both types of change was to have a party capable of winning elections, a project that eventually gained the acquiescence of the members and unions. Although unions qua interest groups are policy-seekers, when they financially and organisationally dominate a major party in a two-party system, electoral considerations are fundamental. No policies can be implemented in opposition, so doctrinal purity is an irrational posture to strike. Imperfect information in the political arena means the party might be able to appease some union demands, but the unions' pure policy preferences are ultimately more likely to constrain than determine party policy.

Vote-seeking party leaders measure their success in terms of electoral performance. When performance is poor, change that increases the autonomy of party leaders becomes more likely. That was the lesson of Labour's years in opposition, with each successive election defeat adding new impetus to the process of centralisation. Normative critiques of electoralism rebuke leaders that sacrifice ideology on the altar of electoral expediency, a charge often made by the Labour left. However, accusing politicians of electoralism is like condemning firms for maximising profits: it may not always be pretty to watch but it is the behaviour we anticipate from rational actors. To get into government parties must offer attractive policies and gain voters' trust.

Everyone in the Labour Party wants to win elections but they sometimes differ over how to do so. It is those that value office-seeking above all else who gain the upper hand inside a party the longer it is in opposition. An unsuccessful party is like a plummeting hot-air balloon: if initial attempts to regain height are unsuccessful, items must be thrown overboard until the fall is halted and height regained. The longer a party is out of office, more policies must be changed; organisational change is often a prerequisite for policy change, as the power-bases of those groups that cling to the old policies are undermined. The personalities associated with those policies may also have to go, which is why Foot resigned as Labour leader in 1983 and his successor, Kinnock resigned in 1992, both doing so after election defeats.

The types of change in which these electoral considerations manifested themselves were centralisation and legitimisation. Although Labour's organisational transformation was not a smooth process following an original blueprint, two stages can nevertheless be identified: the attack on the left in the 1980s, resulting in centralisation; and the weakening of the party-union link in the 1990s, as successive leaders sought to legitimise (and further centralise) the party's structure. Each has consequences for the nature of exchange relations.

The reforms weakening the hard left were straightforwardly redistributive. They included the early moves towards OMOV in candidate selection, and NEC and leadership elections, together with the creation of the by-elections panel. In each case, the aim of the proponents of change (the party leadership) was to reduce the power of CLP activists by centralising power up to the NEC or decentralising it down to individual members. OMOV was partly about changing the way members' preferences were aggregated, giving more power to moderate members. Yet the median Labour Party member (not activist) is a creature of the soft left; it is here that an arguably more important aspect of OMOV comes to the fore. Most Labour members are politically inactive. They may vote for soft leftists if given the chance, but in between membership ballots they are hard to mobilise. Where GCs were once power-bases for the activist left, enabling radicals to meet and plot, atomised members rarely if ever meet face to face. Their aggregated ballots occasionally frustrate the leadership but they mostly remain impotent. They do not constitute a powerful bank of organised opposition to party leaders. Thus, the overall effect of OMOV was to increase the discretionary power of the politicians – not surprisingly, given that it was initiated 'from above'.

By the late-1980s the left was a spent force and Labour's leaders enjoyed considerable policy flexibility, abandoning unilateralism in 1989 and, with union approval, accepting Mrs Thatcher's industrial relations legislation. Yet Labour's electoral performance barely improved, culminating in the catastrophic defeat of 1992. Policy changes were not enough because Labour's problems ran much deeper: the crucial swing voters did not *trust* it. Moderate policies were worthless if too many people suspected that moderation in opposition would be abandoned in government. Distrust of Labour was fed by a number of factors, all played up in the media, including the 'winter of discontent', the traumas of the year-long miners' strike, growing concern about the 'loony left', and a perception that Kinnock had changed his mind on most important issues in British politics. The replacement of Kinnock might have eradicated one source of public mistrust, though it is unlikely to have significantly altered Labour's standing in the 1980s. Some successful attempts were made to counter the 'loony left' image, notably the attack on Militant in 1985–86, though problems later emerged during the Greenwich by-election (see Chapter 5). That left the trade union 'problem', exposed at every party conference, with regular denunciations of the block vote by Labour's opponents. The persistence of union power meant that more than policies had to change. To restore Labour's credibility among voters, the party had to reform its own organisation, freeing it from perceived illegitimate control by sectional interests.

Thus, the second stage of reform pursued by Labour's leaders was the reduction in the power and visibility of the unions in Labour's decision-making structures. The unions' perceived domination of Labour's organisation, together with memories of the 'winter of discontent', combined to create a commitment problem for Labour leaders *vis-à-vis* voters. Party structures are rarely thought to be an important factor in determining a party's level of support. However, institutions and preferences are the joint determinants of party policy. Voters can observe a party's institutions and the stated preferences of powerful intra-party actors, and compare the preferences of the latter to official party policy. If there is a discrepancy they may estimate that control of the institutions by a certain group may lead in the post-election period to a revising of party policy. Anticipating such policy change, voters will discount the likelihood of a party's stated policies being pursued in government. The institutions thus burden the politicians with a credibility problem. This problem was particularly acute for Labour, since its institutions were dominated by trade unions, which are organised interest groups in their own right and whose interests may appear threatened by 'moderate' policies, especially when 'moderation' was defined by a *status quo ante* in which unions had been popularly stripped of many of their old powers. The message hammered home by the Conservatives and their press allies was that Labour could not be trusted to keep its promises, because union paymasters would look for a return on their investments and would take the country back to the strikes, disruption and high tax rates of the 1970s. Labour leaders felt that only organisational reform would show that the unions were not in control of the party. The party-union link had not always been a liability. Labour entered the election campaign of February 1974 arguing that its institutional links with the unions would uniquely allow it to end the industrial disputes that bedevilled the 1970–74 Conservative government. Labour won the election but the 'winter of discontent' in 1978–79 exploded the myth that Labour politicians could control the unions; indeed, the conclusion widely drawn was that the unions were in control. The next two decades saw repeated attempts by Labour leaders to overcome the resulting commitment and legitimacy problems.

Nevertheless, there remained important constraints on the modernisers. Labour's continued dependence on union funds ruled out the prospect of an immediate divorce between party and unions. Loosening rather breaking the link was the order of the day, as modernisers pursued the dual strategy of trying to legitimise the link by defederalising it, while at the same time keeping union leaders out of public sight during election campaigns. Yet even here the modernisers did not get it all their own way, because the attempt to build an internally legitimated party inevitably had distributive consequences. In the electoral college, there were two forms of distributive change: the reduction of the unions' share of the college from 40 per cent to one-third, and the enfranchisement of more moderate individual party members and levypayers. However, the greater impact of OMOV–OLOV lay in the legitimacy it bestowed on elected party leaders. Machinating union leaders were shorn of their 'kingmaking' role, helping to dispel fears that a future Labour prime minister would be beholden to them. Nevertheless, the modernisers' preferred option of an electoral college without any union involvement was rejected. In the realm of parliamentary candidate selection, they did finally see the removal of union influence – nine years after their first attempt. This reform too was marked by the interaction of redistributive and legitimacy considerations: first, to redistribute power away from the hard left and then the unions; second, to create the foundation for a unitary membership structure, with a public battle against the unions in 1993. The very notion of 'one-member–one-vote' evokes democratic values and popular legitimacy, which were watchwords of the party leadership, as it sought to throw off the image of a union-dominated party. (Television news reporters regularly confused the battle for OMOV with the battle against the block vote.) It was also seen in the reforms to Labour's internal policy-making process. The problem here had been the unions' dominance of the party conference through their block votes. Given the reduced authority of the conference, most of the changes were geared towards improving its public image, though some, such as reweighting conference votes and formally abolishing unit voting had distributional consequences. The major change in policy-making was the establishment of the NPF, which assumed many of the powers of the conference and allowed ministers to dominate intra-party policy-making away from the gaze of television cameras.

The twin aims of centralisation and internal legitimation on the basis of OMOV characterised all the major organisational reforms Labour undertook after 1983. In each case, the motive was electoral:

the desire to make the party outwardly more attractive and internally more pliable so as to develop the type of policies it needed to win elections and, equally important, to convince voters that after an election victory its moderate policies would not be at risk from leftwing activists and union barons. On the basis of the 1997 and 2001 general elections, it would appear voters were sufficiently convinced that Labour was no longer under the union yoke. The battle over Clause IV in the face of union opposition was symbolic in this respect, signalling to voters that Labour was consigning old shibboleths to history.

There is little doubt that Labour's poor electoral performance created the conditions for organisational change. Furthermore, it was inevitable that the unions, as the party's major stakeholders, would sanction some changes if they were deemed a *sine qua non* of improved electoral performance. However, organisational change was not an automatic adaptation to 'environmental' pressures. If all party actors had reacted reflexively to poor electoral performance then Labour's 1983 defeat would have been the catalyst for a dramatic transformation. Instead, the unions chose a leader from the soft left, whom they thought would defend their interests. More obviously, Kinnock's reform agenda, particularly OMOV, was constantly resisted. Between the election defeats of 1983 and 1987, very few organisational changes were secured, while leftwing policies remained. The 1987 defeat did spur a major policy review, but again, progress on organisational change was slow. Even after the historic fourth defeat of 1992, powerful interests resisted change, as was shown by the willingness of the big unions to try to defeat Smith over OMOV. It was not until the 1994 election of Blair that most party members and union leaders agreed that far-reaching changes were required, and even then, powerful forces tried to stop the rewriting of Clause IV. The electoral imperative did finally assert itself among a majority in the party but not before four election defeats. The existence of an environmental imperative may *suggest* the need for change but it still requires a coalition of reformers to push through the changes. Organisational changes to produce an efficient electoral machine cannot be 'read-off' from election defeats, because institutional changes have distributive consequences, which can prompt potential losers to resist change. The battle for organisational reform in the Labour Party was fought in the broader context of electoral competition but its rhythm reflected power struggles.

To conclude this discussion of the types of change in the Labour Party, certain other forms of change identified in Chapter 2 are relevant. First, institutional change can be introduced to increase the supply of resources to the party. An example would be the idea that OMOV was partly introduced as a selective incentive to encourage individuals to join/remain in the party (Scarrow et al., 2000). More obviously, subscription discounts were devised to recruit levypayers into CLPs, though the scheme met with limited success and it is questionable how many people joined Labour to participate in internal ballots. Second, institutional change can be introduced to facilitate new communication technologies, as confirmed by the new campaigns and communications structure that was largely autonomous of the NEC and which entailed centralisation. The greater reliance on capital-intensive communications reduced Labour's reliance on activists and permitted a downgrading of the CLP machinery, particularly activist structures such as the GCs. Finally, leadership change can be a spur for party change, which was confirmed by the way in which Kinnock, Smith and Blair each sought to crystallise a given balance of forces on coming to power. Especially interesting was the transition from Smith to Blair in 1994. Labour had not suffered any electoral reverses during Smith's brief tenure – indeed, it was riding high in the polls. However, a sense of urgency and the availability of new leadership selection structures saw the victory of Blair and an abrupt change of direction and tempo. Blair led an intra-party coalition of forces different from that represented by Smith and ensured he was not beholden to union leaders.

These factors provide the main explanation for Labour's transformation. Of less significance for the period under review were redistributive changes instigated from below, particularly after perceived failures in government, though they were evident during the period 1979–83. After Labour's defeat in 1979, it was convulsed by a civil war that resulted in the left winning support for reforms that restricted the politicians' autonomy. Despite some important supporters in the PLP and on the NEC, this coalition for change came largely 'from below', consisting of CLP delegates at the party conference, and leftists in middle-ranking positions in the party and the unions. Many unions supported these reforms because they believed the Labour government shirked on its obligations under the initial terms of the 'social contract'. In the light of such 'betrayals', the left was able to prosper by gaining wider sympathy for a reduction in leadership autonomy: unions and activists remain policy-seekers, and if the government ignores their preferences, electoral success is less meaningful. However, these reforms failed to improve Labour's performance and the defeat of 1983 paved the way for a reassertion of leadership control.

To the extent that the reforms helped Labour to shed its image as a union-dominated party, and to allow the leadership to adopt policies popular with voters, the modernisation project was successful. But what type of party has Labour become and what are its likely relations with the unions? These questions are addressed in the final two sections.

Unitarism and leadership dominance

We are now in a position to assess the structure of exchange relationships in the Labour Party after 1997. The pre-1992 reforms were predominantly, though not solely, centralising in nature, while the post-1992 reforms involved moving away from the federal structure, together with further centralisation. These shifts are illustrated in Figure 8.1. The shaded strip on the left shows the normal historical range of Labour's organisational structure, firmly federal but varying in the degree of centralisation, with the latter greatest when Labour was in government. At the bottom-left is Duverger's ideal-typical indirect

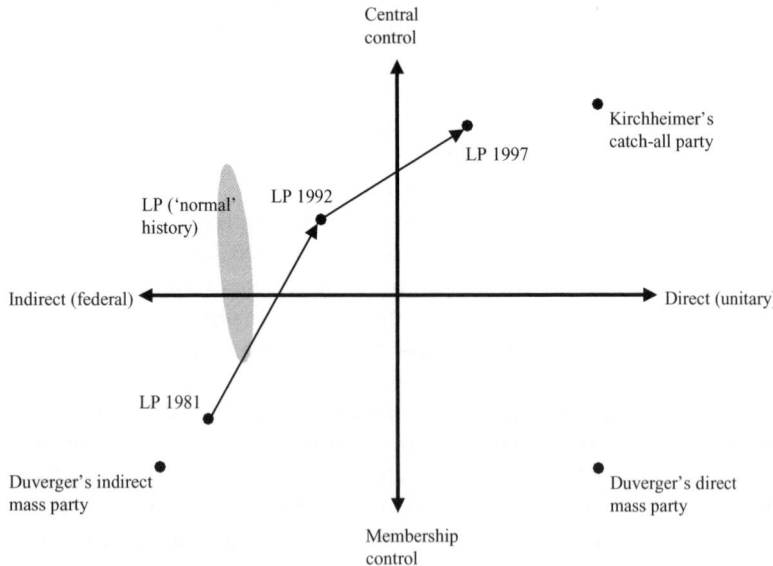

Figure 8.1 Labour's Two Phases of Modernisation
Horizontal plane: Direct (unitary) versus indirect (federal) membership structure
Vertical plane: Distribution of power between centre and party members
LP: British Labour Party

mass party, which Labour often approximated, and at the bottom-right is the ideal-typical direct mass party, with control 'from below' characteristic of both. At the top-right is Kirchheimer's catch-all party, a leadership-dominated structure based on individual membership and with few formal links to interest groups.

It is the latter model Labour increasingly resembles, though it arrived there by a circuitous route. The reforms of 1979–81 increased the degree of federalisation through the establishment of the block vote-based electoral college, but they also devolved power downwards from MPs to party activists and trade unionists. During the Kinnock years, there were numerous moves to centralise power, yet by 1992 Labour still had a largely federal structure.[1] However, Labour shifted strongly towards a unitary structure under Smith and Blair, with OMOV in candidate selection and the electoral college, and the use of membership plebiscites. Further centralisation meant that by 1997 Labour resembled a catch-all party, emphasised by its vastly decreased reliance on union funds. (See main Appendix for a summary of Labour's main shifts from federalism to unitarism.)

The principle of OMOV altered the very nature of the Labour Party. Since 1918, Labour has had a hybrid organisational structure, but while it was for long a mainly federal party with some unitary features, in the 1990s the federal features were eroded (though not abolished) and the unitary features considerably extended. However, it is not simply becoming a conventional mass party. The key feature of the mass party for Duverger was not size but structure, in particular, the network of local branches that mobilised and recruited members, as well as educating the working class. Financially, the mass party's organisation and campaigns were financed by its members, not wealthy donors. In the contemporary Labour Party, electoral strategy is catch-all rather than class-based, and it does not offer political education to members or voters. Local branches persist but rarely to mobilise members. Many branch meetings attract fewer than a dozen members, with councillors and local *notables* dominating proceedings (the same is often true of local policy forums).

Labour started to take seriously the problems of membership recruitment and retention. Membership drives had some temporary success but attention after 1997 shifted to the structures and functions of CLPs. There has been some appreciation that endless centralisation has progressively diluted institutional incentives for participation, and academic observers have argued that the party's grassroots have become 'de-energised'. Some modernisers have suggested a restructuring of

CLPs to turn them into strong campaigning forces, thereby encouraging people into the party and giving it a local presence, which might improve Labour's electoral performance. In a Fabian Society pamphlet, Paul Richards (2000) recommended that Labour become a 'communitarian party'. Richards' pamphlet provided a trenchant critique of CLPs, describing how they are characterised by endless meetings that deal with correspondence, minutes, treasurer's reports, and so on, that are of interest solely to committed activists, but which are extremely off-putting for most members. Richards argued for the abolition of GCs, the wider use of local policy forums and the formation of local 'taskforces' to organise members into local campaigns (2000: 34–6). In place of the traditional party structure, Richards advocated a communitarian structure, named after the strand of social thought developed by writers such as Amitai Etzioni, in which the emphasis is on collective action by local communities. Richards claimed, '[t]he incentive for new members to join, and for existing members to become more active, would be huge if they could see a real benefit ensue from the energy they personally expended' (2000: 28), and he gave a number of examples of such community action, including setting up local crèches and removing graffiti and rubbish from housing estates. Richards noted that Labour used to provide many services and social functions in the 1920s and 1930s, such as cycling clubs. His proposals were presented as a way of re-integrating Labour into local communities. Some of these ideas appeared in an NEC consultation document (Labour Party, 1999), and local policy forums were organised to discuss options for change.

The leadership's plans for wholesale change were largely seen off (at least, for the time being[2]) by the major unions, who view reform of GCs with suspicion, regarding it as a way of reducing their remaining influence in local parties (Ludlam, 2004: 73). Yet there are also a number of more general problems with the proposals. The old mass parties were able to provide successful social and cultural functions to party members and the wider community because they were filling a gap in service provision. Before the war, public services were less extensive than they are now. Furthermore, the provision of leisure services depended much more on local groups and clubs. Nowadays, people can obtain leisure in many other ways that do not depend on joining clubs (for example, television, computer games, clubbing, and so on). The pursuit of leisure is an increasingly privatised affair and individuals lead more atomised lives than in the past (Putnam, 2000). Furthermore, when they do want to become involved in campaigns, there are numerous pressure groups they can join.

These developments constrain the space available for the communitarian party. Richards failed to provide any account of how the local collective action problem could be solved by a party that spends much of its time performing chores. There appears to be a significant mismatch of incentives in the communitarian party. There is surely a very low limit to the amount of time that politically motivated activists will be willing to spend removing graffiti from the walls of council estates. Activists are motivated by a combination of strong purposive incentives buttressed by social incentives and institutionalised rights in the local decision-making process. Although the abolition of GCs can be justified on the grounds that they are largely redundant and enshrine a two-tier membership structure (Richards, 2000: 34–5), they are also the focal point for the party's activist core. Without them activists may become more atomised, which would erode social incentives for activism (such as monitoring by ones peers) and perhaps speed up activist exit. The fact that inactive members do not participate in them may be beside the point if one accepts that activists face different incentives than inactive members or potential recruits. Whereas new or inactive members are mainly motivated by purposive incentives, social incentives are a fundamental component of activist participation, in terms of the enjoyment of participation, commitment to the group and social sanctions against shirkers. If the GCs were abolished, there would need to be an alternative institutional structure in which social incentives could be embedded, otherwise the activists might drift away.

Activists also require a role in decision-making as the price for the time they devote to party work. Labour has been heading in the opposite direction. Whiteley and Seyd (2001) claim that an attraction of a campaign-oriented communitarian party to party leaders is its amenability to leadership control and its removal from the policy-making process:

> Opposition and dissent require organisation and if the grassroots organisation is transitory and linked only to campaigns, it would lack the continuity and institutional memory required to challenge the status quo. From a party manager's point of view the ideal party would consist of a sales force who are willing to go out and promote policies which have been decided elsewhere, while at the same time supporting the party with generous donations of money. (Whiteley and Seyd, 2001)

The problem with this type of incentive structure is that it is akin to expecting employees to work hard while foregoing their wages. It is unlikely to provide a stable equilibrium but will instead prompt activist voice or exit. Whiteley and Seyd say that most members oppose a campaign-oriented model of party organisation in which leaders make decisions over policy and conclude: 'Members join the party and are active in part because they want to change policies and have influence over the future development of the Labour government. Take away that motivation and party activity will decline and members leave.' No amount of institutional alchemy is likely to persuade members to devote time to activism if their views are ignored. Worryingly for the party, an increasing proportion of the membership is coming round to this view (Seyd and Whiteley, 2002: 152).

Even the recruitment of inactive members will become increasingly difficult. Blair's ascendancy to the leadership prompted an influx of new members attracted by the image projected by Blair, but membership has since fallen back. Membership retention is also problematic in the case of members who join for purposive incentives: once the salience of the issue that prompted them to join has died down, or if they have come to the conclusion that it is difficult to exert influence in the party, exit becomes likely. The greater reliance of all major West European parties on purposive incentives for membership recruitment, and the relatively weak staying power of such incentives, mean Labour's problem is not unique.

Historically, Labour's dominant coalition has consisted of PLP and union elites, but that has broken down (see below). The OMOV reforms created the possibility of a new coalition, between the PLP leadership and the individual members. Blair's alliance with party members over the reform of Clause IV was evidence of this coalition, and there are indications that CLP delegates to the party conference are more likely to align with the leadership nowadays than with the unions. On the other hand, party members are also policy-seekers, and the limits of their electoral pragmatism may have been reached. Seyd and Whiteley (2002: 152) found that between 1990 and 1999, the proportion of members agreeing that Labour should adjust its policies to capture the support of floating voters fell from 57 to 37 per cent, while the proportion disagreeing rose from 33 to 45 per cent. However, a PLP-individual membership coalition will inevitably be dominated by the PLP. The old coalition of PLP and union leaders entailed two sets of elites who could negotiate with each other and co-manage internal party affairs. By contrast, the individual members have no separate elites who can bargain with the PLP on their behalf. In the 1970s the left saw the NEC as a means of representing the preferences of the wider party, but now the executive is a greatly emasculated body.

If this situation prevails, Labour is likely to continue losing members; in which case, are Labour's institutions inefficient? Activists and trade unions are certainly less powerful than in the 1980s, though the institutions may still offer significant improvements on non-institutionalised exchange (but with the leadership much better off than the members). The problem is that institutional change may decrease members' utility so much that they reduce their supply of labour or even exit the party. If membership loss and activist apathy damages the politicians' ability to campaign for votes, it will reduce their utility too, perhaps leaving them worse off than before the reforms.

Yet Labour's leadership has not loosened central control over the party nationally.[3] The terms of political exchange between leaders and members have changed as capital-intensive campaigning has lessened the need for a large body of activists. Activists cannot be abolished, as they still provide important services. However, by relying on media campaigns or by making greater use of computers and telephones, as well as by concentrating activists in target constituencies, more effective use can be made of a smaller activist body. Financially, Labour can continue relying on wealthy donors and the unions, and if the latter withdraw their funds, state funding is a genuine possibility. There was never much chance of the membership drives of the 1980s and 1990s creating an individual membership base sufficient to bankroll the party. Labour retains members for reasons of legitimacy, decoration, additional finance and free labour, but with the latter two functions less important than they once were (though not unimportant). The party leadership accepts that centralised institutions cannot attract and maintain a large, active membership but its calculation is that fewer institutional concessions are necessary in an age of electoral-professional parties and media-dominated elections. It will have been proven wrong if the party loses so many members that it cannot function as an effective campaigning machine – but judgment on that must be deferred for the present.

The future of the party-union link

When Philip Gould called his book on the party, *The Unfinished Revolution* (1999), the implication was that the modernisers saw the reformed party of 1997 as merely another stage in its transition rather than its end point. Gould hinted that the party-union link should be further reformed or even ended, yet important obstacles stand in the way of a divorce, most obviously the question of union money, which Labour needs in the absence of comprehensive state funding of parties. In government, modernisers slowly changed their tune, with even Blair defending the link at the 1999 TUC. One of the old uses of the link – and the source of greatest tension – was the habitual request by party leaders to union leaders for wage restraint. Labour's adoption of neo-liberal economics and the unions' acceptance of the end of the old tri-partite structures has removed this source of tension and to that extent made the party-union link less objectionable to modernisers. More-over, the government's economic competence has shown it need not be regarded as untrustworthy simply by dint of the link. Provided there is no return to widespread industrial unrest, the unions need not present Labour with a credibility deficit.

However, after seven years in office, the Blair government is finding its relations with the unions increasingly strained. This pattern of party-union relations is fairly 'normal' because Labour governments have often found themselves failing to live up to union leaders' and members' expectations. The unions have secured some policy gains under the Blair government, such as new laws on recognition of unions by employers, and they enjoy access to ministers (Ludlam, 2004: 74). They do not possess the strength they had in the 1960s and 1970s, and are unlikely to recoup it, though many in the unions have accepted the shift from voluntarism and industrial conflict towards a rights-based workplace culture (Ludlam, 2000: 235). However, in the aftermath of the 2001 general election, the govern-ment expressed its desire to increase substantially private sector involvement in the delivery of public services. Labour was re-elected on a pledge to modernise public services, which the government believed would require a large injection of money and a restructuring of the way services are provided. The government raised taxes to fund the improvements, including a 1 per cent increase in the rate of national insurance, but its fear – and a charge frequently made by Labour's opponents – was that the extra spending would vanish into higher wages while services remained shoddy. New money was there-fore tied to reform, which in practice meant an attack on union pre-rogatives in the public sector. The government saw it as a battle that could not be shirked, because the alternative would be the disintegra-tion of Labour's electoral coalition, as voters punished it for raising taxes but not improving services.

The result has been policies such as the private finance initiative (PFI), whereby private consortia finance, build and maintain hospitals, schools and prisons, which are then leased back to the state over a period of about thirty years. This method saves the government from having to raise the money up-front through higher taxes or increased borrowing, though critics argue that taxpayers repay much more in the long-term since PFI is a buy-now-pay-later credit scheme. The advantage for the government is that it has been able to undertake one of the largest ever hospital- and school-building programmes. The drawback for the unions is that the private consortia offer much-reduced terms and conditions for employees. Unions have complained that PFI and other forms of public-private partnerships lead to two-tier workforces, as public sector staff on better terms and conditions work alongside private sector employees on lower pay and less secure contracts. These criticisms have also been levelled at foundation hospitals, the government's key reform initiative for the NHS. This policy gives greater autonomy to high-performing hospitals, including greater control over the terms and conditions of workers. Health service unions lobbied hard against foundation hospitals and found many allies on the government's backbenches, though parliament eventually voted for the policy.

There has been a rising tide of opposition within the unions to this restructuring of the public sector. Strikes have thus far been fairly infrequent, though during 2002–03 a dispute with the FBU over pay and modernisation of the fire service lasted several months. However, the ability of unions to mount the type of large-scale action that damaged the Callaghan government has been greatly impaired by Thatcher-era industrial relations laws and a halving of union membership since 1980. In 2002, 1.3 million working days were lost to stoppages compared with 29 million in 1979.[4] The position of the unions in the economy has also changed dramatically since the 1970s, with de-industrialisation and the abandonment of corporatism. These changes have reduced the unions' political and economic status, and raise questions about the extent to which a party nowadays can allow itself to be dominated by 'old' industrial interests.

So how have the unions responded this time? The first indication of the mounting discontent has been the election since 2001 of a raft of leftists to the leadership of Labour's biggest affiliated unions, Unison, Amicus the GMB, and the TGWU. Leftists also took over the FBU, the RMT, the CWU and the non-affiliated PCS civil service union. The success of the left and the defeat of Blairite loyalists have resulted in a more robust and critical union response to government policies. The fate of Sir Ken Jackson, former leader of the AEEU, is a warning to union leaders who are perceived to be too close to the government. In 2002, Jackson was defeated by the leftwinger, Derek Simpson, in the race to lead Amicus, the successor union after the merger between the AEEU and MSF. Jackson had a reputation for being 'Tony Blair's favourite union leader' and paid the price for his perceived failure to fight for engineering jobs. Simpson and the other leftwing leaders have shown a greater willingness to consider strike action and to call into question what their unions are getting from their affiliations, not least through reviews of the links with the party instigated by a number of unions. Intra-party institutions are inefficient if they do not provide members with sufficient incentives to remain in the party, normally leading to exit or voice. The latter includes efforts by members to redistribute power through institutional reforms. However, there appears little immediate prospect of any loosening of the constraints after two decades of centralisation and the severe erosion of the unions' constitutional rights in the party. The belief in the unions that they are not getting much for their money explains an increase in talk of disaffiliation: big business and non-affiliated organisations such as the British Medical Association have a greater influence on government policy than Labour's affiliates. In February 2004, the NEC disaffiliated the RMT from the Labour Party after the union permitted some branches to affiliate to the Scottish Socialist Party. The RMT's hard-left leadership had for some years been moving away from the Labour mainstream, but its departure was hugely symbolic: the initial motion passed at the TUC in 1899 to form the Labour Representation Committee was moved by a predecessor union of the RMT. In June 2004, the FBU voted to disaffiliate and some other unions could follow suit, yet it is only the union left that is seriously considering the exit option. Most union leaders appear to believe their interests are better served inside the Labour Party.

Union opposition to state funding for parties is the most obvious indicator of their continued commitment to the party-union link. Greater reliance on state funding characterises many countries, reflecting changes in the relationship between voters, parties and the state (Katz and Mair, 1995). In Britain, state funds have been restricted to Short money for opposition parliamentary parties and full state funding would likely generate considerable public opposition. However, since being re-elected in 2001, Labour has found itself facing an increasing funding crisis, as unions have reduced their donations (see below), at one point leaving the party unable to pay routine bills. A hike in individual membership subscriptions was partly intended to address these problems. The financial crisis encouraged modernisers to raise the prospect of state funding, which in turn prompted union leaders to oppose such a move for fear that it would presage a party-union divorce.[5] State funding would permit the unions to spend their money on their own political campaigns but it would also alleviate the party's need to rely on union money. Given this opposition to state funding, and assuming that union leaders do not want Labour to become even more dependent on donations from wealthy business-men, the only conclusion to draw is that unions do indeed want the party to be in a position of some dependence on their money in return for influence over policy. The historical project of labourism remains the only option for most union leaders.

Part of the unions' calculation is that the alternatives to the party-union link are worse than the *status quo*, but the other part is that their institutional and financial ties still afford opportunities to exert some influence. These links are not just to the party leadership but also to sympathetic individual ministers, backbench MPs and CLP activists, all of whom present potential allies in union campaigns against govern-ment policies. Most unions will continue pursuing their interests by building alliances with intra-party allies, and hope that Tony Blair's successor is more receptive to their demands. At the 2003 annual con-ference, the leaders of the big four unions coordinated their activity, agreeing common agendas and defeating the government in a number of votes. However, passing critical resolutions at the party conference and the NPF does not guarantee influence over government policy. The unions have had to devise new strategies in an era when Labour's intra-party institutions do not offer sufficient grassroots and union control over policy. To understand their recent strategies, it is useful to depict current party-union relations in game-theoretic form, where-by the unions face a choice between continuing to fund the party or disaffiliating and withdrawing their money. The government can choose pro-union policies, which carry electoral risks, or moderate policies, which promise greater electoral rewards (see Table 8.1).

Union funding enables Labour to cover its expenditure but if the unions disaffiliate the government must introduce state funding for parties because it cannot rely on wealthy donors in the long term. However, introducing state funding entails costs, as unions, the Conservatives and the media attack the government. Pro-union poli-cies lead to sedate relations between the government and the unions but may carry electoral costs, whereas centrist policies cause conflict. Such discord has intra-party reverberations if it occurs while unions remain affiliated to Labour. The government's first preference is union funding and centrist policies, while it least prefers pro-union policies and the turmoil of disaffiliation. The ordering of its second and third preferences is debatable: it may prefer the freedom to form centrist policies while maintaining its organisation with state funds; or it might opt for the quiet life of pro-union policies and union funding, with possible electoral costs. The government's preference ranking is thus either $T_G>R_G>P_G>S_G$ or $T_G>P_G>R_G>S_G$. Either way, its dominant strategy is to follow a centrist policy path, whether the unions fund the party ($T_G>R_G$) or not ($P_G>S_G$).[6]

The unions' first preference is affiliation and pro-union policies because although disaffiliation and pro-union policies appears a better option if available, the unions prefer a position inside the party in case policy changes in the future. The unions may even prefer centrist policies and affiliation to pro-union policies and disaffiliation – at least in the short-medium term. Worst of all is disaffiliation and centrist policies, because the unions have no intra-party means of pressuring the government for a change in policy. Hence, for the unions $R_U>T_U>S_U>P_U$ or $R_U>S_U>T_U>P_U$. Either way, the unions prefer to fund the party, whether it has pro-union policies ($R_U>T_U$) or not ($S_U>P_U$). These preference rankings for the unions and the government suggest a single-play equilibrium outcome in the top-right box in Table 8.1 – continued union affiliation and centrist policies, which is precisely what has happened since 2001.

However, as the game is repeated over the months and years, this equilibrium may not survive. The unions receive their second- or even their third-best payoff. Even the government, which receives its highest payoff, faces costs, as intra-party conflict increases. The longer

Table 8.1   Government-Union Relations (post-2001)

		LABOUR GOVERNMENT	
		PRO-UNION POLICIES	CENTRIST POLICIES
UNIONS	FUND PARTY	Intra-party harmony R_U, R_G	Intra-party discord S_U, T_G
	DISAFFILIATE	State funding, pro-union T_U, S_G	State funding, anti-union P_U, P_G

(i_U, j_G) payoffs to unions and government

this state of affairs prevails, the more likely it is that the value of S_U will fall, narrowing the gap between S_U and P_U. Eventually, even moderate union leaders may decide there is no hope in forcing a change in policy and the unions could opt for disaffiliation. A few far-left unions have already arrived at this point. Other unions believe there are currently fewer advantages in breaking the party-union link than in *threatening* to break it. In the short-medium term, these threats gain credence by a process of reducing donations in order to exert financial pressure. As we have seen, the GMB reduced its affiliation level in 2001, amounting to a funding cut of £1 million over four years, while other unions were reviewing their affiliation levels. Labour's parlous financial state, together with its determination to halt the politicisation of donations, encouraged the party to seek a five-year funding deal with the unions worth £40 million. However, the union leaders rebuffed this request, preferring to retain the present annual arrangements, specifically because they permit greater bargaining power. As a compromise, the unions agreed to raise affiliation fees (*The Guardian*, 8 September 2003).

The unions' decision to politicise donations is fairly unique in Labour's history. Even during the 1970s, the unions did not cut funding levels because of their dissatisfaction with government policy. On the contrary, unions such as NUPE increased their affiliation levels so that they could obtain a bigger block vote, which was vital in pushing through the left's constitutional reforms. Nowadays, however, no one seriously believes that the unions could increase their power by passing reforms at the party conference. Union money no longer buys votes that make a difference, so it is used to obtain influence in a different way: by being made contingent on policy delivery. Where that delivery is not forthcoming, donations can be reduced. Labour's original institutions were designed to prevent this political use of finance. The regression from institutionalised political exchange to more direct exchange emphasises how inefficient the institutions now are. Labour leaders are unable to make credible promises to their own members and the latter are unable to enforce their will.

Politicising donations is a sign of the unions' desperation, but it presents them with some pointed dilemmas. Using money as leverage is not a viable long-term strategy. Some union officials were worried that refusing to provide a long-term financial package might simply accelerate moves towards state funding and the breaking of the institutional links between the party and the unions. Using finance as leverage assumes that the government prefers a quiet life with the unions to a state-funded centrist life without them ($R_G > P_G$ in Table 8.1). Developments over the next few years will show whether this assumption is correct. On the one hand, the costs of conflict with the unions could become too great for the government, reducing the values of T_G and P_G. Governments that have been in office for a long time tend to lose cohesion; the Blair government is no different, and it has already suffered major backbench rebellions over the war in Iraq, university tuition fees and foundation hospitals. If such opposition to the government from its own supporters continues during a third-term administration, it may decide to opt for a quieter life. Public service reforms could be scaled down, and state funding of parties may be seen as too provocative. This plausible scenario would see the maintenance of the party-union link and a de-radicalisation of the modernisers' overall reform agenda. On the other hand, the government's electoral prospects depend considerably on noticeable improvements in public services, with reform a prerequisite. Moreover, the government will have noted union leaders' fierce opposition to state funding, which everyone concerned accepts would likely follow any sustained campaign of reduced union donations. The government may decide that disaffiliation and threats to slash funding lack credibility as strategies and are simply short-term tactics that will be abandoned the moment the government starts seriously contemplating state funding.

In which case, what alternative strategies exist for the unions to press their case? Increased industrial action is one possibility but the unions are constrained by tough laws from the Thatcher era and their industrial muscle is much diminished. (Another Thatcher-era policy, wider home-ownership and attendant mortgages, also makes long strikes difficult for union members to endure.) The government has shown itself unwilling to capitulate on reform in the face of strikes, as it showed during the fire fighters' dispute in 2002–03. Intra-party responses are still possible, though, and even if the type of left-inspired institutional reforms of 1979–81 are unlikely, the current 'awkward squad' of union leaders is coming round to the view that their best option is to work for change within the party. One suggestion by Tony Woodley, the new leader of the TGWU, is that the six biggest unions could each affiliate six politically motivated activists to each CLP, or even just to those in safe or marginal Labour seats (*The Spectator*, 2 August 2003). In the context of a plummeting individual membership in the party, this revival of 'entryism' could see unions take over moribund CLPs and determine parliamentary candidate selection, not only through OMOV ballots but also by nominating trusted union officials as candidates. This idea was floated at the same time that smaller unions and leftwing activists revived the Labour Representation Committee, forerunner of the party, to affiliate to CLPs and sway selection contests. By influencing the social and ideological composition of the PLP, unions may hope to alter the government's policy payoffs, increasing the costs attached to centrism (reducing T_G) and increasing the attractiveness of compromise (raising R_G). It may be the case that such proposals are simply signals to the government that the unions are dissatisfied rather than genuine plans of attack; the point is that they indicate a rejection of disaffiliation and a return to the original labourist strategy of securing direct parliamentary representation.

The coming decade will see a continuation of this debate about the ultimate purpose of the party-union link. Modernisers believe institutionalised links with producer interests in industry and the public sector are anachronistic and have the potential to damage Labour in the future. The unions can be a destabilising influence when Labour is in government. The party-union link can create unrealistic policy expectations, which if either accommodated or steadfastly resisted by the party may end up damaging its electoral prospects. Yet one reason why the party-union link survived so long was that Labour had no viable alternative source of funds. A divorce would have bankrupted the party. However, it is no longer impossible to imagine British parties being funded mainly by the state, even though opposition is entrenched. This prospect has the potential to create alternative endgames for future party-union disputes. Further party funding reforms are likely to play a role in determining whether the party-union link survives in its institutionalised form.

Conclusion

The relationship between the Labour Party and the affiliated unions has entered an uncertain phase, with few precedents available to help us predict the outcome. The norms and values that long characterised the relationship are breaking down – to return to the metaphor used in Chapter 1, the ivy on the walls of the old mansion is withering away. The working-class culture and ethos has receded in the CLPs, as the individual party membership has become increasingly middle class. In such circumstances, a methodological framework that emphasises the importance of long-lasting practices is a poor guide to understanding the comprehensive transformation the party has undergone since 1983. Nothing that was said in the course of this book denied the reality of norms and values, or their influence on actors' decisions. Rather, resorting too quickly to this sociological schema, with its bias towards stability, will tend to divert us from the instrumental foundations of Labour's organisation.

The approach used in this book has stressed the rationality underlying the party-union link and Labour's internal institutions. As those institutions failed to provide adequate forums within which different sets of intra-party actors could pursue their rival goals, conflict and change were the inevitable consequence. One hundred years of accumulated traditions was not enough to deter modernisers from seeking a fundamental overhaul of the party and its policies to make Labour electable once more. By the same token, that shared heritage has not stopped trade union leaders from using the money they give to the party as leverage against it. The rational choice approach allows us to see these developments straightforwardly as reasoned responses to changed circumstances. Any future party-union divorce will be exactly the same.

It is important for political scientists to be clear about the theories and methods they use to explain events and institutions. Theoretical and methodological tools should not have restricted applicability to one subset of phenomena, since that fails to take us beyond the realm of description. The rational choice approach is not the only one in political science – and neither should it be. However, its use is spreading in the discipline and it is being applied to a wider array of problems. One advantage of the approach, which has facilitated its growth, is that it offers political scientists a common body of analytical possessions, to which it is easy to add at low cost (Barry, 1991: 191). The present book utilised many different models, some developed by others, to address separate questions. In turn, some of the models developed here can be used to analyse institutions and institutional change in other parties. Rational choice work on the theory of party organisation is relatively underdeveloped. This book has sought to contribute to that body of work.

Appendix: From Federalism to Unitarism in the Labour Party

Year	Event	Details	Effect on Labour Party
1900	Formation of Labour Representation Committee	An extra-parliamentary party dominated by unions. No individual members. Unions and socialist societies elect separate sections to NEC. Unions finance party out of normal union (industrial) funds without members' permission	Strongly federal party structure with completely indirect membership structure
1909	Osborne judgment	A railway worker, W.V. Osborne, objects to his union's funds going to Labour Party. Wins court injunction, upheld by House of Lords.	Union funding to Labour virtually collapses and the party's survival is at risk
1913	Partial repeal of Osborne judgment	Liberal government introduces Trade Union Act 1913, allowing unions to spend money on political activities provided that (a) political and industrial funds are kept separate, and (b) union members have the right to 'contract out' of paying political levy	Shift towards a more direct relationship between individual union members and Labour Party – principle of consent means levypayers can 'contract out' (but apathy ensures not many do – 'negative' consent)
1917	NEC reform	Entire NEC elected by the annual conference (socialist societies allowed exclusive right to nominate candidates for their section)	Undermined federalism by ending exclusive voting rights for affiliated bodies to their own NEC sections

1918	Labour's new constitution	Permitted individual membership for the first time (through CLPs). NEC reform of 1917 upheld	Strong shift towards direct membership elements
1927	Introduction of 'contracting in'	Conservative government introduces Trades Disputes and Trade Union Act 1927 – now union levypayers must state they wish to pay political levy	Increased direct nature of party-union link (requirement of 'positive' consent) and decreased affiliated membership
1937	NEC reform	CLPs permitted exclusive right to vote on NEC candidates for the CLP section of the NEC	Increased federal nature of the party and reversed NEC reform of 1917
1946	Reintroduction of 'contracting out'	Labour government introduces Trade Disputes and Trade Union Act 1946, which brings back 'contracting out'	Increased indirectness of party-union link and raised affiliated membership
1981	Electoral college for leadership elections	Separate union (40%) and CLP (30%) sections (block voting), as well as PLP section (30%)	Federalisation of leadership elections by giving votes to all party stakeholders
1985–86	Political fund ballots	Unions obliged by law (Trade Union Act 1984) to ballot all members on whether to maintain political funds	Strengthened direct link between levypayers and party (because ballots were won); legitimised Labour's union funding
1987	Reform of candidate selection	Introduction of local electoral colleges for selecting parliamentary candidates: min. 60% share for individual members (by OMOV); max. 40% share for unions	Considerable strengthening of direct nature of individual party membership (but not affecting continuing indirect nature of party-union relationship)

1989	Computerised national membership list	Establishment of computerised national membership list enabling individuals to join party at the national level	Strengthening of unitarism: centre can communicate with individual members, including distribution of ballot papers
1989–91	NEC and electoral college reform	Mandatory OMOV ballots for CLP sections in NEC and leadership elections	Strengthening of unitarism and reduction in power of GCs
1993	Rule changes introducing OMOV and abolishing union block votes	(a) Union votes removed from parliamentary candidate selection (pure OMOV). (b) Electoral college – OMOV and OLOV in CLP and union sections. (c) Formal abolition of block voting at party conference and reduction of unions' vote share to 70% (50% in 1996)	Very strong shift towards direct membership structure among both individual and affiliated members; considerable undermining (though not abolition) of federal structure
1995	National membership ballots	Provision for membership ballots on policies or issues decided by the NEC (reform of Clause IV in 1995; draft election manifesto in 1996)	Further shift to unitarism but this time at the national level. NEC control of agenda-setting implies greater central powers
1997	*Partnership in Power*	(a) Reduction in union power on NEC; (b) confirmation of new power of NPF (lower union membership than party conference)	Reduced power for affiliates

Notes

Introduction

1 For competing interpretations of Labour's policy changes, see Coates (2001); Driver and Martell (1998); Hay (1994, 1999); Heffernan (2001); Ludlam and Smith (2001, 2004); Panitch and Leys (1997); Smith (1994, 2000); Smith and Spear (1992); and Wickham-Jones (1995a, 1995b, 1996, 1997, 2000).

2 Throughout this book, the term, 'new Labour', is not generally used, but on the few occasions it is, I have not followed the trend to capitalise both words. The party's constitution still states that its name is 'The Labour Party' (Labour Party, 2003a: Clause I.1). For simplicity, here and elsewhere I have referred to the relevant section or clause of the 2003 edition of Labour's constitution (the most recent at the time of writing) unless otherwise stated.

1 Aims and Methods

1 Some of the papers presented at the conference were subsequently published in Callaghan et al. (2003).

2 For discussions of the rational choice approach, see Cox (1999), Friedman (1996), Green and Shapiro (1994), Shepsle and Bonchek (1997: 5–35), and Tsebelis (1990: 18–47).

3 An individual's *political* history is a different matter, because it can shape his political reputation.

4 Moreover, King et al. (1994: 43) have observed, 'the difference between the amount of complexity in the world and that in the thickest of descriptions is still vastly larger than the difference between the thickest of descriptions and the most abstract quantitative or formal analysis'.

5 Before 1997 there were no regional assemblies (as there are in federal systems) that opposition parties could capture to implement policies and dispense patronage.

6 For rational choice discussions of institutions, see Dowding (1994), Pettit (1998), Shepsle (1979, 1989) and Tsebelis (2002).

7 It could be objected that the UK is not a two-party system, because the Liberal Democrats win about one-sixth of the votes in general elections. However, there is a largely two-party system in the House of Commons. Even in 2001, when the Liberal Democrats achieved the best result by a third party since the 1920s, their 52 seats amounted to only 8 per cent of the total, whereas the Conservatives and Labour together accounted for 88 per cent of the legislative seats. The assumption of two-party competition is a simplification but a justifiable one.

8 In other words, it is majority-preferred to all alternatives. The median-voter theorem applies only to unidimensional policy space; multidimensional

space is usually chaotic, with any point being a potential equilibrium (McKelvey, 1976).

9 Kaare Strøm (1990) uses the term 'vote-seeking' for two-party systems and reserves 'office-seeking' for multi-party systems, where office-seeking need not involve seeking to increase votes. However, these terms are used interchangeably in the present book.

10 The same is generally not true of rational choice debates on this subject.

11 This discussion of the relative contributions of performance, values and support in maintaining the party-union link is based on Brian Barry's account (1978: 94–5) of the role values play in sustaining democracy.

12 Interestingly, Minkin made an identical criticism of Robert McKenzie's depiction of union leaders as a 'Praetorian Guard' to the PLP leadership (Minkin, 1980: 321).

13 In the final chapter of *The Contentious Alliance*, where Minkin criticises proponents of a party-union divorce, he sets out his own reasons for keeping the link. Despite his 'sociological' framework, almost all the important ones are instrumental: the potential electoral costs of a divorce; union ballast for the leadership; union finance for the party; and the party as a political vehicle for union interests (1992: 646–50).

2 Political Exchange and Party Organisation

1 See also Aldrich (1983, 1995), Robertson (1976) and Wright (1971).

2 The following three paragraphs are based on Schlesinger (1984: 380–9).

3 Parties may employ some professional specialists, such as pollsters and designers, but the latter are limited in number. The ordinary foot soldiers – the envelope-stuffers and pavement-pounders – are unpaid volunteers.

4 In the days of party 'machines', politicians could secure services through patronage. Moreover, despite parties' collective goods output, party donors may secure private goods from politicians, such as a construction firm being awarded building contracts by a governing party, to which it donated money. Such rent-seeking behaviour by business donors is a fundamental feature of party politics, but business donors do not generally acquire institutionalised rights within parties (though parties such as Forza Italia, a creation of the media mogul, Silvio Berlusconi, are an exception). Most party members must rely on purposive and social incentives.

5 Social and purposive incentives are important in John Aldrich's model of party activism (1983), which revolves round a calculus of individual participation for prospective activists.

6 Even so, we might still expect ideologically-motivated activists to be fairly radical. Melvin Hinich and Michael Munger (1994) argue that ideologies tend to be non-centrist because they initially arise as justifications of, or reactions to, the *status quo ante*. Centrist ideologies are a mish-mash of leftwing and rightwing ideas, lacking any great coherence. Ideologies offer views of the world based on principles, not the middle-of-the-road compromises characteristic of centrist politics.

7 This section appears in a modified form in Quinn (2002: 208–12).

3   The Pre-Modernised Labour Party

1   Much of the material in the first three sections of this chapter appears in Quinn (2002).

2   Trade union branches also affiliate to CLPs. In between the national- and local-level structures, Labour has a regional structure, which is likely to become more important in the era of Celtic (and probably English regional) devolution.

3   The Trade Union Act 1913 overturned the 'Osborne judgment' and established the right of unions to hold political funds. However, it stipulated that all unions must immediately hold one-off ballots of their members to establish whether the latter wanted their unions to possess political funds, and provisions had to be made to entitle members to 'contract out' if they desired. Under the provisions of the Trades Disputes and Trade Union Act 1927 (introduced by a Conservative government), the law was changed so that union members had to 'contract in' to pay the political levy, otherwise their dues would not be deducted. Inertia and ignorance now worked to Labour's disadvantage and its affiliated membership duly fell. The Attlee government reintroduced 'contracting out' in 1946, and it remains to this day. However, the Thatcher government's Trade Union Act 1984 made it mandatory for unions to hold 10-yearly ballots for members to decide whether their unions should maintain political funds. For a discussion of the impact of successive trades union legislation on funding of the Labour Party, see Ewing (1987: 49–72); see also Fisher (1992).

4   Affiliation fees went into Labour's 'general fund', but the unions also contributed heavily to its separate 'general election fund' (see Webb, 1992a: 21–4). Contributions to the latter by individual unions roughly reflected the pecking order of affiliation size.

5   Something similar happened at the 1993 annual conference, when the divided MSF delegation narrowly decided to abstain in the crucial vote on OMOV despite being mandated to vote against it. See note 6 to Chapter 5.

6   The dominance of the large unions has been reduced since 1996, when the CLPs were allocated half of the conference votes.

7   It is argued in Chapter 8 that unions may have fewer inhibitions in withdrawing funds if they are *all* being antagonised by the party, with few immediate prospects for change through intra-party institutions.

8   See note 2 to Introduction.

9   Throughout this book, the term 'PLP' usually refers to the parliamentary leadership, unless otherwise stated, though strictly speaking, the two are not identical. Backbench Labour MPs do not always obey their leaders, though the whipping system in the House of Commons, together with leadership control over patronage (such as frontbench appointments), *normally* ensures general backbench compliance with the leadership's wishes.

10   See Beer (1982); Brand (1989); Epstein (1962); Garner and Kelly (1998); Kavanagh (1985, 1998); McKenzie (1964, 1982); and Minkin (1980, 1992).

11   Possessing more power may help actors maximise their utility, but so could 'systematic luck' (Dowding, 1996, 2003), which is the non-random advantage bestowed upon an actor by virtue of his position in a social or political structure. Securing more power also entails costs, and at some point, the

incremental increase in costs will exceed the incremental increase in benefits.

12 On the link between decentralisation and free collective bargaining, see Crouch (1982) and Taylor (1991, 2000).

13 A further reform, to allow only the NEC to decide the content of Labour's election manifesto, was narrowly rejected.

14 The letters are conventional game-theoretic notation: T(emptation), R(eward), P(enalty) and S(ucker) payoffs. To determine player A's strategy in a game matrix, the analyst asks: what will A do if player B chooses to co-operate; and what will A do if B chooses to defect? Hence, T must be compared to R, and P compared to S. In a single-play prisoner's dilemma, the dominant strategy is to defect; that is, a player will always defect irrespective of what his opponent chooses to do. The result is that each player ends up with his third-best payoff, whereas cooperation would have brought each his second-best payoff. In Table 3.2, the soft left's cooperative strategy is 'ally with right', while the right's cooperative strategy is 'ally with soft left'.

15 When a game of prisoner's dilemma is to be repeated an indeterminate number of times conditional cooperation can emerge. Repeated interaction gives the players the means to enforce a deal to secure their respective Reward payoffs (top-left cell). If either player subsequently defects in a given round to secure his Temptation payoff, the other player can punish him in the following round by defecting. This tit-for-tat strategy is robust in repeated games of prisoner's dilemma because it ensures that gains from defection are short-lived (Axelrod, 1984). However, in single-shot games, mutual defection is a stable equilibrium.

16 A survey by Seyd and Whiteley (2002: 72) showed that 15 per cent of Labour members placed themselves on the hard left of the party, 44 per cent on the soft left, 30 per cent on the soft right and 11 per cent on the hard right. An earlier survey carried out by the authors (1992) had shown a similar distribution of preferences.

4   Policy-making

1 Nowadays, the *ex officio*, non-voting membership of the conference has expanded to include, *inter alia*, members of the national policy forum (see below), MEPs, Labour representatives in the Scottish parliament and Welsh assembly, and Labour officials of major local government bodies (Labour Party, 2003a: Rule 3A.1(d)).

2 The CAC now has seven members (at least three of whom must be women). Five of these members are elected by the whole conference, and the remaining two are elected by CLP delegates to the conference. The term of office of CAC members is now two years (Labour Party, 2003a: Rule 4C.3).

3 In the late-1970s, the left secured a majority on the NEC, and the platform then came into conflict with the PLP leadership, particularly over the policies of the Callaghan government and Labour's constitutional reforms of 1979–81.

4 At least not until 1997, when it applied to the rolling programme of the national policy forum (see below).

5 'Short money' was named after Edward Short, the then leader of the House of Commons who introduced the measure in 1975.

6 For example, there was a 'contact group' between the NEC and the TUC, in which Kinnock built support for his policies among the major union leaders.

7 The cycle in the 2001–05/06 parliament began in November 2001, with a preliminary meeting of the NPF and was due to end in September 2004 at the party conference.

8 These three sections each elect two members to the JPC, as part of its NPF contingent. The other NPF members of the JPC are the NPF chair and vice-chairs.

9 The eight groups were Britain in the world; Crime, justice, citizenship and equalities; Economy, welfare and work; Education and skills; Health; Quality of life; Trade and industry; and Transport, housing, local government and the regions. They prepared 10 policy documents in two waves (the Crime and Economy commissions each produced two reports).

10 Local policy forums are new structures introduced under *Partnership in Power*. They are open to all individual party members in a given constituency, and usually involve discussion of a specific policy issue in workshops guided by a facilitator.

11 The following two paragraphs are based on information in an internal party document, *Partnership in Power II: NPF Procedural Guidelines* (26 October 2001). See also Shaw (2002) and Seyd (1999). My understanding of Labour's policy-making process has also benefited from personal communication with NEC and NPF member, Ann Black. Her website contains detailed subjective accounts of decision-making at meetings of the NPF. See <www.annblack.com/npf_directory.htm>.

12 One example from the July 2000 NPF was on tax and benefits. The initial amendment stated: 'As we continue to reform tax and benefits, we will further raise the upper earnings limits for National Insurance contributions so that it at least keeps pace with inflation.' It was accepted as: 'We will continue to reform tax and benefits in order to achieve a fairer system that assists the lower-paid.' See <http://www.annblack.com/npf_july2000.htm>.

13 At the NPF meeting of July 2000, 658 amendments were tabled to six policy documents. Most were accepted either immediately or after some negotiation. A total of 38 went to a vote of the NPF, with two winning a majority, seven passing the minority threshold, and 29 being defeated outright. See <http://www.annblack.com/npf_july2000.htm>. In the 2002–04 cycle, five amendments to ten documents will be put to the 2004 conference. The NPF debated 1100 amendments, with most adopted in some form.

14 The stipulation that proposals included in the party programme require a two-thirds majority remained.

15 Seyd and Whiteley (2002: 25, 189, n.6) give the example of the deal at the NPF meeting of July 1999, whereby the unions did not support critical amendments on welfare reform, after party leaders agreed to establish an inquiry into welfare provision. Consequently, the party conference was presented with a document that was supportive of the government. However, a year later, the unions were not satisfied that progress had been made in setting up the inquiry, and used their power on the NPF to demand that a

debate take place at the 2000 annual conference. A motion was passed linking rises in pensions to wages, against the government's wishes.

16   The priorities of the unions have tended to dictate the choice of CIRs. CLP disquiet led to a pilot scheme in 2002 and 2003 to add to the conference agenda CIRs that did not secure a majority of votes among conference delegates but which did win the support of over 50 per cent of CLP delegates. Since the CLP delegates tend to vote for many of the topics that union delegations choose, the effect of the scheme was limited, with only about five CIRs in total debated each year. Nevertheless, the 2003 party conference formally adopted it as a rule change – though strangely, a majority of CLP delegates voted against.

5   The Selection of Parliamentary Candidates

1   There is some variation between CLPs in the rules for allocating GC places, though the formula detailed here is fairly typical. Nowadays, CLPs usually expect to have about two-thirds of their GC members from ward branches and one-third from union branches, though the latter are more preponderant in industrial areas. In 1988, a rule change stipulated that union branches were entitled to a maximum of five delegates per GC, though only the heavily-concentrated NUM was significantly affected (Minkin, 1992: 245).

2   The following division of the candidate selection process into application, nomination, shortlisting, selection and endorsement is taken from Norris and Lovenduski (1995: 53–76), whose discussion informs the present one. For an earlier account, see Janosik (1968).

3   Though in Tsebelis' model, even if the NEC is moderate, GCs may sometimes deselect moderate MPs to signal their unhappiness with the *status quo*.

4   The unions' share of votes matched their share of delegates on the GC up to a maximum of 40 per cent.

5   Some candidates were accused of paying membership fees for individuals who would then become union delegates to GCs, boosting the strength of local unions in electoral colleges. See McSmith (1996: 218–22) and Heffernan and Marqusee (1992: 153–5).

6   MSF abstained despite being mandated to vote against OMOV. Key members of its delegation were persuaded that the defeat of OMOV would hinder the adoption of all-women shortlists, a cherished union policy and included among the rule changes in the NEC's OMOV resolution.

7   Tight central control has also marked candidate selection for the Scottish parliament and Welsh assembly, as well as Labour's party lists for European elections, now conducted by proportional representation (see Bradbury et al., 2000; Shaw, 2001).

8   By comparison, in 1993 an MP's salary was £30,854 plus an office allowance of £39,960 and various parliamentary expenses.

9   For figures on all unions, see Butler and Butler (2000: 162).

10   In June 2002, the left-dominated (and now ex-affiliated) RMT withdrew financial support totalling £44,000 from the CLPs of thirteen MPs (including John Prescott and Robin Cook) in the light of their failure to support

RMT policies. Minkin (1992: 260–7) recounts instances of unions making inappropriate threats to withdraw sponsorship from MPs, most notably the leader of the NUR, Sid Weighell, in 1975. Weighell told a public rally that NUR-sponsored MPs would be instructed to vote against a contested aspect of the Labour government's railways policy. However, the press published details of the speech and Weighell made a full apology. A comprehensive account of sponsorship up to the 1970s can be found in Muller (1977).

11 Nevertheless, the threat of deselection never disappeared entirely. In February 2004, the Blairite MP for Reading East, Jane Griffiths, was deselected by her local party, which replaced her with a local councillor. The cause of the deselection was a breakdown in relations between the CLP and Ms Griffiths, with the MP accused of refusing to meet local officials.

12 On gender, selection and representation in the Labour Party, see Norris (1995a), Perrigo (1995) and Childs (2001).

6   Electing the Party Leader

1 On principal-agent relationships, see Milgrom and Roberts (1992: 126–203).

2 There was some ambiguity: until 1978 Labour's parliamentary leader was the *de facto*, but not the *de jure*, leader of the entire party (Punnett, 1993: 258–9). This state of affairs was changed as part of the reform of the selection mechanism.

3 This section included socialist societies as well as unions, but the latter accounted for 39.5 of the section's 40 per cent allocation.

4 Things are not always equal. One reason why the left did not launch more challenges to Kinnock was that it knew it would be heavily defeated and feared subsequent witch-hunts.

5 Moreover, the turnout rate among levypayers in the 1994 contests was only 19 per cent, a figure broadly comparable to turnout in internal union elections.

6 The candidates also run up considerable costs as they produce campaign literature, and travel up and down the country for meetings. In 1994, Blair's leadership campaign cost £78,000 (Stark, 1996: 122).

7 Opposition in the Labour Party to the war in Iraq, and two cabinet resignations, would have left Blair vulnerable to a 'stalking-horse' challenge under the Conservative Party's old system. The clumsiness of the electoral college ensured that only serious contenders would be tolerated, but none were forthcoming.

8 The Welsh assembly is elected by the mixed-member proportional system, whereby 40 of the 60 AMs are chosen by the plurality system in single-member constituencies, and the remaining 20 are elected through regional 'top-up' lists.

9 The election for Labour's mayoral candidacy was also contested by Glenda Jackson, who was initially favoured, and later dropped, by the party leadership. Jackson won 4.4 per cent of the college, and her supporters' votes were reallocated on second preferences. All percentages cited in the preceding paragraph refer to the second count, after Jackson had been eliminated.

10 Elections became biennial from 2002.

11 The NEC recently modified its standing orders to end the practice of policy motions being tabled at its meetings (which the left had been submitting to attack government policy). Such resolutions are now referred to the relevant policy commission (see Chapter 5).

12 A further seat has been set aside for the Black Socialist Society, once its membership passes 2500 and at least a third of eligible trade unions have affiliated.

13 In 2003, Labour peers were also barred from standing in the CLP section, as were MEPs, and elected members of the Scottish parliament and Welsh assembly.

7   Resources and Political Communications

1 The figures for 1992 and 1997 are from Webb (2000: 232), while the 2001 figures are from Labour Party (2002).

2 Many CLPs also have trade union liaison officers to coordinate between local parties and affiliated union branches.

3 Between 2000 and 2002, Labour's cumulative income amounted to £88.5 million, of which 41 per cent came from donations, a mere 21 per cent from affiliation fees, 11 per cent from membership subscriptions and 14 per cent from commercial activities. Source: Labour Party (2002, 2003c)

4 The three individuals were the Labour peer and supermarket magnate, Lord Sainsbury (£2 million), the publisher, Lord Hamlyn (£2 million) and the philanthropist, Sir Christopher Ondaatje (£2.1 million).

5 For introductory overviews of the debate, see Webb (2000: 38–83) and Denver (2003: 66–94).

6 From 2003, such 'registered' members, as they are called, pay an annual subscription of £12 (compared with the standard rate of £24).

7 It also helped the unions: 'By directing their donations to the center and to safely held Labour constituencies, the unions have ensured very good value for money in terms of their power within the party.' (Pinto-Duschinsky, 1981: 226)

8 A similar version of this illustration is used in Robertson (1976: 33), except that the author plots financial contributions rather than number of activists along the vertical axis.

9 By 1989, under Kinnock the leader's office had 12 members, compared to five under Foot (Minkin, 1992: 417, n.19). Blair expanded the leader's office to about 20 members.

10 Labour's new communications structure is increasingly professionalised, with more paid central HQ staff (rising from 50 in 1970 to 179 in 1998), alongside a long term decline in the number of employed local party staff (see Webb, 2000: 242–7; Fisher and Webb, 2003).

11 The taskforces were attack and rebuttal; coordination; external projection; field operations; fundraising and endorsements; leader's tour; legal; media; membership; operations; and policy briefing (Seyd, 2001: 59, n.8).

12 This threat was brought home during the London mayoral election of 2000 when much of the London Labour activist base refused to campaign for Labour's official candidate, Frank Dobson, against the activists' favourite, Ken Livingstone (see Appendix 1 to Chapter 6).

8   Conclusion: Labour's Modernisation

1   An important shift to unitarism in the 1980s was not prompted at all by intra-party reforms: the trade union political fund ballots involved *individual* union members affirming their unions' links with the Labour Party, and thereby affirming their own status as affiliated members.

2   In September 2003, the NEC circulated a follow-up document to *21ˢᵗ Century Party* (Labour Party, 2003b), which set out problems with local structures and listed examples of best practice among CLPs that have undertaken reform.

3   It has relinquished some control at the regional level in response to the fiascos over the selection of candidates for the London mayoralty and the leadership of the Labour group in the Welsh assembly.

4   Even the 2002 figure was high by recent standards: from 1997 to 2001, between a quarter- and a half-million working days were lost in stoppages per year. The brief surge in 2002 was caused by public sector strikes.

5   A report by the think-tank Catalyst, which has close links to the union movement, came out strongly against full state funding and strict limits on union donations (Ewing, 2002). A rival report by the IPPR (Cain with Taylor, 2002) recommended state funding together with caps on donations, which would demolish the present form of party-union political exchange.

6   See note 14 to Chapter 3 for a brief explanation of game matrices.

References

Alderman, Keith and Neil Carter (1993), 'The Labour Party Leadership and Deputy Leadership Elections of 1992', *Parliamentary Affairs* 46 (1): 49–65.

Alderman, Keith and Neil Carter (1994) 'The Labour Party and the Trade Unions: Loosening the Ties', *Parliamentary Affairs* 47 (3): 321–37.

Alderman, Keith and Neil Carter (1995) 'The Labour Party Leadership and Deputy Leadership Elections of 1994', *Parliamentary Affairs* 48 (3): 438–55.

Aldrich, John (1983) 'A Downsian Spatial Model with Party Activism', *American Political Science Review* 77 (4): 974–90.

Aldrich, John (1995) *Why Parties? The Origin and Transformation of Party Politics in America*. Chicago: University of Chicago Press.

Alesina, Alberto, and Alex Cukierman (1990), 'The Politics of Ambiguity', *Quarterly Journal of Economics* 55 (4): 829–50.

Alt, James E. and Kenneth A. Shepsle (1990) 'Editors' Introduction', in James E. Alt and Kenneth A. Shepsle (eds), *Perspectives on Positive Political Economy*, pp. 1–5. Cambridge: Cambridge University Press.

Arrow, Kenneth J. (1951) *Social Choice and Individual Values*. New York: Wiley.

Axelrod, Robert (1984) *The Evolution of Co-operation*. New York: Basic Books.

Ballinger, Chris (2002) 'The Local Battle, the Cyber Battle', in David Butler and Dennis Kavanagh, *The British General Election of 2001*, pp. 208–34. Basingstoke: Palgrave.

Barry, Brian (1978) *Sociologists, Economists and Democracy*. Chicago: University of Chicago Press.

Barry, Brian (1991) *Democracy and Power: Essays in Political Theory 1*. Oxford: Clarendon Press.

Becker, Gary (1986) 'The Economic Approach to Human Behavior', in Jon Elster (ed.), *Rational Choice*, pp. 108–22. Oxford: Basil Blackwell.

Beer, Samuel (1982) *Modern British Politics: Parties and Pressure Groups in the Collectivist Age*. London: Faber.

Bendor, Jonathan and Dilip Mookherjee (1987), 'Institutional Structure and the Logic of Ongoing Collective Action', *American Political Science Review* 87 (1): 129–54.

Berger, Mark M., Michael C. Munger and Richard F. Potthoff (2000) 'The Downsian Model Predicts Divergence', *Journal of Theoretical Politics* 12 (2): 228–40.

Binmore, Ken (1998) *Game Theory and the Social Contract. Volume II: Just Playing*. Cambridge, MA: MIT Press.

Black, Duncan (1958) *The Theory of Committees and Elections*. New York: Cambridge University Press.

Bradbury, Jonathon, James Mitchell, Lynn Bennie and David Denver (2000) 'Candidate Selection, Devolution and Modernization: The Selection of Labour Party Candidates for the 1999 Scottish Parliament and Welsh Assembly Elections', in Philip Cowley, David Denver, Andrew Russell and Lisa Harrison (eds), *British Elections and Parties Review* 10: 151–72. London: Frank Cass.

Brand, Jack (1989) 'Kavanagh and McKenzie on Power', *West European Politics* 12 (2): 112–21.

Brennan, Geoffrey and Loren Lomasky (1993) *Democracy and Decision: The Pure Theory of Electoral Preference*. Cambridge: Cambridge University Press.

Butler, David and Gareth Butler (2000) *Twentieth-century British Political Facts, 1900–2000* (8th ed.). Basingstoke: Macmillan.

Butler, David and Dennis Kavanagh (1985) *The British General Election of 1983*. London: Macmillan.

Butler, David and Dennis Kavanagh (1988) *The British General Election of 1987*. Basingstoke: Macmillan.

Butler, David and Dennis Kavanagh (1997) *The British General Election of 1997*. Basingstoke: Macmillan.

Butler, David and Dennis Kavanagh (2002) *The British General Election of 2001*. Basingstoke: Palgrave.

Cain, Matt with Matthew Taylor (2002) *Keeping it Clean: The Way Forward for State Funding of Political Parties*. London: Institute for Public Policy Research.

Callaghan, John, Steven Fielding and Steve Ludlam (2003) *Interpreting the Labour Party: Approaches to Labour Politics and History*. Manchester and New York: Manchester University Press.

Calvert, Randall L. (1985) 'Robustness of Multidimensional Voting Models: Candidate Motivations, Uncertainty, and Convergence', *American Journal of Political Science* 29 (1): 69–95.

Childs, Sarah (2001) 'In their own Words: New Labour Women and the Substantive Representation of Women', *British Journal of Politics and International Relations* 3 (2): 173–90.

Chong, Dennis (1991) *Collective Action and the Civil Rights Movement*. Chicago: University of Chicago Press.

Chong, Dennis (2000) *Rational Lives: Norms and Values in Politics and Society*. Chicago: University of Chicago Press.

Clark, Peter B. and James Q. Wilson (1961) 'Incentive Systems: A Theory of Organizations', *Administrative Science Quarterly* 6 (2): 129–66.

Coates, David (1980) *Labour in Power? A Study of the Labour Government of 1974–79*. London: Longman.

Coates, David (2001) 'Capitalist Models and Social Democracy: The Case of New Labour', *British Journal of Politics and International Relations* 3 (3): 284–307.

Cox, Gary W. (1999) 'The Empirical Content of Rational Choice Theory: A Reply to Green and Shapiro', *Journal of Theoretical Politics* 11 (2): 147–69.

Craig, F.W.S. (1989) *British Electoral Facts 1832–1987*. Dartmouth: Parliamentary Research Services.

Crewe, Ivor (1991) 'Labor Force Changes, Working Class Decline, and the Labour Vote: Social and Electoral Trends in Postwar Britain', in Frances Fox Piven (ed.), *Labor Parties in Postindustrial Societies*, pp. 20–46. Cambridge: Polity Press.

Criddle, Byron (1997) 'MPs and Candidates', in David Butler and Dennis Kavanagh (eds), *The British General Election of 1997*, pp. 186–209. Basingstoke: Macmillan.

Criddle, Byron (2002) 'MPs and Candidates', in David Butler and Dennis Kavanagh (eds), *The British General Election of 2001*, pp. 182–207. Basingstoke: Palgrave.

Crouch, Colin (1982) 'The Peculiar Relationship: The Party and the Unions', in Dennis Kavanagh (ed.), *The Politics of the Labour Party*, pp. 171–90. London: George Allen and Unwin.

Demsetz, Harold (1990) 'Amenity Potential, Indivisibilities, and Political Competition', in James E. Alt and Kenneth A. Shepsle (eds), *Perspectives on Positive Political Economy*, pp. 144–60. Cambridge: Cambridge University Press.

Denver, David (2003) *Elections and Voters in Britain*. Basingstoke: Palgrave Macmillan.

Denver, David and Gordon Hands (1998) 'Constituency Campaigning in the 1997 General Election: Party Effort and Electoral Effort', in Ivor Crewe, Brian Gosschalk and John Bartle (eds), *Political Communications: Why Labour Won the General Election of 1997*, pp. 75–92. London: Frank Cass.

Denver, David, Gordon Hands and Simon Henig (1998) 'Triumph of Targeting? Constituency Campaigning in the 1997 Election', in David Denver, Justin Fisher, Philip Cowley and Charles Pattie (eds), *British Elections and Parties Review, Volume 8: The 1997 General Election*, pp. 171–90. London: Frank Cass.

Dowding, Keith (1991) *Rational Choice and Political Power*. Aldershot: Edward Elgar.

Dowding, Keith (1994) 'The Compatibility of Behaviouralism, Rational Choice and the "New Institutionalism"', *Journal of Theoretical Politics* 6 (1): 105–17.

Dowding, Keith (1996) *Power*. Buckingham: Open University Press.

Dowding, Keith (2003) 'Resources, Power and Systematic Luck: A Response to Barry', *Politics, Philosophy and Economics* 2 (3): 305–22.

Dowding, Keith and Andrew Hindmoor (1997) 'The Usual Suspects: Rational Choice, Socialism and Political Theory', *New Political Economy* 2 (3): 451–63.

Downs, Anthony (1957) *An Economic Theory of Democracy*. New York: Harper and Row.

Driver, Stephen and Luke Martell (1998) *New Labour: Politics After Thatcherism*. Cambridge: Polity Press.

Drucker, Henry (1979) *Doctrine and Ethos in the Labour Party*. London: Allen and Unwin.

Drucker, Henry (1984) 'Intra-Party Democracy in Action: The Election of Leader and Deputy Leader of the Labour Party in 1983', *Parliamentary Affairs* 37 (3): 283–300.

Dunleavy, Patrick and Hugh Ward (1991) 'Party Competition – The Preference-Shaping Model', in Patrick Dunleavy, *Democracy, Bureaucracy and Public Choice*, pp. 112–44. London: Harvester Wheatsheaf.

Duverger, Maurice (1964) *Political Parties: Their Organization and Activities in the Modern State*. London: Methuen.

Elliott, Gregory (1993) *Labourism and the English Genius: The Strange Death of Labour England?* London: Verso.

Elster, Jon (1989) *The Cement of Society: A Study of Social Order*. Cambridge: Cambridge University Press.

Epstein, Leon D. (1962) 'Who Makes Party Policy: British Labour, 1960–61', *Midwest Journal of Political Science* 6 (2): 165–82.

Epstein, Leon D. (1980) *Political Parties in Western Democracies*. New Brunswick, NJ: Transaction Books.

Ewing, Keith (1987) *The Funding of Political Parties in Britain*. Cambridge: Cambridge University Press.

Ewing, Keith (2002) *Trade Unions, the Labour Party and Political Funding: The Next Step: Reform with Restraint*. London: Catalyst.

Farrell, David M. and Paul Webb (2000) 'Political Parties as Campaign Organizations', in Russell J. Dalton and Martin P. Wattenberg (eds), *Parties Without Partisans: Political Change in Advanced Industrial Democracies*, pp. 102–28. Oxford: Oxford University Press.

Fielding, Steven (2000) 'New Labour and the Past', in Duncan Tanner, Pat Thane and Nick Tiratsoo (eds), *Labour's First Century*, pp. 367–92. Cambridge: Cambridge University Press.

Fisher, Justin (1992) 'Trade Union Political Funds and the Labour Party', in Pippa Norris, Ivor Crewe, David Denver and David Broughton (eds), *British Elections and Parties Yearbook 1992*, pp. 111–23. London: Harvester Wheatsheaf.

Fisher, Justin (1995) 'The Institutional Funding of British Political Parties', in David Broughton, David M. Farrell, David Denver and Colin Rallings (eds), *British Elections and Parties Yearbook 1994*, pp. 181–96. London: Frank Cass.

Fisher, Justin and Paul Webb (2003) 'Political Participation: The Vocational Motivations of Labour Party Employees', *British Journal of Politics and International Relations* 5 (2): 166–87.

Flynn, Paul (1999) *Dragons Led by Poodles: The Inside Story of a New Labour Stitch-up*. London: Politicos.

Friedman, Jeffrey (1996) *The Rational Choice Controversy: Economic Models of Politics Reconsidered*. New Haven and London: Yale University Press.

Garner, Robert and Richard Kelly (1998) *British Political Parties Today* (2nd ed.). Manchester: Manchester University Press.

Gould, Philip (1999) *The Unfinished Revolution: How the Modernisers Saved the Labour Party*. London: Abacus.

Grafstein, Robert (2000) 'Employment, Party Economic Performance, and the Formation of Partisan Preferences', *Journal of Theoretical Politics* 12 (3): 325–51.

Green, Donald P. and Ian Shapiro (1994) *Pathologies of Rational Choice Theory: A Critique of Applications in Political Science*. New Haven and London: Yale University Press.

Hain, Peter (2004) *The Future Party*. London: Catalyst.

Harmel, Robert and Kenneth Janda (1994), 'An Integrated Theory of Party Goals and Party Change', *Journal of Theoretical Politics* 6 (3): 259–87.

Harmer, Harry (1999) *The Longman Companion to the Labour Party 1900–1998*. London and New York: Longman.

Harrison, Martin (1960) *Trade Unions and the Labour Party Since 1945*. London: George Allen and Unwin.

Hay, Colin (1994) 'Labour's Thatcherite Revisionism: Playing the Politics of "Catch-up"', *Political Studies* 42 (4): 700–7.

Hay, Colin (1999) *The Political Economy of New Labour: Labouring Under False Pretences?* Manchester: Manchester University Press.

Heffernan, Richard (2001) *New Labour and Thatcherism: Political Change in Britain*. Basingstoke: Palgrave.

Heffernan, Richard and James Stanyer (1997) 'The Enhancement of Leadership Power: The Labour Party and the Impact of Political Communications', in Charles Pattie, David Denver, Justin Fisher and Steve Ludlam (eds), *British Elections and Parties Review*, Volume 7, pp. 168–84. London: Frank Cass.

Heffernan, Richard and Mike Marqusee (1992) *Defeat from the Jaws of Victory: Inside Kinnock's Labour Party*. London: Verso.

Hindess, Barry (1988) *Choice, Rationality and Social Theory*. London: Unwin Hyman.

Hinich, Melvin J. and Michael C. Munger (1994) *Ideology and the Theory of Political Choice*. Ann Arbor: University of Michigan Press.

Hinich, Melvin J. and Michael C. Munger (1997) *Analytical Politics*. Cambridge and New York: Cambridge University Press.

Hirschman, Albert O. (1970) *Exit, Voice, and Loyalty: Responses to Decline in Firms, Organizations, and States*. Cambridge, MA: Harvard University Press.

Hirschman, Albert O. (1986) *Rival Views of Market Society and Other Recent Essays*. New York: Elisabeth Sifton Books.

Hughes, Colin and Patrick Wintour (1990) *Labour Rebuilt: The New Model Party*. London: Fourth Estate.

Iversen, Torben (1994) 'The Logics of Electoral Politics: Spatial, Directional, and Mobilizational Effects', *Comparative Political Studies* 27 (2): 155–89.

Janosik, Edward G. (1968) *Constituency Labour Parties in Britain*. London: Pall Mall Press.

Katz, Richard S. (2001) 'The Problem of Candidate Selection and Models of Party Democracy', *Party Politics* 7 (3): 277–96.

Katz, Richard S. and Peter Mair (1995) 'Changing Models of Party Organization and Party Democracy: The Emergence of the Cartel Party', *Party Politics* 1 (1): 5–28.

Kavanagh, Dennis (1982) 'Representation in the Labour Party', in Dennis Kavanagh (ed.), *The Politics of the Labour Party*, pp. 202–22. London: George Allen and Unwin.

Kavanagh, Dennis (1985) 'Power in British Political Parties: Iron Law or Special Pleading?', *West European Politics* 8 (1): 5–22.

Kavanagh, Dennis (1995) *Election Campaigning: The New Marketing of Politics*. Oxford: Basil Blackwell.

Kavanagh, Dennis (1997) 'The Labour Campaign', *Parliamentary Affairs* 50 (4): 533–41.

Kavanagh, Dennis (1998) 'Power in the Parties: R.T. McKenzie and After', *West European Politics* 21 (1): 28–43.

Kavka, Gregory S. (1991) 'Rational Maximizing in Economic Theories of Politics', in Kristen Renwick Monroe (ed.), *The Economic Approach to Politics: A Critical Reassessment of the Theory of Rational Action*, pp. 371–85. New York: Harper Collins.

Kiewiet, Roderick, and Mathew McCubbins (1991) *The Logic of Delegation*. Chicago: University of Chicago Press.

King, Gary, Robert O. Keohane and Sidney Verba (1994) *Designing Social Inquiry: Scientific Inference in Qualitative Research*. Princeton, NJ: Princeton University Press.

Kirchheimer, Otto (1966) 'The Transformation of the Western European Party Systems', in Joseph LaPalombara, and Myron Weiner (eds), *Political Parties and Political Development*, pp. 177–200. Princeton, NJ: Princeton University Press.

Kitschelt, Herbert (1989) 'The Internal Politics of Parties: The Special Law of Curvilinear Disparity Revisited', *Political Studies* 37 (3): 400–21.

Kitschelt, Herbert (1994) *The Transformation of European Social Democracy*. Cambridge: Cambridge University Press.

Koelble, Thomas (1987) 'Trade Unionists, Party Activists and Politicians', *Comparative Politics* 19 (3): 253–66.

Koelble, Thomas (1996) 'Economic Theories of Organization and the Politics of Institutional Design in Political Parties', *Party Politics* 2 (2): 251–63.

Kogan, David and Michael Kogan (1982) *The Battle for the Labour Party*. London: Fontana.

Kreps, David M. (1990) 'Corporate Culture and Economic Theory', in James E. Alt and Kenneth A. Shepsle (eds), *Perspectives on Positive Political Economy*, pp. 90–143. Cambridge: Cambridge University Press.

Labour Party (1990) *Democracy and Policy Making for the 1990s*. London: Labour Party.

Labour Party (1993a) *Labour Party/Trade Union Links: Interim Report of the Review Group*. London: Labour Party.

Labour Party (1993b) *Trade Unions and the Labour Party: Final Report of the Review Group on Party-Union Links*. London: Labour Party.

Labour Party (1997) *Partnership in Power*. London: Labour Party.

Labour Party (1999) *21ˢᵗ Century Party: Members – the Key to our Future*. London: Labour Party.

Labour Party (2002) *Labour Party Annual Report 2002*. London: Labour Party.

Labour Party (2003a) *The Labour Party Rule Book 2003*. London: Labour Party.

Labour Party (2003b) *21ˢᵗ Century Party: The Next Steps*. London: Labour Party.

Labour Party (2003c) *Labour Party Annual Report 2003*. London: Labour Party.

Laver, Michael (1997) *Private Desires, Political Action: An Invitation to the Politics of Rational Choice*. London: Sage.

Lax, David and James Sebenius (1991) 'Thinking Coalitionally: Party Arithmetic, Process Opportunism, and Strategic Sequencing', in Henry Peyton Young (ed.), *Negotiation Analysis*, pp. 153–93. Ann Arbor: University of Michigan Press.

Leech, David (1992) 'Empirical Analysis of the Distribution of *A Priori* Voting Power: Some Results for the British Labour Party Conference and Electoral College' *European Journal of Political Research* 21(3): 245–65.

Lijphart, Arend (1999) *Patterns of Democracy: Government Forms and Performance in Thirty-Six Countries*. New Haven and London: Yale University Press.

Lovell, John (1991) 'Trade Unions and the Development of Independent Labour Politics 1889–1906', in Ben Pimlott and Chris Cook (eds), *Trade Unions in British Politics: The First 250 Years*, pp. 28–47. London: Longman.

Ludlam, Steve (2000) 'Norms and Blocks: Trade Unions and the Labour Party since 1964', in Brian Brivati and Richard Heffernan (eds), *The Labour Party: A Centenary History*, pp. 220–45. Basingstoke: Macmillan.

Ludlam, Steve (2004) 'New Labour, "Vested Interests" and the Union Link', in Steve Ludlam and Martin J. Smith (eds), *Governing as New Labour: Policy and Politics Under Blair*, pp. 70–87. Basingstoke: Palgrave Macmillan.

Ludlam, Steve and Martin J. Smith (2001) *New Labour in Government*. Basingstoke: Macmillan.

Ludlam, Steve and Martin J. Smith (2004) *Governing as New Labour: Policy and Politics Under Blair*. Basingstoke: Palgrave Macmillan.

Lupia, Arthur and Mathew D. McCubbins (1998) *The Democratic Dilemma: Can Citizens Learn What they Need to Know?* Cambridge: Cambridge University Press.

McCormick, Paul (1980) 'The Labour Party: Three Unnoticed Changes', *British Journal of Political Science* 10 (3): 381–7.

McKelvey, Richard D. (1976) 'Intransitivities in Multidimensional Voting Models and Some Implications for Agenda Control', *Journal of Economic Theory* 12 (3): 472–82.

McKenzie, Robert (1964) *British Political Parties: The Distribution of Power Within the Conservative and Labour Parties* (2nd ed.). London: Mercury Books.

McKenzie, Robert (1982) 'Power in the Labour Party: The Issue of "Intra-party Democracy"', in Dennis Kavanagh (ed.), *The Politics of the Labour Party*, pp. 191–201. London: George Allen and Unwin.

McNair, Brian (1999) *An Introduction to Political Communication* (2nd ed.). London: Routledge.

McSmith, Andy (1996) *Faces of Labour: The Inside Story*. London: Verso.

Mandelson, Peter and Roger Liddle (1996) *The Blair Revolution: Can New Labour Deliver?* London: Fontana.

Maor, Moshe (1997) *Political Parties and Party Systems: Comparative Approaches and the British Experience*. London: Routledge.

Margolis, Howard (1982) *Selfishness, Altruism, and Rationality: A Theory of Social Choice*. Chicago: University of Chicago Press.

May, John D. (1973) 'Opinion Structure of Political Parties: The Special Law of Curvilinear Disparity', *Political Studies* 21 (2): 135–51.

Michels, Roberto (1962) *Political Parties: A Sociological Study of the Oligarchical Tendencies of Modern Democracies*. New York: The Free Press.

Milgrom, Paul and John Roberts (1992) *Economics, Organization and Management*. Englewood Cliffs, NJ: Prentice Hall.

Miliband, Ralph (1972) *Parliamentary Socialism: A Study in the Politics of Labour*. London: Merlin.

Minkin, Lewis (1980) *The Labour Party Conference: A Study in the Politics of Intra-Party Democracy*. Manchester: Manchester University Press.

Minkin, Lewis (1992) *The Contentious Alliance: Trade Unions and the Labour Party*. Edinburgh: Edinburgh University Press.

Minkin, Lewis (1997) *Exits and Entrances: Political Research as a Creative Art*. Sheffield: Sheffield Hallam University Press.

Moore, Roger (1978) *The Emergence of the Labour Party, 1880–1924*. London: Hodder and Stoughton.

Muller, William D. (1977) *The Kept Men? The First Century of Trade Union Representation in the British House of Commons, 1874–1975*. Hassocks: Harvester Press.

Nairn, Tom (1964) 'The Nature of the Labour Party – 1 and 2', *New Left Review* 27: 38–65; *New Left Review* 28: 33–62.

Neill, Lord (1998) *Report of the Committee on Standards in Public Life on the Funding of Political Parties in the UK* (2 vols), Cm 4057. London: The Stationery Office.

Norris, Pippa (1995a) 'Labour Party Quotas for Women', in David Broughton, David M. Farrell, David Denver and Colin Rallings, *British Elections and Parties Yearbook 1994*, pp. 167–80. London: Frank Cass.

Norris, Pippa (1995b) 'May's Law of Curvilinear Disparity Revisited: Leaders, Officers, Members and Voters in British Political Parties', *Party Politics* 1 (1): 29–47.

Norris, Pippa (1998) 'The Battle for the Campaign Agenda', in Anthony King (ed.) *New Labour Triumphs: Britain at the Polls*, pp. 113–44. Chatham, NJ: Chatham House.

Norris, Pippa and Joni Lovenduski (1995) *Political Recruitment: Gender, Race and Class in the British Parliament*. Cambridge: Cambridge University Press.

North, Douglass C. (1990) *Institutions, Institutional Change and Economic Performance*. Cambridge: Cambridge University Press.

Olson, Mancur (1971) *The Logic of Collective Action: Public Goods and the Theory of Groups*. Cambridge, MA: Harvard University Press.

Ostrogorski, Moisei (1902), *Democracy and the Organisation of Political Parties*. London: Macmillan.

Panebianco, Angelo (1988) *Political Parties: Organization and Power*. Cambridge: Cambridge University Press.

Panitch, Leo and Colin Leys (1997) *The End of Parliamentary Socialism: From New Left to New Labour*. London: Verso.

Pelling, Henry, and Alastair J. Reid (1996) *A Short History of the Labour Party* (11th ed.). Basingstoke: Macmillan.

Pennings, Paul and Reuven Y. Hazan (2001) 'Democratizing Candidate Selection: Causes and Consequences', *Party Politics* 7 (3): 267–75.

Perrigo, Sarah (1995) 'Gender Struggles in the British Labour Party from 1979 to 1995', *Party Politics* 1 (3): 407–17.

Pettit, Philip (1998) 'Institutional Design and Rational Choice', in Robert E. Goodin (ed.), *The Theory of Institutional Design*, pp. 54–89. Cambridge: Cambridge University Press.

Pinto-Duschinsky, Michael (1981) *British Political Finance 1830–1980*. Washington D. C. and London: American Enterprise Institute for Public Policy Research.

Przeworski, Adam and John Sprague (1986) *Paper Stones: A History of Electoral Socialism*. Chicago: University of Chicago Press.

Punnett, R.M. (1990) 'Selecting a Leader and Deputy Leader of the Labour Party: The Future of the Electoral College', *Parliamentary Affairs* 43 (2): 179–95.

Punnett, R.M. (1992) *Selecting the Party Leader: Britain in Comparative Perspective*. London: Harvester Wheatsheaf.

Punnett, R.M. (1993) 'Selecting the Party Leader in Britain: A Limited Participatory Revolution', *European Journal of Political Research* 24 (3): 257–76.

Putnam, Robert D. (2000) *Bowling Alone: The Collapse and Revival of American Community*. New York: Simon and Schuster.

Quinn, Thomas (2002) 'Block Voting in the Labour Party: A Political Exchange Model', *Party Politics* 8 (2): 207–26.

Quinn, Thomas (2004) 'Electing the Leader: The British Labour Party's Electoral College', *British Journal of Politics and International Relations* 6 (3): 333–52.

Ranney, Austin (1965) *Pathways to Parliament: Candidate Selection in Britain*. Madison: University of Winconsin Press.

Rentoul, John (1995) *Tony Blair*. London: Little, Brown and Co.

Richards, Paul (2000) 'Is the Party Over? New Labour and the Politics of Participation', *Fabian Pamphlet* 594. London: Fabian Society.

Robertson, David (1976) *A Theory of Party Competition*. London: John Wiley & Sons.

Rush, Michael (1969) *The Selection of Parliamentary Candidates*. London: Nelson.

Scarrow, Susan E. (1996), *Parties and their Members: Organizing for Victory in Britain and Germany*. Oxford: Oxford University Press.

Scarrow, Susan E., Paul Webb and David M. Farrell (2000) 'From Social Integration to Electoral Contestation: The Changing Distribution of Power within Political Parties', in Russell J. Dalton and Martin P. Wattenberg (eds), *Parties Without Partisans: Political Change in Advanced Industrial Democracies*, pp. 129–53. Oxford: Oxford University Press.

Schlesinger, Joseph A. (1984) 'On the Theory of Party Organization', *Journal of Politics* 46 (2): 369–400.

Schuessler, Alexander A. (2000) *A Logic of Expressive Choice*. Princeton, NJ: Princeton University Press.

Self, Peter (1993) *Government by the Market? The Politics of Public Choice*. London: Macmillan.

Seyd, Patrick (1987) *The Rise and Fall of the Labour Left*. Basingstoke: Macmillan.

Seyd, Patrick (1998) 'Tony Blair and New Labour', in Anthony King (ed.) *New Labour Triumphs: Britain at the Polls*, pp. 49–74. Chatham, NJ: Chatham House.

Seyd, Patrick (1999) 'New Parties/New Politics? A Case Study of the British Labour Party', *Party Politics* 5 (3): 383–405.

Seyd, Patrick (2001) 'The Labour Campaign', in Pippa Norris (ed.), *Britain Votes 2001*, pp. 43–59. Oxford: Oxford University Press.

Seyd, Patrick and Paul Whiteley (1992) *Labour's Grass Roots: The Politics of Party Membership*. Oxford: Clarendon Press.

Seyd, Patrick and Paul Whiteley (2002) *New Labour's Grassroots: The Transformation of the Labour Party Membership*. Basingstoke: Palgrave Macmillan.

Seyd, Patrick and Paul Whiteley (2003) 'Party Election Campaigning in Britain: The Labour Party', *Party Politics* 9 (5): 637–52.

Shapley, Lloyd S. and Martin Shubik (1954) 'A Method for Evaluating the Distribution of Power in a Committee System', *American Political Science Review* 48 (3): 787–92.

Shaw, Eric (1988) *Discipline and Discord in the Labour Party: The Politics of Managerial Control in the Labour Party, 1951–87*. Manchester: Manchester University Press.

Shaw, Eric (1989) 'The Policy Review and Labour's Policy-making System'. Paper presented to the annual conference of the Political Studies Association of the UK, University of Warwick, April.

Shaw, Eric (1994) *The Labour Party Since 1979: Crisis and Transformation*. London: Routledge.

Shaw, Eric (2000) 'The Wilderness Years, 1979–94', in Brian Brivati and Richard Heffernan (eds), *The Labour Party: A Centenary History*, pp. 112–42. Basingstoke: Macmillan.

Shaw, Eric (2001) 'New Labour: New Pathways to Parliament' *Parliamentary Affairs* 54 (1): 35–53.

Shaw, Eric (2002) 'New Labour in Britain: New Democratic Centralism?', *West European Politics* 25 (3): 147–70.

Shaw, Eric (2003) 'Lewis Minkin and the Party-Unions Link', in John Callaghan, Steven Fielding and Steve Ludlam (eds), *Interpreting the Labour Party: Approaches to Labour Politics and History*, pp. 166–81. Manchester and New York: Manchester University Press.

Shepsle, Kenneth A. (1972) 'The Strategy of Ambiguity: Uncertainty and Electoral Competition', *American Political Science Review* 66 (2): 555–68.

Shepsle, Kenneth A. (1979) 'Institutional Arrangements and Equilibrium in Multi-dimensional Voting Models', *American Journal of Political Science* 23 (1): 27–60.

Shepsle, Kenneth A. (1989) 'Studying Institutions: Some Lessons from the Rational Choice Approach', *Journal of Theoretical Politics* 1 (2): 131–47.

Shepsle, Kenneth A. and Mark S. Bonchek (1997) *Analyzing Politics: Rationality, Behavior, and Institutions*. New York: Norton & Co.

Short, Clare (1992) 'Fixing the Fixers', *Fabian Review* 104 (4): 14.

Smith, Martin J. (1994) 'Understanding the Politics of "Catch-up": The Modernization of the Labour Party', *Political Studies* 42 (4): 708–15.

Smith, Martin J. (2000) 'From Old to New Labour, 1994–2000', in Brian Brivati and Richard Heffernan (eds), *The Labour Party: A Centenary History*, pp. 143–62. Basingstoke: Macmillan.

Smith, Martin J. and Joanna Spear (eds) (1992) *The Changing Labour Party*. London: Routledge.

Stark, Leonard P. (1996) *Choosing a Leader: Party Leadership Contests in Britain from Macmillan to Blair*. Basingstoke: Macmillan.

Strøm, Kaare (1990) 'A Behavioral Theory of Competitive Political Parties', *American Journal of Political Science* 34 (2): 565–98.

Strøm, Kaare (1993) 'Competition Ruins the Good Life: Party Leadership in Norway', *European Journal of Political Research* 24 (3): 317–47.

Stubager, Rune (2003) 'Preference-shaping: An Empirical Test', *Political Studies* 51 (2): 241–61.

Tanner, Duncan (2000) 'Labour and its Membership', in Duncan Tanner, Pat Thane and Nick Tiratsoo (eds), *Labour's First Century*, pp. 248–80. Cambridge: Cambridge University Press.

Tanner, Duncan, Pat Thane and Nick Tiratsoo (2000) *Labour's First Century*. Cambridge: Cambridge University Press.

Taylor, Andrew J. (1987) *The Trade Unions and the Labour Party*. London: Croom Helm.

Taylor, Gerald R. (1997) *Labour's Renewal? The Policy Review and Beyond*. Basingstoke: Macmillan.

Taylor, Robert (1991) 'The Trade Union "Problem" in the Age of Consensus', in Ben Pimlott and Chris Cook (eds), *Trade Unions in British Politics: The First 250 Years*, pp. 173–99. London: Longman.

Taylor, Robert (2000) 'Trade Union Freedom and the Labour Party: Arthur Deakin, Frank Cousins and the Transport and General Workers Union 1945–1964', in Brian Brivati and Richard Heffernan (eds), *The Labour Party: A Centenary History*, pp. 187–219. Basingstoke: Macmillan.

Tsebelis, George (1990) *Nested Games: Rational Choice in Comparative Politics*. Berkeley: University of California Press.

Tsebelis, George (2002) *Veto Players: How Political Institutions Work*. Princeton: Russell Sage Foundation and Princeton University Press.

Ward, Hugh (2000) '"If the Party Won't Go to the Median Voter, Then the Median Voter Must Come to the Party": A Spatial Model of Two-party Competition with Endogenous Voter Preferences'. Paper presented to the annual conference of the Political Studies Association of the UK, London School of Economics, April.

Ware, Alan (1992) 'Activist-Leader Relations and the Structure of Political Parties: "Exchange" Models and Vote-Seeking Behaviour in Parties', *British Journal of Political Science* 22 (1): 71–92.

Ware, Alan (1996) *Political Parties and Party Systems*. Oxford: Oxford University Press.

Webb, Paul (1992a) *Trade Unions and the British Electorate*. Aldershot: Dartmouth.

Webb, Paul (1992b) 'Election Campaigning, Organisational Transformation and the Professionalisation of the British Labour Party', *European Journal of Political Research* 21 (3): 267–88.

Webb, Paul (1995) 'Reforming the Labour Party – Trade Union Link: An Assessment', in David Broughton, David M. Farrell, David Denver and Colin Rallings, *British Elections and Parties Yearbook 1994*, pp. 1–14. London: Frank Cass.

Webb, Paul (2000) *The Modern British Party System*. London: Sage Publications.

Weingast, Barry R. and William J. Marshall (1988) 'The Industrial Organization of Congress; or, Why Legislatures, Like Firms, Are Not Organized as Markets', *Journal of Political Economy* 96 (1): 132–63.

Whiteley, Paul and Patrick Seyd (1998) 'Labour's Grassroots Campaign in 1997', in David Denver, Justin Fisher, Philip Cowley and Charles Pattie (eds), *British Elections and Parties Review, Volume 8: The 1997 General Election*, pp. 191–207. London: Frank Cass.

Whiteley, Paul and Patrick Seyd (2001) 'Party People', *The Guardian*, 27 March 2001.

Wickham-Jones, Mark (1995a) 'Anticipating Social Democracy, Preempting Anticipations: Economic Policy-making in the British Labour Party, 1987–1992', *Politics and Society* 23 (4): 465–94.

Wickham-Jones, Mark (1995b) 'Recasting Social Democracy: A Comment on Hay and Smith', *Political Studies* 43 (4): 698–702.

Wickham-Jones, Mark (1996) *Economic Strategy and the Labour Party: Politics and Policy-Making, 1970–83*. Basingstoke: Macmillan.

Wickham-Jones, Mark (1997) 'Social Democracy and Structural Dependency: The British Case. A Note on Hay', *Politics and Society* 25 (2): 257–65.

Wickham-Jones, Mark (2000) 'New Labour in the Global Economy: Partisan Politics and the Social Democratic Model', *British Journal of Politics and International Relations* 2 (1): 1–25.

Williams, Paul (1983) 'The Labour Party: The Rise of the Left', *West European Politics* 6 (4): 27–55.

Williamson, Oliver E. (1985) *The Economic Institutions of Capitalism: Firms, Markets, Relational Contracts*. New York: The Free Press.

Wright, William E. (1971) 'Comparative Party Models: Rational-Efficient and Party Democracy', in William E. Wright (ed.), *A Comparative Study of Party Organization*. Columbus, Ohio: Charles E. Merrill.

Index

Note: references to tables appear in *italics*, and those to figures in **bold**.